NAPOLEON'S
OF RUSSIA

THEODORE AYRAULT DODGE

FOREWORD BY GEORGE F. NAFZIGER

Frontline Books, London

Napoleon's Invasion of Russia

This edition published in 2008 by Frontline Books, an imprint of Pen
and Sword Books Ltd, 47 Church Street, Barnsley, S. Yorkshire, S70 2AS
www.frontline-books.com

Copyright © Pen and Sword Books Ltd, 2008
Foreword © George F. Nafziger, 2008

ISBN: 978-1-84832-501-2

Publishing History

Napoleon's Invasion of Russia is an extended excerpt from Volume III of
Theodore Dodge's *Napoleon: A History of the Art of War*, which was
published in four volumes by Houghton Mifflin Company (Boston and
New York) and Riverside Press (Cambridge, UK), from 1904–7, as part
of the *Great Captain* series. This edition contains a new introduction by
George F. Nafziger.

British Library Cataloguing-in Publication Data

Dodge, Theodore Ayrault, 1842–1909
Napoleon's invasion of Russia
1. Napoleonic Wars, 1800–1815 – Campaigns – Russia
I. Title
940.2'742'0947

Library of Congress Cataloging-in Publication Data available

For more information on our books, please visit
www.frontline-books.com, email info@frontline-books.com
or write to us at the above address.

Printed and bound in Great Britain by Biddles Ltd, King's Lynn

CONTENTS

FOREWORD

———✦———

THERE have been innumerable authors writing on Napoleon and his campaigns. The best of them are those who can give the clearest understanding of the military aspects of Napoleon's operations, and they are those who have had military experience themselves. Theodore A. Dodge is one of the finest of those military historians with a military background. Having served as an officer in the Union Army during the American Civil War, he brought an insightful and understanding mind to the study of Napoleon's Russian campaign.

Considered the greatest American military historian of the 19th century, he received a military education in Berlin, then attended University College London and Heidelberg University in Germany. When the American Civil War erupted he enlisted as a private and rose to the rank of brevet lieutenant-colonel. He lost his right leg at the Battle of Gettysburg in July 1863. He continued to serve in the Union Army, retiring as a major in 1870.

Dodge started his career as an author and military historian by writing on what he knew, the Civil War. His first work was *The Campaign of Chancellorsville* (1881), which was followed by *Bird's Eye View of the Civil War* (1883). These were followed by *Parrocius and Penelope* (1885) and *Riders of Many Lands* (1894). However, his greatest work was his twelve-volume work *History of the Art of War: Alexander, Hannibal, Caesar, Gustavus Adolphus, Frederick the Great, and Napoleon* (1889). His personal journal was recently published by Stephen W. Sears, under the title *On Campaign with the Army of the Potomac: The Civil War Journal of Theodore Ayrault Dodge.* Dodge lived from 1842 to 1908.

The volume you have in hand is an excerpt from Volume III of *Napoleon: A History of the Art of War*, part of the classic series *Great Captains*. Even though the original work on Napoleon is contained in four large volumes, as it covers Napoleon's entire military career, the level of detail is necessarily limited. Dodge begins with an exploration of the prelude to the campaign, including the influence of the Continental System on the eventual decision to attack Russia. Dodge betrays a touch of his subscription to the concept of the Corsican ogre in his presentation, no doubt due to his studies in England and Germany, where memories of Napoleon were still fresh. Despite this, Dodge recognizes Napoleon as one of the greatest military commanders in human history and, throughout the work, provides a very favourable and insightful examination of Napoleon's military prowess. He provides a favourable commentary on Napoleon's well-thought-out plans for the invasion of Russia, explaining their failure by a variety of causes ranging from Jerome's incompetence, to the distances and the technical difficulties of moving supplies long distances in the days before the motor vehicle and railroad. However, he also has no hesitation to point out Napoleon's failures.

In his discussion of the reasons and preparations for the invasion of Russia, Dodge examines the complex politics of the period from 1811 to the beginning of military operations. He also provides a brief overview of the various treaties and preparation before turning to military operations.

Dodge examines the campaign from the strategic and operational level. Because he is focused on Napoleon as a great captain, he examines only the operations of the central column, which was under the direct control of Napoleon. As a result, the side operations of the Austrian Hilfkorps and of the corps under Oudinot and St. Cyr are not examined. Nor does he discuss anything in the rear of the advancing columns or back in

Germany, Napoleon's logistical base.

In his examinations of the battles, Dodge provides a quick review of several engagements, but not all. He does this so that they can be fitted into the strategic picture. Even his account of Borodino is quite limited. Again his focus is strategic, not tactical. Woven into his discussion of strategic operations, is a steady accounting of the logistical situation and how it was affecting operations from the very beginning of the campaign. The logistical situation steadily grows through his examination of the campaign until it becomes the focus of his discussion in his account of the disastrous retreat.

Dodge's work, *History of the Art of War*, is a classic of 19th-century military literature. It provides the reader with a clear and concise strategic review of Napoleon's Russian campaign. It is the sort of work that should be on the shelves of the serious student of the Napoleonic era.

For the modern reader, this work still has considerable value in that its focus is on Russia and covers one of the greatest events in the history of modern Russia. Russia has been a major player in European military history since Charles XII of Sweden invaded it. One might even call the Battle of Poltava Russia's coming out party, for certainly the crowned heads of Europe suddenly looked eastwards upon hearing the booming cannon and crashing musketry that heralded the entry of a new player on the world stage and the death throes of another world power. The Russian victory at Poltava also heralded the death of yet another major European power, Poland, which would be divided up between Russia, the growing Prussian kingdom and the moribund Holy Roman Empire.

The new player on the European political stage had totally realigned the system of alliances and continues to play a massive role in European politics into the 21st century. When the Seven Years War erupted, Prussia invaded Saxony to snatch its army away from the Austrians. Austria sought help from France, whose crown prince was married to the daughter of the King of Saxony, the first victim of Prussian aggression. This drew France into an alliance with Austria, who had been its historical enemy. As a price for its support, Austria agreed to cede the Lowlands to France, which was a threat to England, France's historical enemy for the previous 600 years. England aligned with Prussia. In response, Austria and France then moved to bring Russia into the war.

Russia's military was powerful, but primitive. They stormed into eastern Prussia and at Gross Jägersdorf brutalized the Prussian Army under Field Marshal von Tehwaldt. However, due to their very poor logistical system, they were unable to capitalize on their success. The Russians had again demonstrated themselves as a power that had to be considered in every calculation of the balance of power in Europe.

When the French Revolution erupted, the Empress of Russia was distressed at the overthrow of the French king and his replacement by a republic. However, Catherine was more interested in pursuing her designs on Poland, which Russia had been steadily consuming for many years. The Russians did not, therefore, offer more than moral support to the Austrians, Prussians and English as they engaged France's revolutionary armies. In 1794, however, Russia negotiated an arrangement with Prussia and Austria, as a result of which Poland was finally eradicated from the map of Europe.

Poland had had long ties with the French and, because of its geographical position, had allied itself with France to balance against the threats to Polish sovereignty by the Holy Roman Empire. France's armies, however, were barely able to hold their own against the Prussian and Austrian armies along the Rhine and in the Lowlands, so when Prussia withdrew from the First Coalition against France and participated in the division of

Poland, the Republican government was happy to simply let Poland disappear, instead of once again engaging the Prussian Army. Prussia was happy to pick up this territory to its east and also had no desire to support Austrian designs on seizing Alsace and Lorraine from France.

The wars continued until Catherine II of Russia died and Paul I ascended to the throne. Paul eagerly threw himself into the Allied cause, joined the coalition, and sent his forces to join the war against France. Russian troops landed in Holland and marched into Italy in 1799. In Holland they were badly handled by the French from the start, but in Italy and Switzerland, Marshal Suvorov inflicted many defeats against the French armies he encountered until he arrived at Zurich. Here he found himself faced by Massena and a converging force of French armies. Suvorov executed a skilful retreat and barely escaped destruction. Paul's anger at the Austrians and English after these two disasters caused him to withdraw from the alliance against the French. Russia would remain out of the wars until 1805 when Austria once again coaxed the Russians into assisting them against the French. The Battle at Austerlitz was a disaster for the Russians and utter catastrophe for the Austrians. Austria signed a peace treaty, but the new Czar, Alexander I, refused to surrender and the war between France and Russia continued until 1807. It only then ended with the signing of the Treaty of Tilsit. Despite Tilsit, Russia was still a competitor for the domination of Europe. It was, in Napoleon's eyes, a hole in his economic blockade of England, France's principal enemy, and a renewed conflict was inevitable.

Dodge provides the reader with the prelude to Napoleon's invasion of Russia, so I will not comment on that. However, I do need to say that Russia, despite its close involvement in European politics, was still an enigma. Little was known about this kingdom as its borders were closed and closely patrolled by

Cossacks. Entry into Russia was not only controlled by limited numbers of passports and entry visas, but maps of any sort were simply not available to a degree necessary to support military operations. Efforts to send spies into Russia were limited, because of the tight border controls. However, Napoleon did avail himself of travellers, frequently Jewish merchants, that could be persuaded to send him information on the conditions and geography of Russia. Napoleon's preparations were as thorough as they could be in 1810–1811. He avidly studied every book he could on Russia and particularly focused on accounts of the Poltava campaign of Charles XII. This was not enough, but it had to do. There simply was nothing more to be had.

Using what was available, Napoleon took every step imaginable, within the technological limits of the 19th century, to prepare for his operations against the Russians. He cannot be faulted for his logistical preparations, but he can be faulted for pushing his logistical system beyond what he knew it could handle. Napoleon's problem was that his geopolitical goal was beyond the technical capabilities of his day.

This is where Dodge demonstrates his strength and the value of his work. Dodge examines all the failures – both by Napoleon and by his generals. He takes the strategic and logistical situation and explains where the campaign went wrong for Napoleon and resulted in one of the greatest disasters in all military history.

Histories of this campaign generally dwell on the deaths of about 500,000 French and allied troops in Napoleon's retreat. They do not mention that the Russian Army suffered heavily and that its losses were close to 50 per cent of its strength. The rigours of the winter showed no favouritism and killed Russian and invader alike.

When 1813 arrived, the remains of the Grande Armée were followed into Poland by the survivors of the Russian Army. The

Prussian King was shaken out of his neutrality and fear of Napoleon by the actions of his generals, whose division serving as part of the Grande Armée defected to and joined the Russians. Forced to rejoin the alliance, Prussia mobilised its army and the 1813 campaign began. Two major French victories, Lützen and Bautzen, forced the Allies to sign an armistice, which was probably Napoleon's second greatest strategic error – after his failure to stop at Smolensk and his decision to push on to Moscow in 1812.

A renewed, reinforced and rebuilt Coalition deployed armies that were more than Napoleon could stop. Victories were followed by defeats, the greatest of which was Leipzig, where the French Army was essentially destroyed. Shattered, but still deadly, the remains of the French Army crossed back over the Rhine and the 1814 and 1815 campaigns quickly followed, ending Napoleonic Europe.

Russia, however, had now stepped firmly onto the stage of European politics. Russia was a power with a seat at the table and with whom the major issues of Europe had to be negotiated.

Napoleon's invasion of Russia lit the fire that would lift Russia to the forefront of world powers. Dodge would not know where this fire would lead, as he did not live to see the formation of the Soviet Union, nor could he have imagined how it would influence the last half of the 20th century. Nonetheless, his analysis of the Russian campaign provides an exceptional picture of the first flickers of that fire. As such, it is an exceptional work and well worth the attention of the 21st-century reader.

GEORGE F. NAFZIGER

CHAPTER 1

THE INVASION OF RUSSIA. 1811 TO JUNE, 1812.

To control England, Napoleon had created his Continental System, which excluded her from European markets, and Russia had maintained it since Tilsit; but Russian good-will grew less, Alexander distrusted Napoleon more, smuggling was rampant, and only force could insure its continuance. The emperor should have himself gone to Spain to finish matters there before undertaking a Russian campaign, but he believed in his lieutenants, and was unwilling to wait. His preparations were enormous, his grasp of the general scheme and the details was extraordinary, but he no longer accurately gauged facts. Austria and Prussia were lukewarm allies, and though suspicious of the other, each furnished a quota. Foreseeing war, Alexander made a treaty with Turkey and raised troops, while England strove to create another Coalition. Napoleon left Paris May 9, the Grand Army being already on the Oder, in eleven corps of over a half million men, fully equipped. In 1807 he had tested the Russian roads, but still believed he could wheel supplies to his moving troops. Alexander collected three armies under Barclay, Bagration and Tormasov, of about a quarter million men, and erected a huge intrenched camp at Drissa. He understood that with a retreating campaign no force could conquer Russia, but had no systematic plan. Napoleon strove to use the Poles without giving them independence. Russia had but three frontier entrances through which she could be invaded from Germany, and until the Dvina-Dnieper line is reached one is not in Russia proper. Each entrance was blocked by troops. The Russian generals disagreed. Chichagov wanted to march up the Danube into Italy, Bagration to hold the Niemen and invade Warsaw, Barclay to defend the frontier. Alexander waited on events. Napoleon advanced on a wide front, to prevent the enemy from guessing his purpose, but proposed to cut Barclay from Bagration. He himself commanded the left, Eugene the centre and Jerome the right. He should have placed Davout on the right: Jerome was no soldier. The Grand Army had long been advancing through Germany, the Austrians and Prussians as flying wings, and on June 24 headquarters was in Kovno. Transportation difficulties were little heeded. The Russians retired from Vilna, burning immense stores, and the French reached it June 28. Jerome's laxness was giving trouble. Napoleon remained too long in Vilna: he would have done better nearer the front. None of his lieutenants was independent, and time was consumed for reports and orders to go to and fro. Matters did not advance, and information was as scant as rations; but owing to the immense theatre, this could not be corrected.

SCANT space can be devoted to the political events which led up to the Russian war. These were the outcome of what Napoleon had accomplished in the past, as they were the foundation of his failure in the future; and as elucidating the military narrative during this, his first great year of defeat, they are briefly referred to.

So long as Napoleon could neither influence nor coerce the British cabinet, and the British fleet commanded the seas, so long was he compelled to oppose his island enemy with his Continental System, and to sustain this by arms. The effect of the System was to oppress the English working-classes, though commerce still held itself fairly well; and while finances were in poor condition, and many failures occurred, for its then population English agriculture was better than to-day. Not only this, but the Continental manufactures were damaged, many towns were ruined, merchandise coming by sea was so expensive as to breed discontent, and articles of English commerce entered France with enormous duties.

Napoleon saw no reason why he should not reign thirty years, and during this time consolidate his empire, for he had back of him a strong body of peasantry, to whom he had assured its holdings of land taken from the ancient feudal owners, and a strong bourgeoisie, whose position under the empire was better than before. Meanwhile the terrors resulting from the Revolution had been forgotten.

Napoleon's Code and administration were strong and sound. The quarrels with the pope had not disturbed the ancient faith, education advanced under a good school system, and finances recovered an outwardly prosperous aspect. He had rehabilitated so far as possible the old nobility, and employed many of its members; he had also created a new nobility, hoping to weld the two into one body; but this proved impossible, despite the prominence given to the titles of his marshals and companions in arms. Paris was made the centre of this great empire, which was upheld by nearly a million men under arms, and was decorated with the spoils of all the countries overrun; and yet, despite the grandeur of the Napoleonic court, the new brand was apparent.

Napoleon had really abolished the privileges of feudalism to the great increase of Continental liberty; abuses were far less, and the poor man could see a future before him; yet this huge structure, outwardly so prosperous, did not possess a healthy body. No country so drained of its working element to furnish soldiers could long prosper, and even the army was no longer the splendid force of Austerlitz, while the French body politic had grown so fast that it might disappear in some new crash. The structure of the emperor's creation was not as solid as it had been. The legislative bodies were more under his control, and less real; the judges were not as independent as they had begun by being, and ministers had become mere clerks to register his will. An independent thinker like Talleyrand was removed from office, and a good servant, however full of faults, like Fouché, was shelved. At the top was much that was unhealthy; but the worst feature was the protest of the lower classes against the constantly growing severity of the conscription; and the far-seeing man could divine that the French Empire depended solely on the life of Napoleon.

In addition to the evils of the Continental System, France had annexed what neighboring states did not carry out its terms. It is a question whether any scheme which should make France extend beyond her so-called natural boundaries could be permanent, and France was striving to overrun Spain, had taken Italy and added to it the Roman states and the Illyrian provinces; she had extended her boundaries along the North Sea and Baltic to a point east of Berlin; she had practically annexed western Germany under the name of Confederation of the Rhine, as well as Switzerland, and had recreated Poland, while the so-called kingdom of Naples was a mere suburb of France. It was only a question of time when this great dream must dissolve. It trenched upon the rights of races.

Next to England, Russia was hardest to control; and her good-will was unfortunately slipping away. Alexander had been more frank at Tilsit than Napoleon, and had better kept faith since, but the treaty was outworn; and when Russia ceased adherence to its terms, the Continental System was bound to break down. That Napoleon intended to recreate Poland as a means of controlling Russia, the treaty of Vienna proved; and to this threat was added the hardship on a grain-growing people, which under the System could not export its chief product.

Napoleon had thus overrun all Europe, except Russia and Great Britain. He could not expect to conquer and control the land of the czar; but he believed that he could force Russia to keep out of European politics by creating a new Poland as a buffer-state for his Austrian and Prussian allies. According to him, Russia had demanded that France should guarantee that the Kingdom of Poland should never be reëstablished — in its nature an impossible thing; and Poland could be peacefully rehabilitated only by ceding to Russia and Austria valuable provinces, a thing Napoleon was not willing to do.

The warmest relations had existed between France and Russia. In fact, the emperor, in May, 1808, wrote to Berthier that too much heed had been paid to Russian requests; but as smuggling grew, amity gave place to irritation, for Napoleon insisted on his System as an article of faith. " The decrees establishing the Continental System are fundamental laws, having their origin in the nature of things," he said. " If English commerce triumphs on the sea, it is because the English are strongest there. It is, however, probable, inasmuch as France is strongest on land, that she can there cause her commerce to triumph; without which all is lost."

The negotiations for a Russian princess as Empress of the French had neither been conducted with diplomatic complaisance, nor to a happy issue; and when Napoleon dispossessed the Duke of Oldenburg, the czar's brother-in-law, he upset even the temperate mind of Alexander. Not because of this, but just a month afterwards, was issued the czar's ukase of December 31, 1810, which was in effect a declaration of independence, and in European courts portended a growing hostility to France and friendliness to England. What France had gained in the Austrian alliance was more than lost in Russian disaffection, and it was not long after Wagram that the emperor foresaw the inevitable clash.

The Tilsit status should have been maintained to give Napoleon time himself to finish the Spanish war; but he feared that in such an interval Russia would tamper with north Germany, or England with St. Petersburg, Berlin, or Vienna. On the other hand, Prussia had proposed an alliance; Austria was by marriage tied to France; Sweden, despite Bernadotte's ill-will, could, the emperor thought, be pacified by helping her to regain Finland; Turkey's peace with Russia had not yet come to a head. To delay with Russia was dangerous; and Napoleon was loth to go to Spain. Diplomacy seemed to retain him in Paris, and he never ceased to believe that the Spanish war would wear itself out. The difficult conditions in Spain would require many months, even for him, to close the war; and what might meanwhile happen elsewhere? Had he gone to Spain, with the forces he could have placed there, England would no doubt have been compelled to leave the Peninsula; once driven out, she could not have again regained her footing there; and meanwhile no great harm would probably have happened. But Napoleon decided that Spain could wait rather than Russia; Wellington had for years been cautious, had generally maintained the defensive, and Napoleon underrated him.

There lacked not prominent Frenchmen to decry a Russian campaign, and, with Charles XII. as an example, to show that Russia could not be brought to terms, should she conduct a retreating campaign. Others approved both the project and the time. Napoleon weighed both opinions, but consulted only himself. He had studied all the pros and. cons; but years of success in overcoming difficulties as they arose had led him into the habit of less closely gauging them. He deemed it certain that Russia would give way long before he reached St. Petersburg or Moscow; and that he could march so far, he never doubted. At least he was willing to take the risk. His failures on the difficult theatres of Egypt and Syria had been obliterated by recent successes, and he believed the Russians would again fight a general battle near their own frontier. Could he but win another Austerlitz on the Russian steppes, would not all Europe be at his feet? The chances seemed to him more favorable than in 1807, when Austria might have fallen on his rear, and have roused Prussia to fresh resistance; for in this campaign he had, from a military standpoint, the right to count on both Prussia and Austria as being helpful; and he overrated Poland.

Of cabals at home Napoleon had no fear: he could govern France from his Russian headquarters as securely as in Paris.

Though France had already furnished her best blood, yet men were still to be had; England would be kept busy in Spain; Austria and Prussia would each furnish a strong corps as a hostage; victual was in plenty, for Russia and Poland had for years not marketed their surplus grain, and Prussia could pay her indemnities in breadstuff; beeves roamed in droves in Galicia; and a well-operated supply-train, organized in battalions, had already been created. The worst that could happen was to fail and retire intact to the Vistula. Napoleon had gauged everything properly except the transport of supplies; in his account he falsely weighed the Russian soil and the Russian roads; and he had forgotten the difficulties of 1807.

Napoleon would have preferred peace on his own terms.

On April 2, 1811, he wrote the King of Wurtemberg, "I believe and I hope, as does Your Majesty, that Russia will not make war." Yet "the King of Prussia let things go to war when war was far. . . . It was the same with the Emperor of Austria. . . . I am not far from thinking that the same thing will happen to the Emperor Alexander. This prince is already far from the spirit of Tilsit. All the ideas of war come from Russia. If the emperor wishes war, the direction of public spirit conforms to his intentions. If he does not want it, and does not promptly stop this impulsion, he will be drawn into it next year in his own default, and thus war will take place despite him, despite me, despite the interests of France and those of Russia. . . . All this is a scene of the Opera, and it is the English who run the machines. . . . Why should I make war? Would it be to reëstablish Poland? I could have done it after Tilsit, after Vienna, this year, even. I am too good a tactician to have given up such easy opportunities. Therefore I do not wish it. Finally, I have the war of Spain and Portugal . . . which occupies enough men and means. I cannot wish another war. . . . Shall we keep peace? I yet hope we shall, but it is necessary to arm."

On April 5, 1811, through the Minister of Foreign Relations, he instructed Lauriston, in St. Petersburg, to talk clearly with the czar, and to say that the emperor "would not make war for Poland . . . that he would not make war except in case Russia, tearing the Treaty of Tilsit, should make peace with England." And next day he wrote in the same vein to Alexander: "Monsieur my Brother, as soon as I learned . . . that the choice of Count Lauriston was agreeable to Your Imperial Majesty, I gave him an order to leave. I do not send to Your Majesty a man perfected in affairs, but a man true and straight, like the sentiments I bear you. And yet I receive, daily, news from Russia which is not pacific. . . . For me, I shall remain the friend of the person of Your Majesty even if the fatality which is dragging Europe should one day put arms in the hands of our two nations. . . . I shall never attack, and my troops will not advance until Your Majesty shall have torn the Treaty of Tilsit."

Inasmuch, however, as the language of diplomacy is a lying tongue, and the emperor was no exception to the rule of that day, it will not do to lay too great stress on his utterances thus made. Some of his less official sayings have more weight. That by his abnormal triumphs Napoleon had lost that hard hold on fact which in earlier life distinguished him from all other men, is unquestionably true. Facts, as the common assertion runs, may no longer have meant to him what they were, but what his imagination desired them to be. Yet it is easy to go too far in this direction; for by taking here and there from Napoleon's voluminous correspondence letters supporting any given theory, one might prove that the emperor had quite lost his balance. From Bayonne, for instance, on July 17, 1808, he wrote the Imperial Librarian: "The emperor also desires that Monsieur Barbier will occupy himself with the following work, with one of our best geographers: get up memoirs on the campaigns which have taken place on the Euphrates, and against the Parthians, beginning with that of Crassus up to the eighth century, including those of Antony, Trajan, Julian, etc., tracing on maps of a convenient size the road followed by each army, with the ancient and new names of the countries and the principal towns, and geographical remarks about the territory, and historical narratives of each expedition, taken from the original authors." And yet this letter does not prove, as has been asserted, that the emperor was contemplating an attack on the British possessions in India. It rather proves that he was anxious to learn how the ancient leaders conducted operations in campaigns over a vast territory. Evidence of this kind may be carefully weighed, but must not be exaggerated. The words that Constant puts into the mouth of the dying Lannes have been used to prove Napoleon's boundless ambition, which many believed would lead him to eventual ruin. Marmont tells us that shortly after Wagram, Decrés, Minister of the Navy, said : " The emperor is mad, completely mad, and will destroy us all ; all this will end in a horrible crash." These quotations contain truth, but too much weight must not be given them. So far as any dared, Napoleon had plenty of people about him to hold him back, but he never wavered in his faith in his destiny : " I feel myself driven towards a goal which I do not know," Ségur quotes him as saying ; " when I shall have reached it, so soon as I shall be no longer useful to this end, an atom will suffice to throw me down ; until then, all the efforts of men can have no effect against me." Nor would he listen, as he had used to do, to those who told him facts which did not chime with his preconceptions ; even to Davout, who sent him a report made by Rapp with regard to an English pamphlet on Portugal, the emperor wrote, December 2, 1811 : " I beg you not to put such rhapsodies under my eyes. My time is too precious for me to lose it in occupying myself with such twaddle."

It is true that Napoleon misinterpreted more things than formerly ; and that he leaned less on actuality. But it will not do to assert that he was drawn on solely by belief in his destiny, or his love of gigantic conflict. This may in part be true ; but for all that, his military skill was fully tested in

1812, and his preparations for the struggle with the Russians were in the highest degree sane. Had he used his opportunities in 1812 with the judgment and energy of 1805, the armies of Barclay and Bagration would have been destroyed in July, and a glorious peace have ended the operations before the Grand Army had reached Smolensk. Indeed, had he arrested his advance here for the winter, he might eventually have won. It is not so much a fact that Napoleon undertook too gigantic a task for his power at its best, as it is that he did not show in its doing his ancient power of body and character. It is equally unsafe to draw too broad a conclusion from Napoleon's weaknesses, for though it is not within human powers to remain unspoiled by such abnormal successes as he had won, yet, up to July, 1815, he continued to be the greatest man by far in Europe.

Meanwhile the master's eye was on everything, civil and military. The diligence and care of detail shown by the Correspondence can be appreciated only by reading several of these amazing volumes, although they cover but a small part of the emperor's daily work. As a rule, the man who writes much, acts little; or conversely, the man who is great in action has little time to write. But Napoleon did both.

At the risk of surplusage, a few items are now and then quoted, all tending to show how carefully this master of war laid the foundations of his success. These are but samples of thousands, and help to illustrate the organization and status of the Grand Army.

On July 23, 1811, he complains to Lacuée of badly made saddles, with short skirts and ill stuffed : "Hold back payments from the contractor culpable of fraud. I disburse much money, I pay promptly, I intend that contractors shall deliver good things. I should prefer to have nothing than to have bad things." On August 27 the emperor sends Mortier three sample shirts : "They only cost 4 francs 7 sous. They seem to me

much finer than those of the Dutch, which cost 6 francs 10 sous. . . .
Make me a report on this." And so with hundreds of details.

Despite his autocratic power, the emperor apparently could not control
the army contractors. He wrote on November 12 to Lacuée : "In the
visit I have made to the different corps of the army, I have found that
the troops were better clad than in the Revolution, . . . but I have been
far from satisfied with them, in view of the enormous sums which they
cost me. . . . Generally speaking, the cloths are bad, and the shakos are
of bad quality ; or sometimes they are of good quality, but badly made
up. It is the same with the knapsacks. No reproaches can be made to
the corps, because they answer to everything that 'the Administration
of War has sent them.' As to the cloths, the greatest portion that I
have seen are much worse than that which I have observed in regiments
which bought them themselves." On November 14 he wrote Clarke
"to issue a circular to the different majors to make them responsible
for the supplies received by the regiments . . . so that they will have
nothing to allege whenever the regiments are in a bad condition. That
the supplies cost His Majesty a great deal, and that the payments are
promptly made ; that the supplies then should be of good quality and
excellent for service."

On November 30 Napoleon wrote Berthier to see that the regimental
flags bore only the names of battles in which the regiments actually took
part : "I give but one flag for an infantry regiment, one for a cavalry
regiment, one for an artillery regiment, one for a gendarme regiment, none
to departmental companies, or Guards of Honor, or otherwise. No one is
to have an eagle that has not been received from the hands of the emperor. Every other corps is to carry a banner." On January 14, 1812,
Clarke was ordered to see that the eagles should be made handsome,
and that the standards attached to the eagles should be inscribed with
all the battles. That the battalion banner was to be made simply, so that
in case it fell into the hands of the enemy it would not appear of much
value.

On November 30 the emperor wrote Berthier to make a narrative of
the campaigns of Ulm, Austerlitz, Jena, Friedland, Eggmühl and Wagram. "It is necessary that you should busy yourself without stopping
with this duty . . . without which nothing will remain of these campaigns." He then ordered him to edit the Bulletins so that they should
be a proper army diary, with the errors corrected, and with suitable
vouchers, showing day by day where each corps was and what it did.

Beyond this Berthier was to begin a more serious work on the campaigns of the Grand Army.

On December 2 Napoleon wrote Davout that the Germans were complaining that the marshal had said at Rostock that he would know "how to prevent Germany from becoming a Spain, and that so long as he commanded there, they would dare undertake nothing." "There is nothing in common between Spain and the German provinces," said the emperor. "Spain would have been reduced long ago without her sixty thousand English, without her thousand leagues of coast. . . . But in Germany there is nothing to fear, even were the Germans as lazy, slothful, murderous, superstitious, and as much given over to monks as the people of Spain. . . . Judge, then, how much there is to fear from a people so well behaved, so reasonable, so cold, so tolerant, so far from all excesses, that there is not one instance of a man being assassinated in Germany during the war. It is annoying . . . to circulate in the country comparisons which can only do harm." Yet Napoleon had misunderstood the German character : he had cowed but not broken it, and it was soon to turn on him with double fury.

On August 31 he wrote Lacuée : "The bread distributed to the troops at Boulogne is very bad. Take measures to remedy this abuse." On the same date to Decrés against employing sailors as servants, while the pay and rations of these men were charged up as if on duty, and on October 7 to Decrés about a navy paymaster who was occupying Marshal Soult's house in Utrecht, while Ney was lodged in the citadel, like a captain : "You do not treat my marshals right. This is not the way to give them consideration and attach them to the service. There is no choice to make between the Marshals of the Empire and the employees of finance."

On October 30 he wrote Davout, ordering the young soldiers to have fire drill : "It is very important that the soldiers should do target firing;" and November 1 about fifty young soldiers illegally imprisoned in Wesel, ordering their cases to be at once examined. On November 3 he wrote Cambacérès, complaining that the prefects of provinces had guards of honor and gave the rank and uniform of colonels to the commanders, and stating that this must be regulated.

It seems that Davout had taken into his staff some officers who had served in Austria, probably in the notion that they would be more useful. On November 30 Napoleon wrote him : "I am entirely opposed to your idea. . . . Leave those men in the regiments where I placed them. I will have in the staff only men who since 1789 have not quitted the French flag." On December 16 Eugene, whose troops had the longest distance to march to join the army, was ordered to see that they started with a pair of shoes on the feet, two pairs in their knapsack and one or two pairs in the train. " By this means one can hope that they will arrive on the Vistula with two pairs in the knapsack and one pair on their feet."

And the following has peculiar interest: —

On January 6, 1812, he indicated to Davout the desirability of the heavy cavalry learning to manœuvre on foot, " so that if they found themselves in a village, and dismounted to file through it, they would know how to work together." He had also discovered that the cavalry should be armed with a good carrying carbine or musket, and had written Clarke November 12 : " I cannot accustom myself to see . . . men *d'élite*, who in an insurrection or a surprise of light troops could be carried off by a partisan, or in a march stopped by a few bad sharpshooters behind a brook or a house. That is absurd. My intention is that each man shall have a gun. Let it be a very short musketoon carried in the most convenient way by the cuirassier. I care little about that." " War is composed of unforeseen events. It is to have small ideas of it to suppose that . . . heavy cavalry can always be kept in such a manner as to be covered." What we soldiers of the second half of the nineteenth century think that we originated, Napoleon, though no man dealt more in massed cavalry charges, or pinned his faith more fully on their momentum, had discovered, viz. : that two pistols did not suffice, that every mounted man must have a firearm which would carry to a distance, and that he must know how to fight on foot. Dragoons were not the only mounted infantry.

In 1811, while Napoleon was making his Russian preparations, although Austria and Prussia privately leaned to the side of the czar, with the fear that the brunt of the struggle would fall upon the fatherland, each chose a temporizing policy. It was only after the campaign of 1812, which proved to both that future wars against Napoleon would be waged on other territory, that these countries were willing to act together. Napoleon's rise to power was due, primarily, to his astonishing military skill, secondarily to the fact that each of his ene-

mies, until after 1812, in seeking his own purpose was afraid
of his neighbor. England had constantly preached the common cause, but the Continental coalitions were broken up by
mutual jealousies. During 1811–12, both Prussia and Austria would have been glad to join Russia, but each was afraid
of the other's staunchness. The Prime Ministers, Hardenberg
and Metternich (the latter of whom distrusted the Russian
Chancellor, Rumantzov), were fully agreed as to the desirability of acting in concert, but each in a way suspected the other.
Austria was still strong; but Prussia had been ground down
at Jena; since then she had fed enormous French armies, had
had her fortresses occupied, and her army limited to forty-two
thousand men. Her king was not a strong man, and had it
not been for the wonderful reforms of Stein and Scharnhorst,
she could not have arisen from her ashes, as she did in 1813.
Because Austria and Prussia could not coöperate, the Russian
campaign became possible.

In February, 1812, a treaty was made by Napoleon with
Prussia, and the land of Frederick paid the uttermost far-
thing of the debt she had incurred by her vacillating policy
toward France from the opening of the Revolution. Austria
could scarcely refuse an alliance when it was suggested.
Metternich, who had been much in Paris, had gauged the
emperor well, and early in 1811 reported to Francis that a
Russian war was certain; but although England exerted her
influence on Austria, the latter saw no outlet except to join
France, while doing a minimum of harm to Russia. Schwartzenberg, Austrian ambassador to Paris, believed in the French
alliance. Napoleon could not invade Russia unless Austria,
which would lie on his flank, were his ally. Metternich, knowing that if Poland was reconstituted, Napoleon would want to
add Galicia to that kingdom, made a claim that, should this
occur, Austria should be indemnified in Illyria, which was

more valuable; this was in a way recognized, and by treaty in March, 1812, Austria agreed to furnish thirty thousand men, to act in a separate body under Napoleon's general direction, and to make war upon Russia only; and this force assembled at Lemberg by the middle of May. Archduke Charles having refused the command, it fell to Schwartzenberg. The secret conditions were, however, such that Austria scarcely considered herself at war with Russia.

In the lukewarm aid of Prussia and Austria lay one reason for the failure of the coming campaign, in the status of Poland another. While Napoleon was ready to use the Poles in any helpful way without binding himself, they were counting on him for the restoration of their kingdom. Napoleon sent to Poland his own agent, de Pradt, and his scheme for reëstablishing the ancient kingdom reads like the previously prepared minutes of a primary meeting. He proposed to have things all his own way. As de Pradt said, Napoleon "never saw in man anything but projectiles made to be launched against his enemies."

Alexander meanwhile, who, though deprecating war, was ready to engage in it rather than to yield any further to Napoleon, said and did little. It had been agreed at Tilsit that Russia might conquer Finland and the provinces of the Danube. The former had been done in 1809. Sweden was weakened by Denmark owning Norway, and her hold of part of Pomerania did not add to her strength. So soon as Bernadotte deemed Sweden's interests to be anti-French, he took that direction, and soon sought Russian help to subject Norway; and when in April, 1812, Napoleon seized Swedish Pomerania, the ground for quarrel was complete. Bernadotte scarcely believed Alexander as staunch as he was; and, uncertain whether he could rely upon the Russians, he also made overtures to England.

Having got Finland, Russia had turned on Turkey. The Russian armies overran Wallachia and Moldavia, and frightened Austria as well as France by approaching the mouths of the Danube. When war with France began to loom up, Alexander saw that he must make peace with Turkey, and in May, 1812, he concluded a hasty treaty at Bucharest, retaining but a small part of his conquests. So dilatory, however, was the action of Turkey, that even at the beginning of August Chichagov was still at Bucharest, just starting his army northward, and was not on hand to help resist the first French advance.

Early in 1812 England and Russia began to draw together, and in midsummer Cathcart started for Russia as ambassador.

Meanwhile a war footing had long been in preparation. On April 20, 1811, in a letter to Clarke, Napoleon directed the organization of the " Army of Germany," and —

On May 7 he wrote Davout : " My Cousin, all the news that is received from Russia is full of protestations by the Emperor Alexander for the continuance of peace and of the alliance. Nothing leads me, then, to think that Russia has the will to commence hostilities. However this may be, all preparations to put your army corps in condition, instead of being slowed should be continued." This letter shows how Napoleon's ideas as to the size of armies had grown. " If your regiments had in line six battalions, that would make a fine brigade, which would allow the composition of your sixteen regiments and the three you are organizing . . . into six fine divisions, each division with three brigades, and each brigade with six battalions. That would make one hundred and eight battalions, or nearly ninety thousand men. That would really be an army."

On June 23 he wrote Clarke: " During the course of July, August and September, all the companies of infantry will be put at full strength of one hundred and forty men, excluding sick, by sending to them refractory conscripts, who will be drawn from Walcheren and other depots. The Observation Corps of the Elbe alone will form an army of six infantry divisions, four brigades of light cavalry, and four divisions of heavy cav-

alry, making a total, including artillery, of one hundred and twenty thousand men, independently of what is used for the garrisons of Danzig,
Stettin, Cüstrin and Glogau. The army of the King of Saxony is ready
to move, twenty thousand infantry and four thousand horse strong. The
army of the Grand Duchy of Warsaw has twenty-four thousand men
of infantry and ten thousand cavalry. The army of Westphalia has
twelve thousand men of infantry and three thousand of cavalry. In case
anything happens, all the troops will be under the orders of Davout.
Thus there are assembled at this moment under his command one hundred and forty-five thousand infantry, forty thousand cavalry, fifteen
thousand artillery, total two hundred thousand men. . . . There is nothing
urgent, but my intention is that should anything extraordinary happen,
this corps, in twenty-four hours, is to start and move to the Vistula."

Here we have the wonderful spectacle of an army of two
hundred thousand men under a lieutenant. The days had
indeed changed since the Great Captain had won Rivoli with
twenty-two thousand men.

Each and all of the details of the service passed under
Napoleon's eye.

On June 23 he wrote Davout, who still remained in Hamburg : "My
Cousin, so large a quantity of horses has been bought in France, as much
for Spain as to remount the corps of the interior, that France is exhausted
of horses. You must seriously work to make purchases in Hanover, Mecklenburg and Holstein." And on July 7 he wrote that he noticed sergeants
and corporals of less than two years' service. These men were all to be
sent back to the ranks, and to be replaced by sub-officers from Fontainebleau, or by men drawn from old regiments. And again, July 20 :
"Watch closely so that no sergeant or corporal shall be made who has
not been at Wagram, that is to say, who has not seen war. . . . It is
ridiculous to see colonels make sergeants out of soldiers of six months."

So far there had been no breach with Russia. There
had been vague complaints and explanations ; each monarch
dreaded a rupture. Alexander complained of the increase of
Polish territory, Napoleon of infractions of the Treaty of Tilsit. On the face of things the Continental System was begin-

ning to bear fruit, and from Napoleon's standpoint it was the moment all the more stringently to enforce it. If Russia would not do so in good faith, Napoleon could see naught but war; for should Russia act with England, a worse contest must ensue. He was in no mood to abate jot or tittle of his requirements; and it was because smuggling went on in Pomerania, especially at Stralsund, that he had, in January, 1812, occupied this Swedish territory. This aggression, the heavy increase of the garrisons of Danzig, Stettin, Cüstrin and Glogau, and especially the alliances with Prussia and Austria, demonstrated to Alexander that war was certain. Yet Napoleon made one more effort to get what he wished without war, and sent Colonel Chernishev, one of Alexander's aides, who had long been in Paris, with a pacific mission, agreeing to add no more territory to the Grand Duchy of Warsaw, and to give indemnities for recent seizures; but with scant faith left in Napoleon's promises, Alexander deliberated some weeks.

A final effort was made to bring about an understanding with England. During 1811 Napoleon had considered an attack on Ireland or England, going so far as to plan for three hundred ships to carry forty-thousand men across the Channel. " Nothing more easy," said he, " than to destroy the navy yard at Chatham." This attack, however, did not argue an intention to give up the struggle against Russia, so much as it did a desire to divert the attention of Great Britain from the Peninsula. England had been desirous of peace, but she has never claimed much less than the lion's share, and in any peace she expected to have her own way. Many Englishmen appreciated the good bred of the French Revolution, but the British character was not one to be overridden by even a Napoleon, and England confided in her naval strength and insular safety. Napoleon never gauged England at her true worth. In working out results of the Revolution, his gigantic imagination created too big a scheme. Even had England been quite reasonable, as she was not, the maintenance of the Treaty of Amiens or of any later peace, until one or other had been crushed, was practically impossible. Once roused, it is hard to quiet British antagonism; Napoleon was equally uncompromising, and the "irrepressible conflict" between Gaul and Briton was bound to go on.

England's policy had been to create and maintain a coalition against France which would hang together, and in a minor way, this was Wellington's policy in the Peninsula. If the conflict was kept up until all Napoleon's enemies would hold together, the Napoleonic scheme could be crushed. Extravagant in her outlay of men and money at sea, England has always been parsimonious in sending land troops to the Continent; but at this time she paid enormous bills for the troops of other nations. Had the sea controlled the Continent, England would have sooner triumphed, but in the end the sea did its full share. If we cannot blame England for opposing the Continental System, neither can we blame Napoleon for clinging to it. England had merely met a man of transcendent ability and equal doggedness. Within his limits Napoleon did his best to avoid war, and on April 17, 1812, he yet again made overtures for peace, on the basis of the independence and integrity of Spain under the existing dynasty, the rehabilitation of Portugal under its old rulers, Murat to keep Naples, the Bourbons Sicily, the rest to stay on the basis of "let him keep who can." In a way he cared little who was monarch in Madrid. But the capture of Ciudad Rodrigo and Badajoz encouraged the British and made this proposal unsatisfactory; and towards the end of April both Russia and England declined to treat.

Napoleon left Paris May 9 for Dresden. He gave no official notice of a great campaign, though everybody knew the facts, until the 1st Bulletin of the Grand Army, of June 20, was published in France two weeks later. The people accepted blindly whatever he saw fit to order, and as the war would not be on the soil of France, and meant probably new triumphs, there was little open comment.

According to universal testimony, after his hard work in preparing for the war, the emperor was peculiarly cheerful and confident. In Dresden he gave audience to the rulers of Austria, Prussia and other allied potentates, who willingly or unwillingly were about to fight his battles. By nature keen at gauging values, he was not now abreast of the real restlessness of all, and the hatred of some, of those who formally bowed to his will. Almost the only reliable ally was the King of Saxony, who had full compensation in the Grand Duchy of Warsaw.

The army was already on the Oder. As a last mission to Alexander in May, through the French ambassador at St. Petersburg, remained fruitless, and Bernadotte demanded too much for his coöperation, Napoleon contented himself with the allies he had, and left Dresden May 29 for headquarters at Thorn, on the Vistula. Poland was ready to second him; but the Turks, who had formerly proposed a diversion on Russian territory, were already making peace.

Preparations were complete. In June, 1811, two hundred thousand effective had already stood in Germany, and for months the so-called Observation Corps of the Elbe, of the Rhine and of Italy, in reality large armies, had been afoot. No detail with regard to this force escaped Napoleon's eye; and his power to organize was as superlative as his power to direct on the battlefield. He had studied the new theatre he was about to enter. His librarian, Barbier, had collected books and maps exhibiting eastern Russia in detail, and such histories of Charles XII.'s campaigns as could be had. "The emperor demands a history of Courland and everything which can be found, historical, geographical and topographical, about Riga, Livonia, etc.," his secretary wrote Barbier, January 7, 1812.

With maps of Russia proper Napoleon was less well equipped. The Russian government had recently completed a map of the empire, on a scale of about eight miles to an inch, and a copy had reached his hands. From St. Cloud, November 25, he wrote Berthier: " I have a very fine map brought in from Russia. It will be necessary for you to procure yourself a similar one." Defective in many ways, this map was none the less of the greatest use : nothing procurable in any other fashion could have done as much. Yet on July 7 Davout complained that he had but seven maps in his corps, and was obliged to make, for the light infantry officers, sketches which there was no time to prepare properly.

On the 3d of March the Grand Army ready for the invasion of Russia was thus organized : —

The Emperor, and his Chief of Staff, Berthier.

Headquarters and Staff.		4,000 men.
The Guard.	Old : Lefebvre. Young: Mortier.	
Div. Cdrs.	Delaborde, Roguet, Claparède, Curial.	
	Cavalry, Bessières.	
Div. Cdrs.	Walther, Grenadiers ; Guyot, Chasseurs ; St. Sulpice, Dragoons.	
	Durosnel, Guard ; Colbert and Krasinski,	
	Light Horse. Artillery, Sorbier.	47,000 "

Corps		No.	
I.	Davout	Div. 1 Morand.	
		" 2 Friant.	
		" 3 Gudin.	
		" 4 Dessaix.	
		" 5 Compans.	
Light Cav., Pajol, Bourdesolles.			72,000 "

Corps   No.

II. Oudinot.   Div. 6 Legrand.
                                  "   8 Verdier.
                                  "   9 Merle (Swiss).
        Light Cav., Corbineau, Castex, Doumerc.   37,000 men.

III. Ney.   Div. 10 Ledru.
                                  " 11 Razout.
                                  " 25 Crown Prince
                                         (Wurts).
        Light Cav., Mouriez.   39,000 "

IV. Eugene (Junot 2d).   Lecchi (Roy. Gd.).
                                 Div. 13 Delzons.
                                  " 14 Broussier.
                                  " 15 Pino (Ital.).
        Light Cav., Guyon, Villatte.   45,000 "

V. Poniatowski.   Div. 16 Zayonchek (Pol.).
                                  " 17 Dombrovski (").
                                  " 18 Kamieniki.   36,000 "

VI. Gouvion St. Cyr.   " 19 Deroy.
                                  " 20 Wrede.
        Light Cav., Preysing.   25,000 "

VII. Reynier.   Div. 21 Lecoq (Sax).
                                  " 22 Funck (").
        Light Cav., Gablenz, Thielemann.   17,000 "

VIII. Vandamme.   Div. 23 Tharreau (Hes.).
                                  " 24 Ochs (Westph.).
        Light Cav., Hammerstein.   18,000 "

IX. Victor.   Div. 12 Partounneaux.
                                  " 26 Daendels (Ger.).
            (came up later) " 28 Girard (Ger. Pol.).
        Light Cav., Fournier.   33,000 "

X. Macdonald.   Div. 7 Grandjean.
                                      Gräwert — later
                                         Yorck (Prus.). 32,000 "

Aust. Auxs. Schwartzenberg.   Trautenberg.
                                      Bianchi.
                                      Siegenthal.
                                      Frimont.   30,000 "

Cavalry Reserve.

Murat	1 Corps Nansouty.		12,000 men.
(Belliard,	2 " Montbrun.		10,000 "
Ch. St.).	3 Grouchy.		10,000 "
	4 Latour-Maubourg (Sax. Pol.).		8,000 "
	Total,		475,000 "

XI. Corps, Augereau.	Div. 30 Heudelet.	
In reserve.	" 31 Lagrange.	
	" 32 Durutte.	
	" 33 Destrées.	
Cavalry Cavaignac.	" 34 Morand.	47,000 "

The divisions of Durutte, 16,000, and Loison 13,000, plus 65,000 unattached men, joined the Grand Army as reinforcements during the campaign.

On August 1, from the notebook of the emperor, there appear to have been, as aides of the Chief of Staff, 1 gen'l, 1 adjt com^t, 2 cols, 3 majs, 6 capts, 2 war coms, and several other officers. In the General Staff were also 3 gen's of division, 19 gen's of brigade, 15 adjts com^t, 1 col, 21 majs, 30 capts, 14 geog. eng's, 3 offs. of gendarmes. Commanding towns within the domain and on the communications of the army, were 17 gens and 4 lesser officers. At headquarters, 9 admin. off's. The General Administration had 9 aides, 23 war com's and 9 assts, 3 review inspectors. The Hospital Service had 47 assts and 5 com's. The General Staff of the artillery had 13 aides, from gen's to capt's, 18 officers with the great park, 13 with the bridge equipage, and 10 with the siege equipage. The General Staff of engineers had 10 officers from col's down, and 4 in charge of the engineering park.

In the 1st Corps, Davout had 50 officers, from gen's to com's of war, attached to his staff. The other corps was similarly equipped. In the divisions, Morand, *e. g.*, had in his several brigades 16 staff officers. This average held good generally.

On June 25, Davout was equipped with guns and ammunition, as follows: —

	In Divs.	In Res.		In Divs.	In Res.	In Park.
12 pdr. guns.		12	caissons		54	18
6 " "	50		and other	75		38
3 " "	64		wagons.	95		8
6 in. mortars.		4			12	8

	In Divs.	In Res.		In Divs.	In Res.	In Park.
5 in. mortars.	20			40		40
			Inf. caissons.	147		40
12 pdr. ball cartridges.					2,400	1,000
6 " " "				9,000		4,400
3 " " "				20,000		1,800
6-in. mortar "					600	4,000
5 " " "				2,400		2,200
Sundry "				5,000	500	1,300
Infantry "				5,500,000		750,000

The other corps were similarly equipped.

There followed the Grand Army twelve hundred guns (two hundred came up later), three thousand caissons and artillery wagons, six pontoon-equipages, and four thousand commissary wagons, outside the regimental supply. All told, twenty thousand vehicles formed part of the army.

According to the morning reports on file in the War Ministry, the numbers on the dates given were about as below: —

June	25	Davout	70,000 men	11,000 horses	150 guns.
June	1	Oudinot	40,000 "	10,000 "	104 "
July	1	Ney	34,000 "	7,000 "	72 "
July	1	Eugene	46,000 "	10,000 "	116 "
July	16	Poniatowski	33,000 "	9,000 "	48 "
June	30	St. Cyr	23,500 "	4,000 "	58 "
June	30	Reynier	19,500 "	7,000 "	50 "
June	25	Vandamme	17,000 "	2,500 "	34 "
August	30	Victor	25,000 "	4,000 "	42 "
July	1	Macdonald	28,000 "	4,500 "	74 "
July	4	Schwartzenberg	35,000 "	13,000 "	
July		Murat	34,000 "	34,000 "	
July	31	Guard			78 "

Any one familiar with morning reports knows how infinitely varied is their manner of making. The difference between present for duty and aggregate is a great percentage, and between them is room for much honest variation.

Chambray gives the total who crossed the frontiers of Russia as five hundred and thirty-three thousand infantry, ninety-six thousand cavalry, and twelve hundred and forty-two guns. There were one hundred and eighty thousand horses. Even some of the figures from the French archives are not considered accurate. "Situations" are often carelessly made. But the numbers given will serve.

Transportation was organized on the largest scale, and artisans of all kinds accompanied the army. On December 31, 1811, Napoleon wrote Maret: "I should not be disinclined to organize a battalion of military transportation like those in France. Could one get, in Warsaw, horses, harness and wagons? In how many months could these wagons be made? Would the Grand Duchy furnish the men? How much would it cost? This would have to be done under the color of the Grand Duchy, so as to save appearances." Bignon was also ordered to find out all about army subsistence, and to see what could be done to organize a transport service from Thorn, Plotsk, Warsaw and Zamosc on various points. Davout was ordered to arrange with Poniatowski to organize military transports such as was done in the Friedland campaign: "I suppose that wheat and oats will be in abundance this year," said the emperor. Nothing was neglected, and indeed had Napoleon not forgotten his first Russian campaign, and the fact that there are no roads worthy the name in Russia, he would have better succeeded in his victualing. No known source, and no known manner in which breadstuffs, wine and brandy could be gathered, was left untried: contributions came from everywhere. But with the marching columns were later too many wagons, and far too many servants. This was in part necessary in that food was not easy to procure, and officers were allowed a carriage apiece to carry rations. More women were permitted in camp than should have been. The general staff was so enormous that Napoleon in person moved with a smaller body he called " Little Headquarters " — the entire headquarters equaling a division. At the very outset it seemed as if the impedimenta would destroy the expedition. Still, had Napoleon been able to bring on a battle near the frontier, or had he kept within his first plan and not gone beyond Smolensk in 1812, there would have been no failure in the sense of what actually did happen.

In the Grand Army the battalions were supposed to have an average of eight hundred men, but by irregularity in furnishing troops, and later the attrition of service, this number fast dwindled. In the cavalry arm more than half the men were French, in the artillery nearly three fourths were so; but of the whole infantry more than half were non-French. Of this enormous number of foreigners, about a fifth were Italians, and the others were half Germans, half Poles ; and there were Swiss, Spanish, Portuguese, Croat and Illyrian battalions. The contingents of Prussia and Austria operated by themselves, on either wing. It would seem as if so heterogeneous a mass could not be held together, but soldiers are soldiers, and discipline is discipline, and once launched on a campaign, the men in the ranks will, under good leadership, go ahead, whatever their nationality. The French element was enough to leaven the lump, and though there had been trouble for years with " refractories," for absconding conscripts had been hunted down all over France, there was none with the bulk of the army during the campaign. Macdonald wrote Maret that his third battalion men fought as well as the others. No part of the Russian failure can be traced to the unwillingness of the men to do their duty, although this was not quite true of some of the marshals and higher officers, nearly all of whom were weary of war and anxious for rest.

In addition to his personal surroundings and numberless

minor aides and officials, Napoleon had among his executives :
Berthier, Chief of Staff; Generals Lebrun, Mouton, Duros-
nel, Hogendorp, Rapp, aides-de-camp; Dumas, Intendant
(quartermaster and commissary) General; Lariboissière, commanding artillery; Chasseloup, engineers; Eblé, pontoons;
Sanson, topographical engineers; Degenettes, chief of med-
ical service; Daru, Secretary of State; Maret, Minister of
Foreign Relations; Caulaincourt, Grand Equerry and commander of great headquarters; Duroc, Grand Marshal; Méne-
val and Fain, private secretaries; Jomini, historiographer.

Of the commanders of the several corps, Davout and Ney
were those who had done the most important work in past
campaigns. Massena had retired from failure in Spain with
broken health; Soult was still there. Oudinot, Bessières, St.
Cyr, Victor, Junot, were each in his sphere excellent. Macdonald and Reynier were too far off to control easily. Vandamme, much to the regret of the Wurtembergers, was sent
home for an alleged absence without leave. Berthier still
remained the efficient mouthpiece of the emperor. Eugene
and Jerome were in command because of their relationship,
but Eugene was an able leader.

Logistics to-day is simplified by railroad transportation, and
communication by telegraph; and in gauging all Napoleon's
campaigns, we must never forget that every ounce of food,
equipment and munition had to be moved over execrable roads
on wheels, on sumpter animals, or by the men themselves; and
that every order or report had to be carried on horseback.

On February 9 Davout was ordered into marching shape :

" All that is to be very secret. Your movement depends on the day when
that of the Observation Corps of Italy shall be unmasked. It is necessary
that you should be on the Vistula before the thaw, and before the couriers
who shall announce that the Corps of Italy has unmasked its movement
shall have arrived in St. Petersburg. . . . Issue all orders which demand

no confidence, but confide to no one that you are about to march. On the contrary, spread the rumor that everything is being adjusted."

On March 10 the emperor wrote Berthier : "Communciate my annoyance to Junot that he should have reached Munich before his troops, and that thus he unmasked my movement two days too soon. The result of which was that the Russian courier, who would not have left until March 2, did leave February 29. I desire that he shall not go to Dresden, and that he shall remain constantly with his troops, marching with the first division."

On March 16 there were issued to Berthier orders about Davout's movements, so that on April 10 or 12 headquarters should be in Thorn. "Let me know if you have a cipher with Davout. If you have none, establish one with him, and with all the army corps, because it is my intention to have orders in cipher reach them for the most important movements."

During the early months of 1812 this gigantic force had been advancing towards the Vistula, and Napoleon never ceased accumulating food, which he recognized would be the chief difficulty.

He wrote Davout May 26 : "I cannot too much recommend you to take the most efficacious measures to keep with you the least baggage possible, and that all the clothes, shoes and saddles that the corps have with them should be sent to Marienburg and Danzig, so that all the caissons may be employed and charged with flour, bread, rice, vegetables and brandy, beyond what is necessary for the ambulances. The result of all my movements will reunite four hundred thousand men on a single point. There will then be nothing to hope for from the country, and you must have everything with you. The baggage left behind can rejoin after the first expedition." And to Eugene : "The whole army will end by being concentrated on one same field ; each corps, crowded elbow to elbow upon the other, will soon have exhausted the supplies of the country."

Sufficient victual was got together ; but the difficulties of distribution were not overcome. There was no precedent ; what apparently should succeed did not ; and failure was the result.

Bavaria fed Eugene's troops moving from Italy to join the Grand Army, and cleared the snow from the Alpine roads.

Saxony suffered less and gained more than any other vassal state. Being isolated, Austria did not suffer; Bavaria, Baden and Wurtemberg bore their burden with questionable patience; Prussia, nominally independent, was ground down by the moving army; everything was seized, from the peasant's wagons and horses to his very food; her strong places were occupied, and in every fashion she suffered more than any country. Napoleon's purpose to control the whole theatre of operations is shown in his issuing a decree by which " every insult made to my soldiers in the territory of the Grand Army is made subject to the judgment of the French military commission." The word "insult" covered a multitude of sins.

As, in the Jena. campaign, Napoleon had not started with a sufficient pontoon-train, so now he was doubly careful. On May 26, 1812, he wrote Davout: " Everything is subordinate to the arrival of the bridge equipage, for my whole plan of campaign is founded on the existence of this equipage, well harnessed and as mobile as a gun."

There had been constant communication between czar and emperor. Alexander was neutral, resolved solely on defense; Napoleon wished to bring the matter to a head. Alexander listened, but said little. In April he sent a note suggesting that if all French troops were withdrawn from Prussia, so as to leave a neutral zone between them, he would do what was reasonable in commercial matters; to which Napoleon made no reply. The Grand Army kept on moving through Germany, and before the grass was grown enough to forage the horses, was most of it near the Russian border.

Although negative in utterance, Alexander had been active in preparing resistance. Like every other country, Russia had its parties. The war party was for getting Austria and Prussia as allies, and for promising Poland national freedom, with the czar as king, if she would join Russia; another party, led by

Chancellor Rumantzov, desired to keep up the French alliance
and the *status quo ;* the peace party, still aiming to get Con-
stantinople, desired any reasonable means of staving off the
war, delayed preparations, and made Austria and Prussia
suspicious of Russia's constancy.

Napoleon had not gauged Alexander's character with accuracy; naturally amiable and yielding, with his mind once
made up he was immovable, and it is not impossible that the
Prussian Stein, who, fallen under Napoleon's displeasure, had
been expatriated and was now at the Russian Court as a sort
of unofficial adviser of the czar, may have fostered this per-
sistence. Alexander kept abreast of Napoleon's movements,
and had the intelligence to understand that if he met a
French advance by constant retreat, it was beyond the
power of any European army to force him to anything: if
Charles XII. had been conquered by the vast territory of
Russia, Napoleon could be met in the same way. That such
would be the method was assumed by many all over Europe.
Alexander had said that he would retire into Siberia before
yielding, and we know that he was ready to abandon St. Petersburg, as he did abandon the more sacred Moscow. Still,
this was only a policy, not a plan; the Russian generals
expected to fight; and as it happened, the unpreparedness of
the Russian armies at the beginning brought about a defensive campaign. It has been said that Wellington's resistance
to the French hosts by erecting the lines of Torres Vedras
had led Alexander to this policy, but the conditions obtaining
in the two countries are so essentially different that the czar
must have seen the fallacy of comparing them. The lines
may, however, have suggested the Drissa camp.

On March 25 Napoleon wrote to Berthier: "The language
of Davout is then to be very pacific; he is to avoid every reconnoissance or military movement beyond the Vistula. None

of his patrols, even, must go as far as Osterode." And on April 25 Davout was notified that the czar had made fresh propositions, and that if the Russians made no other move‑ ment than to occupy the right bank of the Memel (Niemen), he was not to consider hostilities as commenced.

On May 31 Napoleon was at Posen. By long marches the troops had reached the Vistula; Davout was at Elbing and Marienburg, with Macdonald and the Prussians out at Königsberg; Oudinot at Marienwerder ; Ney at Thorn ; St. Cyr and Eugene at Plotsk ; Poniatowski at Warsaw; Van‑ damme at Gora Kalvaria ; Reynier opposite Novo‑Alexandria ; and Schwartzenberg at Lemberg. This front of four hun‑ dred miles was designed to keep the Russians uncertain whether the main advance would be from Elbing against Kovno, or from Warsaw against Grodno, or from the Lublin country against the line of the Bug, and thus tend to separate their armies. The purpose succeeded.

The numbers of the Russian forces are hard to determine. Clausewitz estimates the total at six hundred thousand, of which not much over two thirds were effective; and there were only under the colors : —

First Army in Lithuania	90,000	men.
Second Army to the south of it	50,000	"
Third Army in Volhynia	30,000	"
Cossacks	10,000	"
Total in first line	180,000	"
Reserves	80,000	"
Finland Army	20,000	"
Moldavia Army	60,000	"
In garrison and detached	80,000	"

According to Buturlin, whose account is official, but not necessarily accurate, —

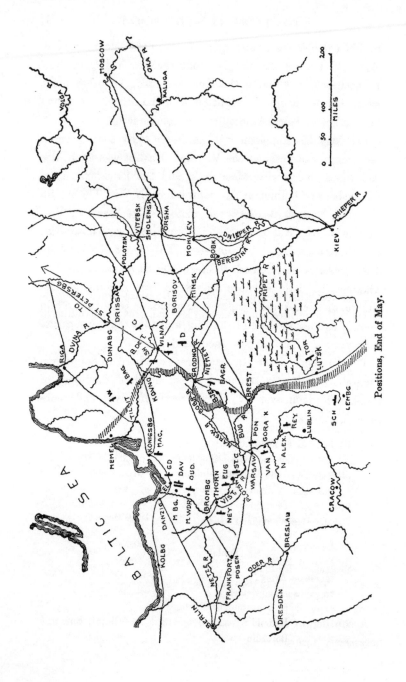

Positions, End of May.

Barclay's paper strength was	111,000 foot.
	20,000 horse.
	13,000 artillery.
	9,000 Cossacks.
The effective was	127,000 men.
Bagration's paper strength was	43,000 foot.
	7,500 horse.
	4,000 artillery.
	4,500 Cossacks.
The effective was	48,000 men.
Tormasov's effective was	43,000 men.
Of which more cavalry.	
Reserves on Dvina and Dnieper	30,000 men.

Thus less than a quarter million Russians were ready to meet half a million invaders under the greatest captain of modern times.

In organization and numbers, the principal Russian armies were approximately as follows: —

First Army, under Barclay de Tolly, consisting of

1st Corps. Wittgenstein	23,000 men.
2d " Baggavut	16,500 "
3d " Tuchkov	18,600 "
4th " Shuvalov and Ostermann	13,500 "
5th " Grand Duke Constantine	20,000 "
(Reserve of Guard)	
6th " Doctorov	17,000 "
Cavalry Reserve under Ouvarov	3,000 "
Korv	4,000 "
Pahlen	3,000 "
Cossacks under Platov	7,000 "

Total about 130,000 effective, with 600 guns.

Second Army, under Bagration, consisting of

| 7th Corps. Raevski | 16,500 men. |
| 8th " Borozdin | 15,000 " |

Reserve	12,000 men.
Cavalry Reserve under Sievers	3,500 "
And Cossack corps	4,000 "
Total about 50,000 effective.	

Third Army, under Tormasov, consisting of

Corps of Kamenski	10,000 men.
" Sacken	6,000 "
" Markov	12,000 "
Cavalry Reserve of Lambert	8,000 "
And Cossacks	4,000 "
Total about 40,000 effective.	

Back of these were thirty thousand reserves, some coming up. The excess of cavalry indicated by Buturlin was serving with the several corps.

The Army of Moldavia and the Finland Corps were shortly to be released from their duty and added to the active forces facing the Grand Army. As Alexander knew all about the French preparations from illicit information obtained in Paris, the troops he put into fighting line seem inadequate.

Barclay de Tolly was a staunch if not a great soldier. Eugene of Wurtemberg says : " He was a man whose efforts had constantly as object to remain faithful to duty. His cold and calm nature created for him few friends among the Russians. With regard to his high military capacity the opinions were much divided, but what his adversaries could not deny to him, without injustice, was his coolness and prudence in danger, his irrepressible perseverance, the exemplary order which he had maintained, as well among authorities called to conduct affairs, as in every part of his troops." Bagration was a fighter, like Ney. Tormasov and Chichagov were good leaders, and Kutusov we remember in Austerlitz days ; but none was able to cope with Napoleon. The Russian chiefs had unlimited power, with right of life and death over their troops, and the inhabitants of the countries occupied. Clausewitz was of small rank, and both he and Gneisenau were ignorant of Russian, and apart from jealousy, unsuited for command. There seemed to have been no specific plan of campaign : Alexander had decided to play a waiting game.

The Russian troops were raised by requiring from each land-owner a certain number of serfs. These princes would be apt to send the least useful men, and Russian intelligence

Barclay de Tolly.

was low. Rudely born and nurtured, inured to a hard climate, healthy as a rule, they were able to bear hardships on short rations as no soldier of middle Europe could do. Frederick's campaigns had shown of what the Russian foot was capable. Enlisted for twenty-five years, his relatives and early life were forgotten, and his regiment became his home. Severe disci-

pline, and the habit of implicit obedience impressed on the
serf, gave him a constancy unknown in other armies; his flag
was his one thought, desertion was unknown, and in times of
extreme danger he would instinctively seek safety near the
regimental standard, having learned in battles with the Turks
that every one who skulked or fled was liable to be cut down
by hordes of cavalry. Transported to other lands he was the
equal of any soldier; on his own territory he was, in a fashion,
incomparable. So far as the Cossacks went, the hard little
runt of the steppes was well ahead of any horse of middle
Europe for the purposes of a Russian campaign; the coarse
forage on which a civilized horse would perish was their daily
food. The Cossacks were to surprise at night the quarters of
the enemy, pillage the convoys, stop the couriers, and do all
the harm possible, but so soon as they met large forces, they
were to fall in on the army and menace the enemy's flanks
and rear. On July 5 an order by Reynier instructs the soldiers " that the . . . Cossacks are dangerous only when they
fall on troops who are dispersed without reserve. One should
always, therefore, march in the greatest order and ready for
any attack." The Russian heavy cavalry horses were accli-
mated, and better fed than the French.

Roughly speaking, the Russian frontiers ran from the
Baltic, north of the Prussian fortress of Memel, to the Memel
(Niemen) River half-way to Kovno, up river to Grodno, down
the Bobr and up the Narew west of Bielostok to the Bug, and
up this river to Brest Litovsk and beyond, and thence along
the border of Galicia. That portion of the Niemen from
Grodno to the sea was the scene of the most important early
part of this campaign. Its channel is sunk, and there are not
many places where it can be crossed, even with pontoons.
There were bridges at Tilsit and at Grodno; at Kovno only
a ferry; between Grodno and Kovno not even this. The

river was navigable some distance above Grodno. As he had the initiative, and occupied the fortress of Memel, Napoleon was able to use the Niemen for transporting supplies. From Lomberg, where Schwartzenberg lay with his Austrians, to the fortress of Memel, the irregular frontier was about five hundred miles long.

East of the Russian frontier were the old provinces which, in the partition of Poland, had fallen to Russia. Lithuania had a small and poor population, and was full of woods and marshes; the roads were few and wretched, and the soil such that wagons or troops could not move across the country. The Bielostok country was better, but south of the Brest Litovsk-Bobruisk line, marshes made campaigning impossible.

Poland had been so vast that until you reach the Dvina and the Dneiper, you are not in a country quite Russian. Taking the Niemen as the first line, these two rivers form a second line of defense to Russia proper. The Dvina from Vitebsk runs northwest to Riga, and its only bridges were at Vitebsk and Dünaburg. Between Vitebsk and Orsha the Dvina and Dnieper are but fifty miles apart, and through this opening lies the easiest road to the heart of Russia, Smolensk being the first great city in the gap; and here everything is Russian. The Dnieper is navigable far above Smolensk, and the bridges here and at Mohilev were most important. Like a great ditch, the Beresina, with bridges at Borisov and Bobruisk, closes the gap between the Dvina and Dnieper, but in summer time this river is fordable in places.

Thus, for the main part of the Grand Army, there were but three roads leading across the Russian frontier, at Kovno, Grodno and Brest Litovsk. These cities being a hundred miles apart shows the vast extent of the theatre of war.

In his defensive scheme Alexander had begun to fortify Riga, Dünaburg, Bobruisk and Kiev, and had built a bridge-

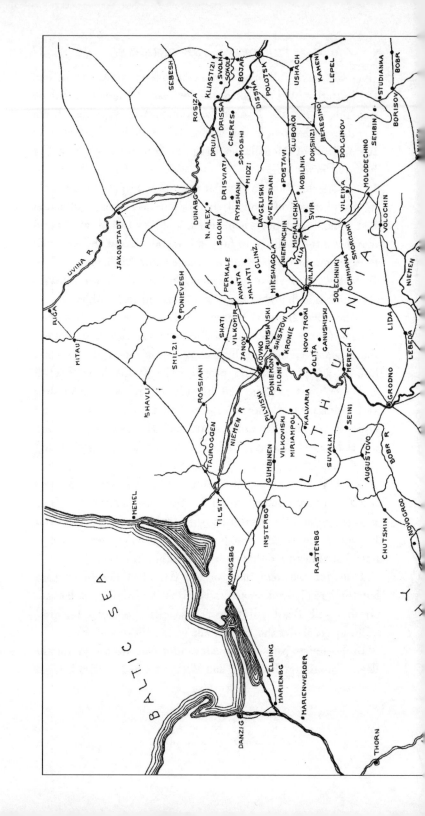

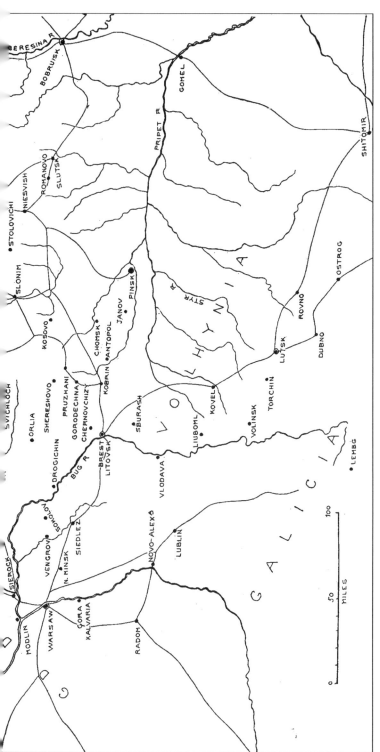

Western Russia

head at Borisov; but most of this work was only half done. At Drissa was a huge intrenched camp, but being on no highway and liable to be turned, it lacked strategic value. The enormous frontier to be covered could not be defended cordon-fashion; nor is it necessary to stand across a road to hold it, for a position enabling the defender to fall upon the flank of an advancing army is the safest defense of any great route.

From a military point of view, the retiring scheme of the Russians against a stronger and more able foe was the best, for the farther this foe advanced, the weaker he would become, from length of communications and difficulty of transportation, while the Russians were gaining strength with every day's retreat upon their reserves. But the czar had to look at some political questions. If a system of retreat was adopted, the Polish provinces would fall away from their allegiance, and the opposition of the anti-war party might be grave, as well as the effect upon friendly nations. A defensive position on the Dvina might do, although the camp at Drissa was ill-placed; but for political reasons the czar established his first depot as far forward as Vilna, and this brought initial disaster. As 1812 opened, the Russian troops were spread all over the five hundred miles from the Baltic to Volhynia; but when in May the French approached the Vistula, the troops drew together into two large bodies, under Barclay and Bagration, with headquarters at Vilna and Lutsk. These two groups were separated by the morasses of the upper Pripet, and their distance from each other was due to the broad front of Napoleon's advance. When it became apparent that Napoleon was to manœuvre on the Niemen, and the czar secretly learned that the Austrians were half-hearted, he strengthened Barclay's army from Bagration's; and as the campaign opened, the former with a hundred and thirty thousand men was near Vilna, with his right at Shavli and his left at Lida; Bagration with fifty thousand men had come up to Volkovisk; and Tormasov with over forty thousand men, not yet fully organized, took his place at Lutsk.

Barclay had the corps of Tuchkov and Shuvalov in front of Vilna, and Baggavut's corps on the Niemen below Kovno; Constantine was in reserve at Sventsiani, and Doctorov at Lida kept touch with Bagration; the cavalry was partly with Baggavut, partly in rear of the left; Wittgenstein was beyond Rossiani as a flying right wing. The Cossacks were advanced towards Grodno, as if to threaten the French advance in flank, but they were unequal to the task. In battle worthless, they later, as light troops, proved invaluable. Bagration lay between Grodno and Brest Litovsk. The First and Second Armies thus stood astride the three roads to St. Petersburg and Moscow.

Napoleon had no preconceived ideas of a plan of campaign, but he was certain that no army the Russians had raised could resist him in battle. Metternich states that the emperor told him in Dresden that in his first campaign he should overrun all of old Poland and not go beyond Smolensk; and in his proclamation Napoleon says nothing to his troops of cities to conquer and sack, as he might have done. He proposed to besiege Riga and Dünaburg, so as to control navigation up to Vilna; but as he could scarcely suppose that the Russians would meet him on the Vistula with a divided army, had he made a plan, he must have changed it. He was conducting what is now called a "war of armies" on an unknown terrain.

Nor was the case different in the enemy's camp: each Russian commander had an idea of his own. On peace being concluded with Turkey, Chichagov wanted to march from Moldavia up the Danube through Illyria into Italy; Bagration, while holding the Niemen, desired to invade the Grand Duchy

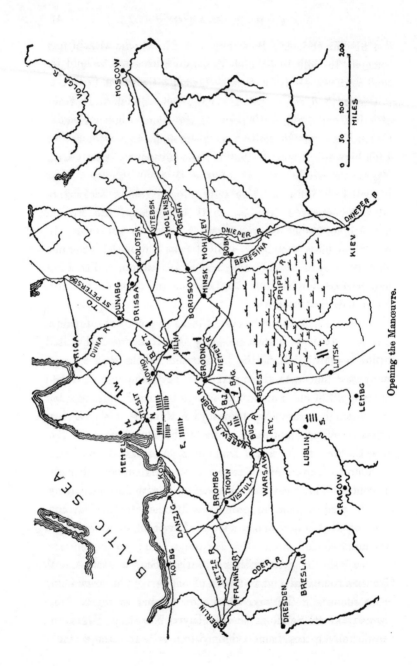

Opening the Manoeuvre.

of Warsaw; Barclay was for awaiting the French oncoming on
Russian soil, and then fighting; Phull's idea was to hold in
force the camp at Drissa, so as to debouch therefrom upon the
flanks of the French should they advance beyond it. Kneso
beck advised ravaging the country, constantly fighting small
affairs but refusing battles, and drawing Napoleon so far
from his base as to be in danger. Gneisenau believed in
many fortifications for stopping and annoying an enemy
flushed with victory. Alexander was proposing to play a
game of retreat.

The information Napoleon had secured about the Russian
armies was necessarily more limited than that of the Russians
about him. He knew Barclay's general location, and that he
had been reinforced from Bagration's army; but he did not
know that Tormasov was replacing Bagration: he imagined
the latter still on the march to join Barclay by way of Brest
Litovsk. It was on this assumed state of facts that he
formed a plan for breaking in between Barclay and Bagration, by an advance through Kovno on Vilna. He had at
first supposed that this would turn the Russian right flank;
but although later news proved the Russian army too far
north, on either supposition he was manœuvring strategically
so as to turn the enemy's flank, as at Marengo, Ulm, Jena,
Friedland, or, as at Montenotte or Burgos, to break through
his centre, in each case with his mass. The main blow would
be delivered by him in person, with the Guard, Davout,
Oudinot, Ney, and Nansouty's and Montbrun's cavalry, say
two hundred and twenty-five thousand men; and in connection with this Eugene, with his own and St. Cyr's corps and
Grouchy's cavalry, eighty thousand effective, was drawn on
to Rastenburg, to advance thence on a more southerly line,
via Suvalki on Seini, as an echelon on Napoleon's right, to
contain any forces from Grodno, and to tear asunder still

farther the gap rent in the Russian line by Napoleon. Still another echelon was to consist of Jerome's army at Warsaw and on the Narew, to which belonged Poniatowski, Reynier, Vandamme and Latour-Maubourg, eighty thousand men. Reynier's task was to keep up a touch with the Austrians. Jerome's rôle was to feint on Lublin, to join Schwartzenberg, and thus draw attention from the French left, which was to deliver the main blow. As Napoleon wrote him, June 5, from Thorn: "In this trade and on so great a theatre one succeeds only on a well-established plan and with elements fully in accord. You must therefore study your orders well, and do here neither more nor less than you are told, especially in what is combined movement." But as conditions altered, Jerome's task was shortly changed to a pursuit of Bagration. The extreme right and left of the French army were protected by Macdonald and the Prussians at Rossiani, and by Schwartzenberg, who from Lemberg had come north to Lublin. Napoleon described the operation in a note of June 10 to Eugene: "The march of the army is a movement that I am making by my left, in constantly refusing my right."

The Russians, Napoleon thought, might themselves advance on Ostrolenka or Sierock, or indeed on Warsaw, in which case Jerome would stand on the defensive on the Narew or Vistula, to protect Eugene's communications on Thorn; and the latter would wheel to the right and take the advancing Russians in flank, and Napoleon from Vilna fall upon their rear.

In order to explain the business to Jerome, whose ability he had every reason to doubt, the emperor wrote him on June 5 : —

"I think I have made you understand what you had best do at the opening of the campaign. First, make believe that you are going to enter Volhynia, and hold the enemy the most possible on this idea, while, turning his extreme right, I shall have gained on him twelve or fifteen marches in the direction of Petersburg. I will be on his right wing. I will cross the Niemen and will seize Vilna, which is the first objective of the campaign. . . . . When this operation is unmasked, the enemy will take one of the two following steps: he will rally in the interior of his state so as to find himself in force to deliver battle, or he will himself take the offensive. Thus, while the extremity of the right would be turned, he might march on Warsaw." And again he sent a dispatch on June 11, 1812, to Berthier, to write to Jerome that "he is always to hold to his line of operation on Modlin, keep constantly assembled, and correspond with the viceroy, so that the latter may fall on the right flank of the enemy. That this movement of attack by the enemy, which is quite natural and which has been foreseen from the beginning, can have no influence on my offensive operations; that the important thing is that the right shall not commit itself against superior forces, and shall manœuvre assembled from position to position ; that if the greatest part of the Russian army were present in this flank attack, nothing could ever happen to the right, which would always have for refuge the intrenched camp of Modlin and the left bank of the Vistula. But that just as soon as such a movement of the Russians shall be decided, I will fall with all my army on their right flank and on their rear. That it is very difficult that the enemy should expose himself thus to an entire loss; yet if he should do it, the march already traced must make the king understand what he has to do."

On the same day, writing Eugene, he tells him that Jerome might retire into the intrenched camp of Modlin, but that Eugene's line of operation being on Thorn, he would have nothing to fear from this state of things.

In thus holding back his right, the emperor had the additional idea of preventing Bagration from retiring too soon, which would make it easier for the French left to cut him off from Barclay. If, however, when left behind, Bagration threatened Napoleon's flank, Eugene and Jerome would be ready to fend him off. As a fact, the Russians never definitely intended to strike Napoleon's flank as he advanced on Vilna ; Bagration was under orders to move in retreat, and

Platov's Cossacks were ordered back via Lida and Smorgoni. None the less, the precaution was a proper one.

This strategic plan, one of Napoleon's best conceptions, was to be a refusal of the right in echelon, while the left in mass should break through the enemy's centre, thrust aside the right, and move promptly on the communications of the left and centre. Ségur calls it a strategic manœuvre similar to what Leuthen was as a tactical manœuvre, conducted over a front of two hundred miles and a number of days, instead of six miles and a couple of hours; but the two plans, each perfect of its kind in conception, one strategical, the other tactical, can hardly be made the subject of comparison.

From the Vistula, during the first half of June, the French left wing corps thus advanced towards the Niemen, and Eugene through East Prussia. Napoleon spent much time in inspecting and encouraging the troops, reviewing them at Königsberg, Insterburg and Gumbinen. On June 22 headquarters was at Vilkoviski. Here he issued a

PROCLAMATION TO THE GRAND ARMY.

Soldiers! The second war of Poland has begun. The first was finished at Friedland and Tilsit. At Tilsit Russia swore eternal alliance to France and war to England. To-day she violates her oaths. She will give no explanation of her strange conduct until the French eagles have recrossed the Rhine, thus leaving our allies to her discretion. Russia is drawn away by fatality; her destiny is about to be accomplished. Does she believe us degenerate? Are we no longer the soldiers of Austerlitz? She places us between dishonor and war. The choice cannot be doubtful. Let us then march forward. Let us cross the Niemen and carry the war on her territory. The second war of Poland will be glorious for French arms, like the first, but the peace that we shall conclude will carry with it its guaranty, and will put a term to the fatal influence which Russia has exercised for fifty years on the affairs of Europe.

This proclamation, cast in the same mould, has scarcely the true ring of those of former days. Its claims are not as exact, it lacks the blare of the trumpet. Yet it had its effect on the French troops.

From Vilkoviski, on June 23, at 2 A. M., the emperor rode out towards the Niemen at Kovno for a reconnoissance, accompanied only by Engineer General Haxo, and at daylight determined that the best place to cross was at Poniemon, just above Kovno, at a large bend in the river. He had not ascertained that only pickets held the further bank, and retiring to his bivouac, he issued unnecessarily detailed orders for the passage.

Haxo.

Count Soltyk gives us a pleasant picture of the emperor here. Some Polish lancers were in bivouac near the river. The emperor drove thither, and borrowing from its owner the Polish uniform which apparently fitted him the best, changed his suit in the road, and then rode forward to the river, where he used his glass for some time and made inquiries as to the lay of the land. When he came back to the bivouac, some refreshment was brought him, of which, in merry mood, he partook in the middle of the road, and asked the surrounding officers whether the Polish uniform suited him. After eating, he resumed his own suit and rode farther down the river.

The several corps now stood: the Guard at and in the vicinity of headquarters; Davout in front of the forest of Pilvishki, with Oudinot in his rear; Ney in front of Mariampol;

Murat with Nansouty and Montbrun within sight of Kovno, and Grouchy at Piloni; Eugene within a march of Kalvaria, St. Cyr not far behind. Thus the left wing was well massed and covered by Murat's cavalry, while Macdonald and the Prussians formed a flying left wing at Tilsit. On the French right, Jerome and Poniatowski were in Chutshin, Vandamme at Novgorod, Latour-Maubourg out in front at Augustovo; Reynier was near Novo-Minsk, and Schwartzenberg south of Siedlez. The enormous front was measurably reduced, and the right wing could coöperate to a certain extent with the left. Late on the 23d, the bridges at Poniemon were begun by Eblé under Napoleon's eye; by midnight two were completed, and Davout began the crossing. Later, a third one was thrown, a fourth at the ferry, and a fifth at the mouth of the Vilia. By noon of June 24 Napoleon took up headquarters in Kovno. Since the days of Peter the Great, no enemy had trodden the soil of Russia proper; and here was the hugest force of modern days, assembled from Germany, France, Italy, Spain, deluging its territory, under command of the leader who had destroyed the armies of all the other Continental powers. How would Russia meet it?

From Kovno Napoleon sent out reconnoissances in every direction, accompanied by geographical engineers, who were to remit, twice a day, sketches of the country. Each party, on June 24, was given sharp instructions: —

" It is necessary also that Murat shall be certain that his light cavalry has beaten the whole country between the Vilia and the Niemen, and that it shall be assured : first, that the enemy has no bridge on the Vilia, and second, that there is there neither infantry nor post. I desire that the geographical engineer attached to the king shall not lose a moment in sending you a sketch of the whole course of the Vilia, and of that of the Niemen to the confluence."

Napoleon found that his Russian map, however useful,

did not give the small details of cross-roads, villages, forests, streams, etc., so necessary for the movement of troops. Yet while vigorously reconnoitring, the emperor was prudent. To Berthier, June 25, he gave instructions to write to Murat: —

" Before making a step in advance, the chess-board must be better cleared up. It is especially very necessary to be entirely master of the left bank of the Vilia. The viceroy cannot be up in line for two days. There can be no question of an immediate march on Vilna. To direct so great a movement the emperor will go there personally. Moreover, our left flank must be perfectly secure." " Write to Ney to reconnoitre seriously Janov, to send there a good column of infantry and cavalry, and if it is necessary, to sustain this column with his whole army corps ; to know everything that is taking place there . . . and to fully assure himself that the enemy has no bridge nor any posts on the left bank of the Vilia. That I much want a positive report thereon." And to Davout, June 26, he wrote : "Assemble your troops and take some rest. Reconnoitre a good position in case the enemy marches on you. . . . Call in all your detachments so as to assemble your army. You must be on guard against an operation coming from Vilkomir. In any case, I am sending Ney to Skomli and Oudinot to Janov. The result of this operation will commence to clear up our position, and let us well understand the chess-board."

The question of victual had already become difficult; large supplies were coming by water to Königsberg, whence they were to be wagoned forward to the marching armies; the shipping up the Niemen and Vilia was not yet organized ; but Napoleon was unaccustomed to wait, and was used to campaigning where some kind of food could always be got. He had ordered the several corps to collect two weeks' rations as they marched through old Prussia, and the doing of this caused vast suffering to the land. Every team that could be seized on the farms that they passed was taken along behind the army; thousands of peasants were compelled to drive them; but the main part of the victual, following the army in endless trains, could not be got along fast enough, proved to be of no avail, and mostly fell a prey to the train-men.

The evil was a crying one, and the emperor, on June 4, instructed Berthier to write Davout that—

" when you ordered him to procure twenty days' victual, you meant that that was to be done regularly, and without foraging the country; that terror and desolation are in Poland from the conduct of the Wurtem-bergers. . . . He is to take the most prompt measures not to devastate the country, else we shall find ourselves as we were in Portugal." And on June 22, at Vilkoviski, an order was issued "to keep the army in the greatest order and to prevent the disorders which commence to desolate the country."

Each army corps was to have a provost-commission of five officers to try every straggler, every marauder, every pillager, and every one who molested the inhabitants of the country, all of whom were to be executed in twenty-four hours. Little patrols were organized to scour the country and pick up stragglers. Similar bodies were created elsewhere.

Napoleon aspired to be looked on as the savior of Lithuania; but by mistaken management, too much freedom was given to the serfs, who rose in many places, elected the richest of their number as chiefs, and became so turbulent that the nobles turned against the French, and increased the difficulty of victualing.

The right wing was now ordered on Grodno. Having been held back to contain Bagration, and if possible keep him from retreat, it was now essential for it to follow, when he should fall back in consequence of Napoleon's proposed manœuvre, and push him back on the left wing, which could then overwhelm him. The emperor was not aware that Bagration had already received orders from the czar to retire. From Königsberg, as early as June 15, he wrote Jerome:—

" As soon as I shall have crossed the Niemen, I shall perhaps resolve to advance on Vilna. I shall then present my flank to the army of Bagration. It will then be essential that you should follow him up closely so that you may take part in the operation I shall make against that army. If I should succeed in separating it from other Russian troops, so as to fall on its right flank, you should be able to attack it at the same time that I do." And on June 21 he wrote: "You are to lean on the centre. In case the enemy turned your right, your line of operations would be on Königsberg. Try to have the Poles reach Augustovo the 23d, and send a vanguard on Grodno with a lot of light troops. Send forward your bridge in that direction. It is probable that I shall give you the order to move on Grodno with all your army. . . . You will be in continuity with the army, so that everything can act together as a mass, and we will then operate against Bagration according to the position he will occupy."

On June 25 and 26 the Niemen crossing was ended. Napoleon and the Guard were in Kovno, Davout in Rumshiski ; Murat out on the Vilna road at Shismori. Oudinot, to reconnoitre the country and form the left, was pushed out across the Vilia towards Janov, near which place he ran across Wittgenstein's rearguard. Although Napoleon was anxious to capture Vilna, for navigation extended up so far, and it was a good point to create a big depot, he was anxious to trace the Russian whereabouts before advancing too fast ; and he wrote Davout, June 26 : " The army is only just concentrated, and one must not march against a yet complete army as one would against a beaten army." The French were still concentrating on the Niemen, and Napoleon abode by his principles of the past sixteen years, and would not advance until he had in hand a sufficient mass. But one thing was notably lacking — his personal supervision ; not only his bodily strength failed to respond to his mental activity, but the territory to be covered was so vast that his staff could not do his work for him, and what he well projected lacked much in the execution.

As Barclay had assembled at Vilna only two corps and the

Guard, his position was critical. If he remained there, he must face superior numbers; if he crossed the Vilia to join his right wing under Baggavut and Wittgenstein, he would be cut off from his left wing under Doctorov at Lida. If he retired on Polotsk, his right wing would be cut off. Thus beset, he determined to destroy his vast Vilna magazines, containing breadstuffs, and especially oats, which would have been treasure-trove to the French, and to retire via Sventsiani on the Drissa camp, and here rally the right and left wing columns on the centre. Orders were issued to this effect; and others were sent Bagration to retire on the Dvina via Vileika or Minsk.

When at Vilna, the czar had issued a proclamation to the army stamped with quiet determination; and in another to the nation he used the words: " I will not lay down my arms so long as one soldier of the enemy remains on the soil of my empire." He also sent one of his aides to Napoleon to say that he would still negotiate, if the French recrossed the Niemen ; but the emperor looked on this as weakness, or a device to gain time, and even failed to treat the officer with diplomatic equipoise.

On June 26 Murat, the Guard and Davout began the march towards Vilna, and on the 28th reached this town, with Napoleon in the van, which marched the sixty miles in three days, meeting only isolated Russian outposts. As flankers, across the Vilia, Ney advanced via Mieshagola, while Oudinot swept farther, via Shati, and, failing to cut them off, drove the rearguard of Baggavut and Wittgenstein out of Vilkomir, after a lively fight; the Russian corps rejoined their chief, and Macdonald from Tilsit was advancing via Tauroggen and Rossiani. By this time, over execrable roads, Eugene got across the Niemen at Piloni, where a pile bridge was being made, Jerome moved under pressing orders towards Grodno, which Latour-Maubourg had already reached, and Poniatowski and Vandamme were at Augustovo in Jerome's left rear. Reynier, whose orders to cover Warsaw until Schwartzenberg took his place had necessarily delayed him, had got to Sambrov, and Schwartzenberg to Siedlez, to close up Jerome's right and rear.

Owing to the difficulties of distance and country, Napoleon's orders were becoming impossible of execution. On June 20 Berthier wrote Jerome: " The emperor orders that the 5th Corps shall begin its march the 22d, to be at Augustovo the 25th, and that the 8th shall march the 23d to move on Raygrod, having with them twenty days' rations." The distance was over eighty miles, and the rain had spoiled the roads : Jerome reached Grodno on the 30th. Napoleon's belated orders had left him too long in Warsaw for him to join in the proposed pursuit of Bagration. Perhaps these movements were as rapid as could be expected without the master's eye ; but Napoleon's hope to anticipate the Russian commanders was not fulfilled. Both armies had retired ; for Barclay's orders from the czar were to retreat from the French advance, and Bagration received similar ones when the French crossed at Kovno. This of itself broke up Napoleon's excellent plans. On June 28 Barclay was at Niemenchin, with his right at Perkale and his left at Oshmiana ; and though Bagration was yet at Volkovisk, it looked as if he might escape the trap. Barclay's objective was Sventsiani, and calculating that Bagration could reach this place before the French advanced too far, ignorant indeed that the emperor's object was to cut Bagration off, he sent him word to join the main army at this place. What he ascertained of the Russian movements puzzled Napoleon, but he kept on with his own operation, which he knew was strategically correct, and was confident would succeed.

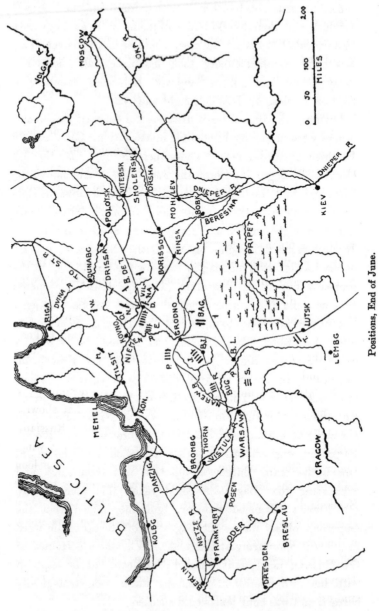

Positions, End of June.

By July 2 Barclay had gathered his army at Sventsiani, without any fighting except Wittgenstein's. Doctorov was farthest off, and had difficulty in rejoining the army. A rear-guard and the Cossacks near Grodno were cut off, and obliged to march south and join Bagration. Barclay reached Drissa July 11. Murat followed along, supported by Ney and Oudinot.

The emperor took up headquarters at Vilna, and there he remained many days, striving to bring order out of chaos, issuing orders to his distant lieutenants on belated information received from them, or on news from the enemy which was more so: he found the direction of operations over so vast a territory different from anything he had yet encountered, and far more uncertain.

On June 29 Napoleon headed Murat, with Friant, Gudin, Nansouty and Montbrun, on Niemenchin; and Davout, with the three divisions left him, on Michalichki and Ochmiana, thus splitting the head of the Grand Army into separate columns so as to reconnoitre a wider space in his front, to keep apart the two Russian armies which he believed he had thrust apart, and to close the road to Smolensk. Had he been able to do the latter, the campaign of 1812 would have terminated in a marked success, for up to this moment Napoleon had shown a much broader view of the strategic situation than the Russians.

Davout soon ran across evidences of Barclay's left wing, under Doctorov, on the way to Ochmiana; this Napoleon took to be the head of Bagration's army marching towards Sventsiani; and on July 1 he instructed Davout, to whom Grouchy was ordered to report, to advance on this body, while Jerome, as he believed, was pushing on its rear, and Schwartzenberg was getting where he could turn its left. Doctorov had already caught the alarm, filed to the right, and escaped by a thirty-mile march, July 1, on Svir. Eugene had got concentrated at Kroni; next day Jerome, with Poniatowski, Vandamme and Latour-Maubourg, had fully reached Grodno, where he found only a Cossack detachment,  which fell back on Lida; Reynier was passing Sokoli, and Schwartzenberg was opposite Drogichin on the Bug. Oudinot was following Wittgenstein. On this day Barclay had reached Sventsiani with the right at Soloki, and the left under Doctorov all but cut off by Davout. The Russian objective was now Drissa, but Bagration, who was at Slonim, was still in danger of being hemmed in between Davout and Jerome, for Barclay's plan to have him join at Sventsiani had been a miscalculation.

Doctorov.

By the evening of July 1 the Guard was still in Vilna, Macdonald had reached Rossiani, Oudinot Vilkomir, and Ney Glinziski; Murat was at Niemenchin, Davout at Ochmiana and Michalichki. From the little information he could gather and the probabilities, Napoleon was convinced that Bagration could still be cut off unless he headed via Minsk towards the Dvina, until, on July 2, the body opposite Davout proved to be Doctorov. This left him in dense ignorance as to Bagration's whereabouts, and he hurried up Eugene towards Vilna, finding fault with his delay, — " notified of the general movement, it is ridiculous that he should have stayed without moving at Piloni," — although the viceroy had been marching over country roads as deep as the worst in Virginia. "It would be difficult," he wrote July 7, "to conceive an idea of the obstacles which this road presented, entirely formed by the trunks of pine-trees placed upon a marshy soil." Corduroy roads were common in Russia, as they are in every new country. The advance had been seriously interfered with by a violent storm on June 29, followed by a five days' rain. Possible bad weather must always be one of the calculations in campaigning; and although this storm did not arrest the troops, it did nearly stop the teaming. The ill-fed horses fell by the thousands, there was no bread, and between starvation and the danger of punishment for pillaging, the soldier did not hesitate. The entire country was ravaged.

Although puzzled by lack of information, Napoleon's effort still was to cut off and destroy Bagration's fifty thousand men, which would leave Barclay at his mercy. But this could be accomplished only by the push of the 1796 Bonaparte. Had his physique been that of his earlier years, he would have ridden to Davout's column — what was forty miles to him? — and ascertained the actual facts; he would have so disposed Jerome's forces, or have had them so commanded, as to hurl them on the rear of Bagration, while Davout cut off his head of column. But the emperor was no longer that Bonaparte. In the midst of his life of hard work, he had found time to indulge his passions, not always in the most creditable way; and now the result of overtaxing his vitality by pleasure, in addition to constant labor, had become apparent in bodily ailments which made him unready to move about, and especially to remain many successive hours in the saddle. His endurance of fatigue and weather had much diminished; the exceptional heat of this July had almost equaled that of Egypt, where many of the rank and file committed suicide — as they began again to do here. Napoleon was no longer the thin, nervous, active general of a dozen years before; instead of seeing things himself, he remained in Vilna directing affairs by couriers, upon information both late and partial; and as might have been expected, his work was ill done.

It may be said that this criticism of the emperor's bodily strength is unwarranted; but there is no reproach intended to be conveyed. Every man must lose his activity sooner or later. The question before us is only whether the growing loss of daily and hourly physical vigor, of the ability to get about, and of the insistence on seeing things with his own eyes, did or did not seriously affect the Great Captain's later campaigns. There is no intention to hold Napoleon responsible for bodily ailments, although much has been written by others on the subject. One purpose of this History of the Art of War, from Cyrus' day down, is to discover to what degree the personal element influences the operations of war. The great captain's equipment consists of intellect, character and opportunity, each to an exceptional degree and all working together. To ascertain how much each has counted in any given operation, and whether each remains at its best, is part of the problem before us. From this point of view the frequent dwelling upon the emperor's inability, from whatever cause, to do as much work as he had formerly done, is a necessary step in our study. That some may not agree in the conclusion drawn is no reason why the fact should not be pointed out.

Nor was this the worst evil. If large and distant bodies were to be subject only to general direction from headquarters, their leaders should be the best men to be had. But here Jerome, solely because he was his brother, had been placed at the head of three army corps; and Jerome was not only devoid of military talent, he was a lover of his ease. How could Napoleon expect him to do the wise, energetic thing? In 1805 he had written Soult from Milan: "There are no princes in the army. There are soldiers, officers, colonels, generals, and the commanding general who must outrank and stand above all." But now the upholding of the dignity of the new imperial family he had created made him forget all this. Later, indeed, he placed Jerome under Davout; but the harm had been done.

On July 3 Napoleon learned that Bagration had crossed the Niemen four days before, at Mosti, as if heading towards Vilna, and this led him to suppose this Russian army at Lida on that day, retiring via Volochin on Molodechno; and he assumed that he was being pushed by Jerome via Minsk.

But Jerome was still in Grodno, closing up his column and looking after subsistence; while Reynier was at Bielostok, and Schwartzenberg crossed the Bug at Drogichin. On this enormous theatre of war the emperor's calculations were all going astray, while owing to the unusual difficulties, only an accurate dovetailing of all the separate manœuvres could save the campaign from failure. Meanwhile Davout was standing at Ochmiana expecting that Bagration would approach his way, and afford him the chance of falling upon him. But Bagration was at Novogrudok, marching eastward to a junction with Barclay, who had reached Davgeliski, with wings out at Rymshani and Postavi. Murat was at Sventsiani, in touch with the Russian rearguard. Eugene, with St. Cyr in his rear, had reached Novo Troki on the way to Vilna, where Napoleon and the Guard still remained. Ney was at Maliati and Oudinot at Avanta; Macdonald still at Rossiani, with orders to march to Ponievesh. As Barclay had manifestly got beyond reach, Napoleon proposed to halt his centre and left a few days and push the operation against Bagration; for if the French head of column could be thrust between the two, the problem was still solvable.

Bagration had been warned not to get cut off from Minsk,

and had left Volkovisk on June 28. It is nearly ten days' march to Minsk, but on June 30 he received the absurd orders to march straight to Drissa. Barclay should have known that Davout barred the way, while Bagration might not. The latter was bridging the Niemen when he heard that Hetman Platov

Hetman Platov.

had met Davout and was at Volochin. How much force Davout had he could not tell, but though it was probably less than his own, Jerome was following him up; and recognizing that he must make a considerable circuit, he sent word to Platov, who had been joined by the infantry rearguard cut off from Doctorov, to hold head to Davout for a while, and he filed off for Minsk. Platov was unable to hold Davout, and rather than attack for mere temporary gain, Bagration kept on via Niesvish towards Bobruisk, so as to reach the Dnieper at Mohilev. By this time Jerome's van had struck Bagration's Cossack rearguard, which fended it off, and Bagration kept on his way. It seems that each side overestimated the force of the other.

This rapid retreat of the Russians from his advance first led Napoleon to fear that he could not bring them to battle; but if he could only keep the two Russian armies apart, he might be able to handle each separately; and it seemed — as was the fact — that Barclay was taking a false direction. If they could be kept from joining, a time would come when each could be attacked.

As in 1807, the soldiers were getting weary of this long march in a naked country, and to encourage them by putting a goal before them, as well as to lead the Russians to accept battle rather than have the enemy winter on Russian soil, Napoleon announced that he would stop his advance at Smolensk, and prepare to occupy the land he should so far have overrun.

French Line Carbineer.

CHAPTER 2
VILNA TO VITEBSK. JULY, 1812.

THE heat was great. The army suffered as never before. Rations could not keep pace with the army, and there was little on the road. Fed on rye straw, horses fell by thousands. The men had no mills to grind the grain they found, and living on boiled rye porridge brought on dysentery. These conditions at the opening of the campaign argued ill. Davout was to head off Bagration, whom Jerome should pursue, but Bagration by a circuit escaped them both, and Napoleon's long pause at Vilna had nullified his first plan. He now began another to contain Barclay by a front attack while turning his left, but he still tarried at Vilna, awaiting news. In mid-July Barclay was in the Drissa camp faced by Murat, Davout was trying to head off Bagration, Jerome was far behind, the Prussians were on the left at Riga, and the Austrians facing Tormasov on the right. Barclay was striving to draw in Bagration. Alexander went back into Russia to rouse the people, and instead of standing for battle, Barclay moved towards Vitebsk. Jerome was placed under Davout, but the harm could not be undone. Napoleon left Vilna July 16, hoping to anticipate Barclay at Vitebsk, but failed. Thrown back by Davout at Mohilev, Bagration made a circuit to Smolensk, and Barclay, after a battle July 25–26, retreated July 27–28 on Smolensk, where he joined Bagration. Napoleon's second plan had miscarried. The condition of the army was pitiable; it was put into cantonments for a few days at Vitebsk, and Napoleon again told the army he would not advance beyond Smolensk.

THE hardships and difficulties of the Russian climate and terrain had begun to be severely felt. The train could not be got up. Ney's artillery had not been brought forward for lack of horses. On July 4 the emperor had Berthier write him "that the situation of his army corps seems most alarming from the point of view of the artillery. It is necessary for him not to make a step farther until his artillery has rejoined him. Without artillery his corps would be much compromised." The cavalry was getting dismounted. Napoleon wrote Clarke,

July 8 : " I do not think it very necessary to augment recruiting for the cavalry; for in this land one loses so many horses that with all the supply of France and Germany, we shall have great difficulty in keeping the actual effective of the regiments mounted." On July 13 Sébastiani reports that the day before he lost forty-two horses from fatigue : " It is in bad taste, I feel, to make such observations at a moment when we should redouble our activity," said he, but without some rest he would lose half of his animals. Excessive rain had spoiled the roads, rations were slack, and the men, as usual, took to plunder, a poor resource in this sparse region, especially just before harvest. Murat reported July 2 : " The weather is awful. The soldier has absolutely nothing, and finds nothing. All the villages, or rather all the farms, are abandoned." And about the same time Deroy wrote that " an officer of Italian mounted artillery, who was here a few days ago, assured me that he had not touched bread for twelve days, and that the horse battery had been transformed into a foot battery, so as to haul the pieces with the saddle-horses." This was not the rich valley of the Po or the Danube, with a village and food every few miles. Straggling depleted the ranks : from the Niemen to the Dvina St. Cyr daily lost the equivalent of a battalion. Orders against plunder arrested no man ; and all this, at the inception of the campaign and in midsummer, argued an evil future. It is amazing that the emperor did not heed the warning.

Not every one understands what the supply-train of a great army means. Although the Revolutionary armies, in fruitful countries, had cut it down materially, the emperor had grown to permit officers pack-horses and carriages far beyond regulations ; the non-combatants were a host ; and for every three men in the Grand Army, there was, including the artillery and ammunition-train, at least one animal. Picture to yourself how much roadway a four-horse wagon or a dozen pack-mules need; calculate the number of beasts and wagons required for the Grand Army and the space they would occupy; remember that the main roads were deep in mud and the side roads impassable; and you will understand what feeding the men meant, particularly as the Russians ate out the land they left, and destroyed the magazines they abandoned; and as, unmindful of the hungry fellow soldiers trudging behind them, pillagers uniformly destroy what they cannot consume, more was trodden under foot than eaten.

On this subject, on July 3, the Crown Prince of Bavaria wrote the king : "The successive dissolutions of the troops into a mass of brigands is the worst and most dangerous consequence that we can fear. Seeking for food gives occasion to this, and it is brought about by the complete cessation of all dispositions taken to assure victual." And with regard to some fault found by Napoleon with his cavalry, he continued : "The 25th of last month, in filing at the head of my division in front of Kovno, I met the emperor, who ran to me with a little suite. Without preamble he commenced to tell me that there were great disorders in my division, that he would write on this subject to Your Royal Majesty, that some generals had allowed themselves undue liberties, that he had a mind to have them shot, and that they might go, as he had no need of them. This was said in a raised voice, and so rapidly pronounced, in part screamed, that an answer was for the moment absolutely impossible." Speaking of the French soldiers, the crown prince says : "In general, I have remarked that in some of these regiments, from top to bottom, there is no authority exercised. Between superiors and inferiors there is far too much familiarity, and a show of comradeship reigns and is habitual there. The soldier is so ill brought up and coarse, that since he has been with French generals he passes before me without saluting, unless recalled to his duty. This is not to be denied and explains many excesses."

The Correspondence of these days is full of orders for the erection of bake-ovens, of which the need daily grew. In many towns means for baking was found, but the army suffered as never before. On July 9, in an order from Vilna, the marching ration was ordered cut down to ten ounces of bread, two ounces of rice, one pound of meat; the biscuit was to be reserved and the bread eaten first. In the last days of a march the ration was to be nine ounces of biscuit, two ounces of rice, one pound of meat; and the men by no means got this. Constant orders were issued to keep up the roads.

On July 2 the emperor wrote Berthier : " My Cousin, charge a general officer of your staff to occupy himself solely with the organization of the routes of communication from Vilkoviski to Kovno, and from Kovno to Vilna. From Vilkoviski to Kovno there should be two commandants, and two little garrisons of twenty-five men, with one or two gendarmes. They will protect the post, do the policing, and send regularly news of what happens. They will make the inhabitants repair the broken roads, fill up the bogs, repair and keep up the bridges. From Kovno to Vilna four commandants must be established, and four garrisons of twenty-five men." Then follow instructions as to the duties of these posts. And on the same subject, on July 4, he wrote him : " My Cousin, a single road cannot suffice for an army like this. Moreover, I desire to let the road from Vilkoviski to Kovno rest, so as to give time to reorganize and repair it. Present me a project to establish a road by way of Königs-berg, Labiau, Tilsit, in following the left bank of the Niemen. By this means it will be easy to give promptly oats to the horses and bread to the troops." This too was followed by full details.

These orders were much to the point; but the trouble was that they could not be carried out. In other campaigns, the emperor's orders had been such that they were, after a fashion at least, feasible; but here more than half of the orders having to do with the logistics of the army were not executed at all. The emperor's will was law; but even the law fails at times ; and this grew rapidly worse as the campaign went on.

The operations of Davout on the upper Niemen now became important. On July 4 Napoleon reinforced him with a Guard division, while Morand at Michalichki reported to Murat. He also ordered Berthier, July 5, to write imperatively to Jerome to get afoot : —

"You will make him understand that I am extremely discontented that he did not put all his light troops under the orders of Poniatowski on the heels of Bagration, to annoy his corps and arrest his march. That, arrived at Grodno the 30th, he should have attacked the enemy at once and pursued him sharply. You will tell him it is impossible to manœuvre worse than he has done. . . . That from his having departed from all the rules and his instructions, has resulted that Bagration will have all the time needed to operate his retreat. . . . Tell him that, had Poniatowski but one division, he should have sent it. . . . That Davout is to-day, the 5th, with a part of his corps in advance of Volochin, but will not be strong enough to stop Bagration. . . . You will tell him that the fruit of my manœuvres, and the finest occasion that has been presented in the war, have been lost by this singular forgetfulness of the first ideas of war."

Next day the emperor placed Jerome's whole command under the orders of Davout.

"Vilna, July 6, 1812. His Majesty orders that in case of the reunion of the 5th, 7th, and 8th army Corps, and of the 4th Corps of cavalry reserve, with the corps commanded by Davout, the command shall devolve upon Davout, as the most ancient general. The emperor orders His Majesty the King of Westphalia to recognize Davout as superior in command, so long as the army corps are united."

But Jerome was not alone at fault: Napoleon's mistake of Doctorov's corps for that of Bagration had led to giving him conflicting orders; and although Jerome had been remiss, what was to be expected of a new made king and a newer made general? Jerome had been told to obey orders specifically, whereas, could the emperor himself have been at hand, he would have risked the improbable attack by Bagration on Warsaw, and have sent Jerome eastward to trap him a week earlier than he did. Jerome was no soldier, and when he had contradictory orders, could not judge which was the more important to obey. Still, he had to pocket his scoldings. Berthier wrote him, July 3: "You must not fall into the snare of the pompous enumerations" (of troops) "which the

Russians make. There are always two thirds to take away." And on July 7: "His Majesty does not find your letters couched in a military style. You should receive the reports of your generals and of your vanguard colonels, and after reading them, you should send the originals to the emperor." He "reads these volumes of reports; and it is there he gets the information according to which he directs his troops."

By July 4 only Latour-Maubourg's cavalry had left Grodno, and by the 8th had reached Lebeda. Meanwhile Davout had marched via Volochin and reached Minsk the same day, when Bagration was at Niesvish. Napoleon kept on prodding Jerome to speed, and would listen to no excuses from him or his lieutenants.

"My Cousin, answer Poniatowski," he wrote, July 9, to Berthier, "that you have put his letter under the eyes of the emperor. That His Majesty is very discontented to see that he speaks of pay, of bread, when it is a question of pursuing the enemy. That His Majesty has been all the more surprised because he" (Poniatowski) "is alone on his side with small numbers; and that when the emperor's Guards, who have come by forced marches from Paris, instead of having half-rations, are without bread, have nothing but meat" ("no meat," says this letter, as given in Fabry), "and do not murmur, the emperor has been able to see only with pain that the Poles are bad enough soldiers, and have a poor enough spirit, to bring up such privations. That His Majesty hopes that there will be no more talk of this."

Bricks without straw was a sad enough cry; but war without bread is a worse one!

Under this whipping up, Jerome's two corps reached Novogrudok July 11 and Niesvish the 14th, after exchanges on the 9th and 10th with Platov's Cossack flankers; and Davout, fearing, without Jerome's aid, to fall on Bagration, whose force he estimated at sixty thousand men, remained at Minsk on the 12th, lest if he reached Igumen, Bagration should file in his rear to a junction with Barclay. Though ignorant of the

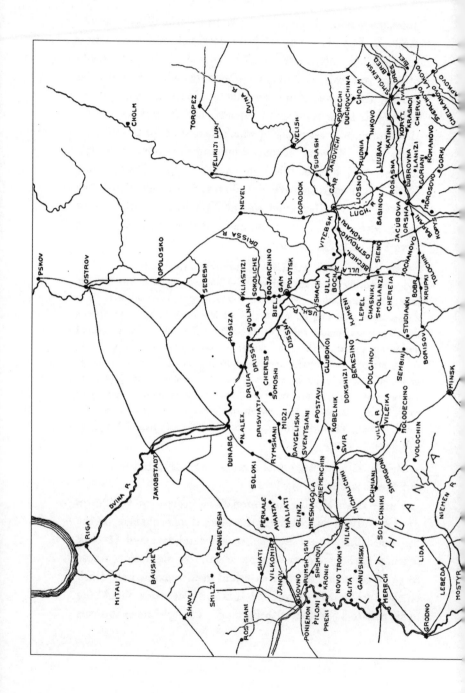

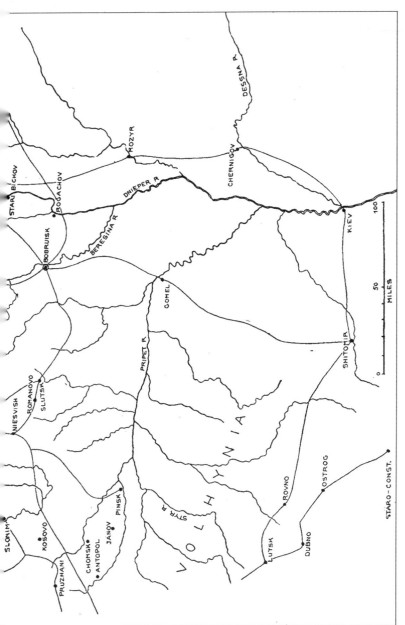

West Central Russia

enemy's whereabouts, had he been allowed to keep all his divisions, he might have advanced with part and echeloned the others back on Minsk, thus covering his rear, while feeling out in front in search of Bagration ; but the distances, the lack of news, and Jerome's slowness made it hard for him to act. Bagration, from Volkovish on the 28th, had reached Slutsk on the 13th, beyond danger of being held up by Davout and Jerome, though whether he could join Barclay in season to stand at the Dvina was yet problematical. The letters and orders seem to show that Davout was doing good work, although the emperor blamed him for laxness. He certainly had kept his divisions in fair condition under the circumstances. On July 12 he reported to the emperor that he had reviewed the *élite* companies (grenadiers and voltigeurs) of Compans, Dessaix and Claparède, in which there were few absent, but that of the *élite* of the 33d Light Infantry only a third was present. " I had these corps file past, butt of musket in air, and the brigadier-general and the colonel at the head, in front of all the other *élite* companies. I ordered that an example should be made in each company of all those who were behind, plying the trade of brigands."

During these days Schwartzenberg had advanced to Pruzhani, and Reynier to Slonim, their eyes fixed on Tormasov's army in Volhynia.

Constrained thereto by Jerome's slowness, Napoleon had ordered Eugene up to Davout's aid in the effort to get at Bagration, and the viceroy left Novo Troki July 7 and reached Solechniki, St. Cyr, the day before, being still at Ganushiski. Like all the rest, Eugene came in for his share of criticism :

"Generally speaking, you do not write enough," said the emperor, July 4 ; "and when you are isolated, you do not do what is necessary to tie yourself with headquarters, and get promptly news and orders." And on the 19th : " Have a care to place posts of correspondence, to which you will give the order to have horses, so that your correspondence may be quite rapid, and that you may transmit me your reports at the rate of two leagues an hour. If they cannot find horses, they are to furnish their own."

The escape of Bagration was not the only disappointment. Instead of standing for battle, Barclay had retired, July 11, to his intrenched camp at Drissa. The works here were not good, nor had bridges been completed; and the position was strategically unsound, because a retreat on Drissa separated Bagration and Barclay. Had the conditions permitted a prompt French advance from Vilna towards Vitebsk, Barclay would have been pushed up north, where he was useless, and Bagration could have been handled singly.

The alleged reasons for Napoleon's fatal pause at Vilna were, in part, to hear from the manœuvre against Bagration, when on a smaller theatre the news would have come sooner; in part to organize the government of Lithuania, which was a lieutenant's work; in part, after holding Eugene back, to wait for him to come up. The most potent actual reason was lack of victual; it was essential to organize water transportation to Vilna, for the line of advance during all 1812 ran through this town, although when the Grand Army was at Smolensk, much material came from Warsaw, via Brest Litovsk and Minsk.

Despite Napoleon's best labors, Lithuania could not be got in hand. Whatever he did either oppressed the peasants, or annoyed the nobles, or frightened the Jews, who then, as now, held the keys of commerce. In a country where warring armies move, license is always the law, and when the soldiers robbed the peasants, the peasants robbed their masters and the Jews. Most of the adherents of the emperor soon lost their patience; and it cannot be said that the efforts to get the whole-hearted help of the Poles were successful, although that country, in the hope for eventual freedom, did everything it could for the French cause.

When Barclay's retreat called for fresh dispositions, Napoleon, as a second manœuvre, planned to contain the First Army by a front attack, with Murat and the cavalry, Ney and Oudinot, while, with Eugene, part of Davout and, if he came up, Jerome, he himself would move on Polotsk and Vitebsk, and strive there to reach the Russian communications both with St. Petersburg and Moscow. But he still dwelt at Vilna until the Bagration question could be cleared up, and would not begin the fresh operation.

"My intention is not to have so great a matter engaged in without my presence . . . and not yet to manœuvre on the Dvina," he wrote Berthier, July 6. And the same day Berthier was ordered to write to Murat: "Let him know that I do not intend to move on Dünaburg, but that, meaning to operate with my extreme right, we are far from being ready for it. We must regulate ourselves on the events happening to Bagration. If one can have an affair with him, beat him, throw him into the Pinsk marshes, or oblige him to retire on Mohilev, one may arrive before him at Vitebsk. . . . Make him understand that my intention is to manœuvre to turn the enemy by my right, because on his right the passage of the Dvina is no longer anything, the river being fordable ; that in marching on Smolensk one menaces Moscow, and that in moving on Polotsk one forces the enemy to evacuate all the country to within four or five marches of St. Petersburg. This evacuation would have an advantageous effect " (for us) " on the morale of the Russians, . . . and instead of a little war of rearguard affairs and skirmishes " (*chicanes*), " it would give rise to great flank movements."

This is excellent strategic reasoning, but the work done thereunder savors little of the tremendous activity of Austerlitz and Jena. Both in Spain and Russia, the emperor's map strategy was perfect, but his logistics lacked the winning quality.

Matters progressed slowly, and on July 14 the Grand

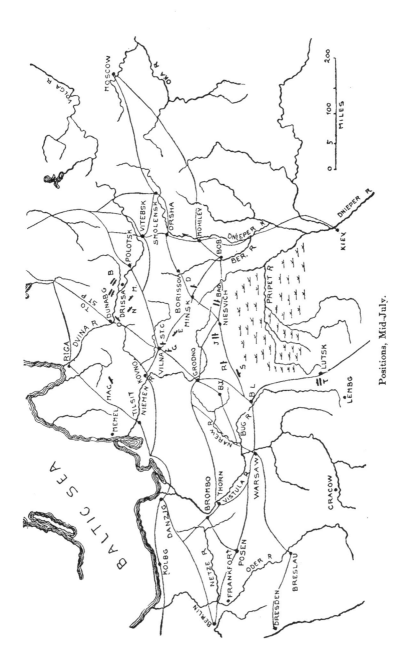

Positions, Mid-July.

Army and the Russian forces stood thus: Murat had advanced via Midzi towards Drissa and had reached Somoshi, with Nansouty and Montbrun out at Druia and Cheres. Ney had joined Murat at Drisviati, and Oudinot was marching up river from Dünaburg. Macdonald had reached Smilzi, acting as a flanking corps to protect the Niemen, watch Riga, threaten a diversion below Drissa, collect breadstuffs in Courland, and finally to besiege and take Riga, to secure future winterquarters by holding the navigation of the Dvina. Eugene was at Smorgoni, the Young Guard at Kobilnik, St. Cyr and the Old Guard in Vilna. Jerome had got to Niesvish with Latour-Maubourg out at Romanovo; Schwartzenberg was at Pruzhani and Reynier at Stolovichi, thus opening the Grand Duchy to a raid by Tormasov. Davout had just left Minsk to march on Mohilev.

On the other side, Barclay had vacated his intrenched camp, and crossed to the right bank of the Dvina; Bagration had left Slutsk for Bobruisk. Tormasov's army had been completed and stood at Lutsk, ready to invade Poland and cut the French right wing communications. Not until July 10 had Napoleon's attention been seriously called to this Third Army, and next day he wrote Berthier to have Jerome detach Reynier to cover Poland : —

" Answer Jerome that you have received with astonishment his letter of July 9. . . . That the order of the 30th is positive, that it was expressed in these terms : ' You are to direct yourself on Minsk. Reynier, without losing sight of covering Warsaw, will direct himself on Niesvish.' This means that the first object of Reynier is to cover Warsaw, that the second, if the enemy should withdraw all his troops from Volhynia and there was nothing more to fear for the Grand Duchy, would be to march on Niesvish."

This is unfair criticism.

By mid-July Napoleon's first excellent plan had completely

failed. Jerome's long stay at Grodno, owing to incompetence, conflicting orders and the enormous theatre, and Davout's at Minsk, expecting Jerome to coöperate and Bagration to march his way, had enabled the latter to escape the toils laid for him and make good his retreat via Bobruisk. Moreover, Tormasov now came into the problem as a distinct threat to the French right, to counteract which a speedy success of the French left was essential.

The Russian generals had been acting on no consistent scheme. When Barclay retired to Drissa and ordered Bagration thither, he did not foresee that his lieutenant would have to fray a passage through the French army. Long before the war, the Drissa camp had been erected as a defense to St. Petersburg; but if it were turned by the French reaching the Dvina above it, Barclay would be compelled to fight a superior force alone; and if he were defeated, Bagration would certainly be so, and the road to the heart of the empire be opened. Yet he could scarcely leave the St. Petersburg road open, small chance as there was of Napoleon's marching thither. Between the two plans, the Russians were preparing failure. All that Napoleon needed to profit by the situation was speed; and this, owing to the immense environments, to the question of victual, and, it must be acknowledged, his own lessened incisiveness, was conspicuously absent.

Alexander remained with his army. He had with him his old military instructor, Phull, who had originated the camp at Drissa, in which Barclay had but half-faith, pointing out to the czar that the French would not seek the Russians there, but that these would have to debouch from it and seek the French. There were jealousies in the Russian army, which even the czar could not allay. Although Clausewitz says Phull passed in Prussia as having much genius, and the czar always remained grateful to him, he was a foreigner, and was hated by the

real Russians. Even Barclay, though born in Russia, was of
Scotch descent, and was not quite trusted. He soon noticed
the French intention of turning the Russian left at Drissa
and cutting the First from the Second Army. "It is for that
reason that I have considered it necessary to make a march
on the road to Polotsk," he said to the czar, while Alexander
of Wurtemberg suggested taking up a strong position at
Vitebsk. In any case, the speedy reunion of the two armies
now became essential. As opinions differed, so antagonisms
grew. While the czar was at hand, Barclay was not supreme,
and although he saw the weakness of the position, he could
not leave Drissa. But shortly Alexander left the army to
organize the national defense; and no sooner was Barclay in
command than he abandoned the camp and started through
Polotsk on Vitebsk to a junction with Bagration. It has
been questioned whether the formal consent of the czar had
been given to this operation; but it may be assumed, and the
documents rather support this view. His common sense must
have shown him the necessity of joining his two main bodies,
that is, for Barclay to move on Smolensk and draw in Bagration. As a rule, he exhibited the same crude but just and
comprehensive idea of the requirements of war that was
shown in our own Civil War by Abraham Lincoln. Each
had to control difficult politics in order to wage efficient war.
Alexander was constantly vexed by the ill-feeling between
Bagration, who wanted to fight, irrespective of caution, — "I
do not understand your wise manœuvres," said this officer:
"mine consist in seeking the enemy and beating him," —
and Barclay, who wished to draw him in to the main army.
As late as November he wrote to Barclay: "Very grave
faults committed by Bagration, in consequence of which the
enemy forestalled him at Minsk, Borisov and Mohilev, forced
you to leave the banks of the Drissa to move on Smolensk.

Fortune favored us there, for against all probability, the junction of the two armies was made there."

In his effort to organize a national system of defense, Alexander began to erect intrenched camps in many parts of the empire, and fully aroused the Muscovite national spirit of resistance by an appeal of July 9 : —

"Russian Warriors, you have finally reached the end you proposed to yourselves. When the enemy dared cross the limits of our empire, you were on the frontiers to observe him. Until the entire assembly of our army, we needed by a temporary and indispensable retreat to restrain the ardor with which you turned to arrest the march of the enemy. All the corps of the First Army are now reunited in the positions chosen beforehand. Now a new occasion presents itself to show your approved valor and to win the reward of the labors you have sustained. Let this day, signalized by the victory of Pultava, serve you for example. Let the memory of your victorious ancestors incite you to glorious exploits. With a powerful arm they threw to earth their enemies. You, in marching in their steps, strive to overturn the project of the enemy directed against your religion, your honor, your country and your families. God, who sees the justice of our cause, will send you his benediction."

A proclamation, probably inspired by Stein, was also issued by the Russians addressed to the German soldiers, warning them to return home. "You know the Russians too well to believe that they are fleeing before you. They will accept battle, and then your retreat will be difficult. They say to you as comrades : 'Return home *en masse*, do not believe those perfidious words that you are fighting for peace. No, you are fighting for the insatiable ambition of the sovereign who does not want peace.' "

The latter appeal had no effect.

While Alexander was thus employed, Barclay left Wittgenstein with twenty-five thousand men at Drissa to hold the communications with St. Petersburg, and promptly moved up the Dvina on Vitebsk. He reached Polotsk July 18, at the time Napoleon arrived at Glubokoi. A few days more and he would have been too late.

When, on July 9, Napoleon gave up the hope of heading off Bagration, he had changed Eugene's direction to one on Dokshizi, thence to move on Polotsk or Vitebsk, as circumstances might dictate, intending himself to join this column with the Guard, while Murat, with his big reinforcement, was to contain Barclay at Drissa, and follow him towards St. Petersburg, should he retreat thither as a consequence of the French operations. He quite disapproved a stroke made by Oudinot at Dünaburg, as Berthier wrote July 16, because it led him to a distance. "You have greatly annoyed the emperor by your movement on Dünaburg. His Majesty charges me to tell you that he hopes that such a thing will not again happen," wrote Berthier. Davout's task was to keep on pushing Bagration, if possible, across the Dnieper. Could this be punctually accomplished, the line of the Dvina might still be won, and Barclay and Bagration cut apart. Of the earlier project, mentioned July 6, to hold Barclay at Drissa, surround him with the whole army, and compel him to fight, there is no further mention. That he would not attack the enemy in his intrenched camps, but turn these and assail him on the march, he wrote Berthier, July 15; and next day, in the hope that Barclay might attack Murat when alone, he wrote that he intended to cross the Dvina between Dissna and Vitebsk, which, by turning their left, would compel the Russians to leave their camp to cover St. Petersburg, or else to attack Murat or himself. In so vast a land as Russia, strategy becomes more difficult than when the theatre is closed in by seas or neutral countries which trace a limit to operations; and moreover the Russians possessed advantages, for though the roads were poor, there was a network of them everywhere, leading through the enormous forests, or over the vast plains, from town to town, which they from knowledge and habit could utilize, when the French could not.

At the opening of the campaign, the emperor forbade small detachments. "The Russian army having a great amount of light cavalry, we must be careful not to make reconnoissances, or to beat the country with little patrols of fifty horse. If the country is open and uncovered, at least a brigade, or about fifteen hundred horse, is necessary." In a broken country, foot should be added. On July 14, from Vilna, he found fault with Latour-Maubourg: "Since when can a chief who has made war in Poland follow the enemy's rearguard, where he knows there are six thousand Cossacks and four thousand men of regular cavalry, with only a division of light cavalry? . . . His Majesty is extremely discontented that personally he" (Latour-Maubourg) "had not been with his vanguard; that when a division of cavalry charges, he should be there."

Napoleon could state his own case with force, if not always with accuracy. From Vilna, July 1, in answer to the approaches of the czar, he wrote: —

"Monsieur my Brother, I have received Your Majesty's letter. The war which divided our states was terminated by the Treaty of Tilsit. I had gone to the conference of the Niemen with the resolution not to make peace without obtaining all the advantages which the circumstances promised me. I had in consequence refused to see the King of Prussia there. Your Majesty said to me, 'I will be your second against England.' This word of Your Majesty changed everything. The Treaty of Tilsit was its corollary. Since then Your Majesty desired modifications made to this treaty. You wished to keep Moldavia and Wallachia, and carry your frontiers to the Danube. You had recourse to negotiation. This important modification to the Treaty of Tilsit, so advantageous to Your Majesty, was the result of the convention of Erfurt. It seems that, towards the middle of 1810, Your Majesty desired new modifications to the Treaty of Tilsit. You had two means to reach this, negotiation and war. Negotiation had succeeded at Erfurt : why this time did you take a different means? You made considerable armaments, declined the road of negotiation, and seemed to desire to obtain modifications to the Treaty of Tilsit only by the protection of your enormous armies. . . . I also had recourse to arms — but six months after Your Majesty had taken this step. . . . Your Majesty first assembled his armies and menaced my frontiers. Your Majesty first left for army headquarters." Napoleon then recites that he had sent Lauriston to St. Petersburg, and that Alexander, and even his minister, had refused to confer with him. "I understood then that the die had been cast. . . . I marched on the Niemen with the intimate sentiment of having done everything to spare humanity these new ills. . . . Your Majesty may say many things, but you will say to yourself that during eighteen months you refused to explain yourself in any manner . . . until I had evacuated the territory of my allies. . . . War then is declared between us. Even God cannot make that which has been not to have been ; but my ear will always be open to negotiations for peace. . . . If Your Majesty desires to finish the war, you will find me disposed so to do. If Your Majesty is decided to continue it, and if you wish to establish a cartel" (for the exchange of prisoners) "on the most liberal basis, . . . Your Majesty will find me ready for everything. . . . You will find me full of friendship and of esteem for your fine and great qualities, and desirous of proving it to you.   NAPOLEON."

It cannot be gainsaid that the emperor here puts a bad case well.

The war of 1812 in America might at an earlier moment have had some influence on the Russian question ; but opening as it did while Napoleon was in Vilna, he was too far advanced to utilize this outbreak against England in lieu or in support of the Russian invasion, as a lever by which to further his projected isolation of that country. Properly made use of, it might have been of assistance to his projects; but anything he did would have been engulfed in the failure of the Russian campaign.

Meanwhile Poland had declared herself free and the old Confederation reëstablished ; but Napoleon did not fully approve this act, fearing to make Austria discontented, and prevent a future settlement with Russia. He desired to use Poland, but not let Poland hamper his own conduct.

The days Napoleon wasted at Vilna caused much future complication. Plausible reasons are given for the delay, but in his former campaigns no reasons were valid which excused the loss of a day, and now the days were priceless. The weather had been rainy, the roads were bottomless; if the days were hot, the nights were cold, as Poniatowski wrote July 22; stragglers were an army in themselves; with only green rye as forage, the horses had died wholesale. Batteries were stalled, squadrons afoot; five hundred caissons and one hundred guns were already left behind; Mortier was ordered, July 13, to "let his artillery march at its ease, even if it arrives a day or two late. That is preferable to seeing it lose horses," — a variation from the orders to Ney ten days before. Difficulties in no sense change facts. Much of the Vilna work could have been left to others; the strategic situation could not. Had Napoleon accompanied Davout and the Guard from Vilna on Minsk, he would surely have headed off Bagration, and with Jerome's assistance — or with that of a better leader — have beaten him. Or had he personally advanced on Barclay with the Guard, Eugene and Davout, he could have reached Polotsk on the 12th and have thrown Barclay back on Riga, and this would have ended the campaign. The loss of seventeen days in Vilna was the error of Napoleon's military career most fraught with ill results.

Late on July 16 he left Vilna, headquarters remaining behind under Maret, and reached Sventsiani next forenoon. Hearing that a Russian detachment had crossed on the 15th at Druia and attacked Montbrun, he inferred an offensive manœuvre by Barclay, and ordered the leading corps to delay; but on learning that the attack was partial, this order was shortly countermanded. On the 18th Napoleon reached Glubokoi with the Guard, St. Cyr two marches in the rear, and Eugene on the right at Dolginov; while Oudinot was just

below Drissa, Murat and Ney moving on Dissna, with Nansouty and Montbrun in their front; and Grouchy was at Bobr
reconnoitring out towards Orsha on the Dnieper. The advance went on. Eugene was ordered towards Kameni on the
road to Vitebsk, and the left wing to be drawn in up the
Dvina; Davout to reach out from Mohilev towards Eugene,
and to bring up in reserve Jerome's wing. The Grand Army
was assembling for a passage at the excellent Dvina crossing
near Bechenkovichi, and though aware that Barclay had already moved up river beyond Polotsk, the emperor expected
to anticipate him at Vitebsk and force battle.

Like all the rest, Davout came in for his share of faultfinding. The emperor felt that he had not been as energetic as usual in his work against Bagration; and though he
had taken part of his divisions from him, and given him a
big task with the rest, he expressed his discontent.

On July 20 he told Berthier to write him : " That I cannot be satisfied
with his conduct towards Jerome. That I only gave him the command in
the case where the assembly had been made, and the two armies being
on the battlefield, one commander became necessary; instead of which
he published this order before the assembly was made, and when he was
scarcely in communication by a few posts. That having done this, and
after having learned that Jerome had retired, he was to keep the direction
and send orders to Poniatowski. That I do not know to-day how my right
is getting on ; that I had given him a proof of the greatest confidence
that I have in him, and that it seems to me that he has not done himself
justice."

Yet Davout took it all in good part, and seems to have
been alive as to what it was necessary to do. From Igumen,
July 15, he wrote Pajol : —

" It is essential to have prompt news of Bagration. Jerome day before
yesterday was at Niesvish, and announced that he was pursuing the enemy
with his sword in his ribs. It is therefore probable that he is marching
to-day on Slutsk. The distances are too great for us to take part in any

affair which might occur there, but we must give the utmost disquiet to
the enemy, and be ready to act against Bagration according to what he
may do. If Bagration wishes to pass by way of Bobruisk, I can, I think, on
his march by the flank do him much harm. If he wishes to pass the Beresina lower down, it is important for me to anticipate him on the Dnieper."

On the same day Berthier was instructed to put Poniatowski in command of Jerome's force, the latter declining to
serve under Davout. Some one had to be wrong, and it was
never Napoleon. From now on, the old reliance upon Davout's
capacity and good-will seems to lessen, much to the emperor's
eventual loss. Davout wrote Poniatowski, July 24 : —

" I see that His Majesty has given you command of the right wing.
I know that this command is in very good hands, and the esteem that
we bear each other, as well as our devotion to the service of the emperor,
is a sure guarantee of our good understanding in our operations. I will
lay bare to you my ideas and will let you know my situation, so that you
may take action according to your own information or mine." Where
upon follow full details of the status.

In consequence of the fresh manœuvres, the situation on
July 24 was this : From Glubokoi via Ushach Napoleon had
reached Kameni ; Murat, with Nansouty and Montbrun in the
van, and Ney close behind him, marching via Dissna and Ulla,
and Eugene via Kameni, followed by the Guard, had all come
on to Bechenkovichi ; St. Cyr was at Ushach, and Oudinot
at Dissna watching Wittgenstein, who had reached Drissa,
and was ready to cross the Dvina and attack anything in his
front, as a diversion. Macdonald had reached Jakobstadt July
21, and at Bauske thrown back on Riga a Russian detachment. Poniatowski was coming along to reinforce Davout, who
had just crossed swords with Bagration. Reynier was back
at Chomsk, Tormasov at Pinsk, Schwartzenberg at Slonim.

Fearing that the French would anticipate him at Vitebsk,
or on the road to Smolensk, Barclay had made speed, and by

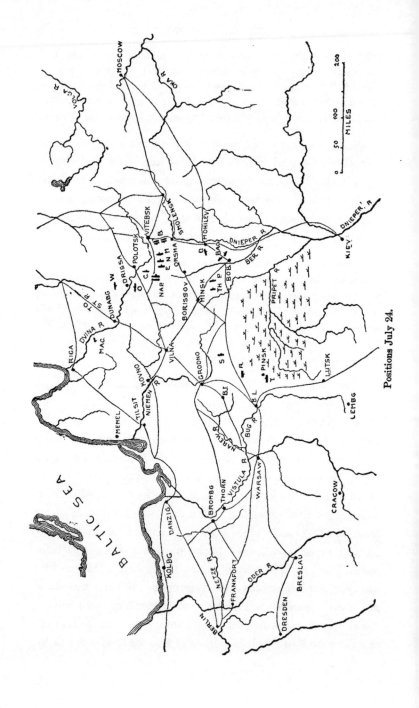

Positions July 24.

July 23 had in part reached Vitebsk. He would have marched to Orsha; but the French were so close at hand that he had to send Ostermann to Ostrovno to retard them and enable him to draw in his rearguard under Doctorov. The French mass was now concentrated at Bechenkovichi, ready either to cross and give battle, or to march on Vitebsk; and Napoleon wrote Eugene, July 24, that it was important to secure this latter town to rest the troops, but that the safe crossing was the main point.

Davout had reached Mohilev July 20, with Grouchy at Kochanovo, keeping touch with Napoleon. He had a difficult task, as he knew little of the enemy, and had to keep communications open on the left to Orsha and on the right to Beresino. Tried by what the rest of the army had accomplished or failed in, he was doing well. Bagration, who had reached Bobruisk two days before, was marching in two divisions on Mohilev. He could either force his way north through Mohilev, or file off towards Mstislavl; but as his orders named Orsha as objective, he determined on the former plan, and on the 23d, with his first column under Raevski, he attacked Davout. The French position was astride the Bobruisk road, on a high bank in rear of a marshy brook, with the left on the Dnieper and the right on a wood where stood a strong detachment. It could have been turned, but Bagration feared that Davout would cut him from his second column, and made only a frontal attack. The contest was sharp — both commanders were fighters of the first water. At one moment it looked as if the French line would be broken; but by putting in his reserves, Davout held his own, and Bagration, exaggerating his forces, and finding the road thus closed, left Platov with his Cossacks to delay pursuit, and marched back to Stari Bichov, crossed the Dnieper, and marched via Mstislavl on Smolensk. Davout would have exceeded his orders in crossing the Dnieper to again head him off. In this battle of Mohilev each side had some twenty thousand men, and the loss has been stated as high as three thousand killed and wounded on each side, although Napoleon put it at one hundred French

Bagration.

and one thousand Russians. Davout wrote Poniatowski, July 26: "I see that the battle of the 23d put great confusion into their projects, but they will follow them in part, and my first manœuvre is not to let myself be separated from the emperor, who to-day must be in Vitebsk. Raevski's two divisions must be looked on as *hors de combat*."

Davout had crossed the Vistula with seventy-two thousand

men, of whom twenty-eight thousand had gone to Murat,
leaving him forty-four thousand men; and that these had
dwindled to one half without a battle shows the stress of the
march on insufficient rations. The same condition obtained
in all the corps. On July 20 the crown prince wrote : —

" The resources offered by the country are very feeble. They have
been devoured by the preceding troops, but one can pick up here and
there something. Mills are wanting to make flour, because on these roads
there are only water-mills, of which the use is very slow, and which only
yield a sort of paste." On July 24 Kerner wrote: "Stockmeyer's battalion
has only one captain. There are several battalions where in all there
are but four or five officers who are well. . . . The country is too bad, the
troops too numerous, the marches too continuous. When we arrive at a
camp, every one is too tired for either man or horse to move a limb. Misery will therefore remain great. It will augment by the continuance of
the marches, because the men will always be exhausted. Each night of
rest does extraordinary harm, and costs us many men sick and horses dead.
Each day when it rains, soldiers are found dead in the bivouac before we
leave." And five days later he wrote: "The marches having continued
without stopping for eleven days, one easily sees that the soldier's strength
has much diminished. Misery has brought on many suicides, and our column resembles more a transport of sick than of warriors. . . . If Ney
demanded from the French divisions which precede us, even after a fashion, a little order, all the corps could be well nourished, but all those who
go before us can, without being prevented, pillage and burn everything."

The condition of the country and population is indicated
in an itinerary from Vilna to Glubokoi, divided into stretches.
In the first stretch of forty miles were forty houses and one
farm; in the next of nineteen miles were seventy houses,
a castle and a near-by farm; in the next of thirteen miles
were forty houses, some hamlets and small farms; in the
next of sixteen miles were twelve houses, several farms and
many near-by houses; in the next of sixteen miles were
twenty houses, one inn, one mill, one castle, one church and
a number of houses far apart; in the next of twenty-four

miles were fifty houses, one convent, one church and several farms.

Bagration had done well. Platov had helped him much, but it was Jerome's slowness that saved him. He was able to reach Smolensk two days after Barclay. On July 24 Davout was still at Mohilev, with Poniatowski coming up, too late to be of present use. Vandamme's corps, now Junot's, was at Krupi, and Poniatowski's at Igumen; Latour-Maubourg was near Bobruisk. The staff of the right wing was dissolved, and the two corps were placed under Davout.

Reynier, ordered back to protect Poland against Tormasov, and starting July 14 from Stolovichi, had reached Chomsk July 24. Opposite him, Tormasov had left Lutsk, and reached the Pripet headwaters on the front Pinsk-Janov-Brest Litovsk about the same time. Schwartzenberg, advancing towards Niesvish to join Davout, had got to Slonim. On July 22 Napoleon ordered Berthier to write Reynier that "I do not prescribe anything to him; that his principal aim is to cover the Grand Duchy; that a good manner of covering the Grand Duchy is to enter Volhynia, to make confederations everywhere, and to get the country into insurrection; that all that is left to his prudence." In the same spirit, on July 26, the emperor told Berthier to write Oudinot that "he alone can decide what he can do; that he therefore has *carte blanche*, but he is to take all means to correspond promptly with us." He was too far off to control his right and left wings.

On this same July 24 Napoleon had ridden to Bechenkovichi, and found Eugene throwing a bridge, and a cavalry party that had waded the river in touch with the enemy's rearguard. Joining the cavalry, he rode with it until satisfied that Barclay had been faster than he, had crossed his head of column, and was well on the way to Vitebsk; but recognizing with chagrin that his turning manœuvre had failed, he still hoped that the Russians would stand for battle to save Vitebsk. The country was good for defense, as there were forests and ravines which retarded the development of troops, and cavalry could not act to the best advantage; and on the 25th he pushed Murat with Nansouty along the left bank of the Dvina, and Montbrun along the right bank, towards Vitebsk. At Ostrovno, July 25, Murat ran across Ostermann in position in the woods. The Russian foot sallied out to attack the French horse, but was thrown back by the sharp French charges; the enemy then essayed to turn both French flanks; but when Delzon's division came up to aid Murat, Ostermann withdrew to the forest lines back of Ostrovno. Next day Murat renewed the combat, hoping to break through; during the night fresh troops under Konovnitsin had replaced Ostermann, and held their ground behind a ravine and leaning on woods. The French left, thrown around the Russian right, was met by the reserve and hurled back; but Roussel's division finally turned the Russian left, and the corps withdrew on Tuchkov at Komari; and this place was held until Napoleon came up, when, pushing Eugene through the forest, the Russians retired slowly in echelon. At a loss of about twenty-five hundred men on each side, Ostermann had retarded the French two days.

As Napoleon informed Berthier, July 25, the prisoners stated that the enemy was waiting at Vitebsk; indeed, Barclay felt that his junction with Bagration was accomplished, but he stayed there a few days to rest his troops. Lest too smart an attack, however, should incline Barclay to further retreat, the emperor instructed Murat not to demonstrate too strongly; for no strategic means was left of compelling the Russian army to stand; nor could Barclay fight at Vitebsk if Davout headed off Bagration and occupied Smolensk, as he feared he might.

To Eugene Napoleon wrote July 26 : " My Son, I have written to Murat to advance near Vitebsk with wisdom and precaution, and without engaging any other affair than a big combat of the vanguard. He can attack a corps of ten or twelve thousand men, but not enter into a general combat without being well prepared. Either the enemy wants to fight or does not want to fight. If the enemy wants to fight, it is very happy for us. He might be prevented from so doing by not being joined by one or two of his corps. There is then no inconvenience in letting him make his assembly, because otherwise it might be for him a pretext not to fight."

It was Napoleon's habit to make the best of everything, to give a rosy hue to affairs, even for his intimates. On July 26 he wrote Maret : " The country is fine, the crops superb, and we find everywhere means of living." This plan worked well for a while, but its consequences were fatal, for although at first his cheeriness encouraged his subordinates, the real situation soon became known to all, and bred a feeling of uncertainty. The evil grew as the campaign went on.

On July 26 the advance on Vitebsk continued, and the French van came into presence of the whole Russian army, which had been marshaled south of Vitebsk and behind the Luchessa stream. Here was the opportunity so long sought : Napoleon could put one hundred and twenty thousand men in line to Barclay's eighty thousand, and the Russian position was bad, as it could be turned by the left and the road to Moscow be seized. Success was certain if the rear corps could be got up. The Russian outposts were pushed back of the brook, and the French head of column deployed in front of the enemy ; but as the army was advancing along a single road, and what he deemed a sufficient force could not be got up during the 26th, Napoleon merely demonstrated, deferring an attack until he had concentrated. He felt certain Barclay intended to fight and would remain in position. Such, indeed, had been Barclay's purpose, for not only was constant retreat affecting both army and nation, but he had ordered Bagration in by way of Orsha; he did not know his whereabouts; and farther retreat was compromising his lieutenant. But the stars in their courses fought against Napoleon: during the night of July 26–27 Barclay received Bagration's report that he had been stopped at Mohilev by Davout, and had changed his route to one by way of Mstislavl on Smolensk; and the necessity of fighting the superior French single-handed was past. Still, as there was not time left for the Russians to withdraw under cover of darkness, on the 27th both armies remained in presence. All the more convinced that Barclay would now stand for battle, Napoleon, instead of attacking this day, busied himself in bringing up forces to make the work decisive, reconnoitred the enemy's position and formed his plan; no doubt on the morrow he would have destroyed the Russian army; but early on the night of July 27–28 Barclay quietly and skillfully decamped, and by morning was marching in three columns far along on the roads to Rudnia and Porechi. So cleverly had he done this that Napoleon could not even ascertain by which road the bulk of the Russian army had marched, though that Smolensk was their objective, there could be small doubt. Not a straggler was left behind, and every village was abandoned. His disappointment must have been keen, although he permitted no one to see it.

On July 29 he cheerfully wrote Maret: " We entered Vitebsk yesterday. The enemy is beating in retreat on every side. I have moved as far as Surash to follow him, but as he has divided to follow several roads, it is not possible to reach him. The general opinion is that he is moving on Smolensk to cover this town. These last affairs have lost many men to the enemy. His loss is estimated at seven or eight thousand men; several of his generals have been killed or mortally wounded."

On leaving Vitebsk, Barclay had received notice that the emperor purposed to cut him from Smolensk, and that Davout would head thither, and he sent Doctorov by way of Rudnia to occupy the town. " The entire safety of the country now depends on the rapidity with which our troops shall occupy Smolensk. Remember the marches of Suwarrov and accomplish such," he said. Entering Vitebsk, the emperor pushed Ney on Rudnia and Murat out towards Gaponava. At the Smolensk fork Murat got in touch with the Russian rearguard, and by night all his cavalry, with Eugene and the Guard close behind, reached Gaponava, the emperor accompanying the column. He was so little certain whither Barclay had retired, that on the 29th the Russians got to Rudnia and Porechi, followed only by cavalry, and Eugene advanced on Surash.

Accompanied by the Guard, Napoleon returned to Vitebsk, conscious that Barclay had escaped him. His failure had been due to lack of his ancient habit of pushing his subordinates by his personal presence and example. As, after Eggmühl, he had for the first time declined to pursue a broken enemy, so here at Vitebsk he had hesitated in attacking an enemy drawn up to meet him, and had permitted a whole day to pass without the attack he would in earlier days have delivered; the enemy had escaped, and the long march from the Vistula to the Dvina had been robbed of all result. It may be said that he was wise, at this distance from his base, to wait for all his troops. True, if you like, but was it not possible to hurry them up? In former campaigns they had marched night and day. The army was exhausted and ill-fed, but the old Bonaparte had a way of getting it along; and while no other commander could have done better with half a million men on this enormous theatre, we are accustomed to demand more of Napoleon than of others. If to march faster than the Russians was not possible, his clear vision should have foreseen the fact, and other measures should have been adopted. The entire Russian campaign depended for success on the superior speed he had theretofore always shown.

The army was rapidly decreasing. The emperor had crossed the Niemen at Kovno, Piloni and Grodno with three hundred and sixty thousand men on a front of eighty miles; he now stood from Polotsk through Vitebsk to Mohilev with two hundred and thirty thousand men on a front of one hundred and fifty miles. The advance of two hundred and fifty miles in five weeks, seven miles a day including halts, had lessened his fighting force by over a third, — in some bodies more, for the Wurtemberg division, from July 15 to August 11, diminished by just a half, — and the object of the campaign, viz.: to keep his own force concentrated and separate that of the enemy, had been quite reversed. Barclay and Bagration joined hands at Smolensk August 3. The one purpose of the advance in echelon by the left had been to cut Barclay and Bagration apart and to fall on the flank of either, or both in turn. First went lost the hope of surrounding Bagration; then the hope of keeping him from joining Barclay; last the hope of beating Barclay in a frontal attack. Apart

Polish Footman.

from the vast theatre, the first loss seems due to the growing incapacity of the emperor for bodily exertion, which did not permit his being personally at the critical points; the last rather to an increased habit of mental indecision, perhaps originating in physical ailments. "Fortune is a woman; if you fail her to-day, look not to find her to-morrow," he once said. On the 27th he failed the goddess at the Luchessa; on the 28th she was no longer with him.

To the dispassionate observer to-day it is evident that, in

operations of no greater speed, the French could accomplish nothing in this vast land if the Russians played a waiting game; but by Napoleon this view of the prospect was not even considered; he still believed he could reach and destroy the enemy at Smolensk.

At Vitebsk everything was seized for the army, and hospitals were established in the convents. July had been rainy; scant or bad food had multiplied sickness; the usual rations were still in the rear, transporting from Königsberg to Kovno, under control of Admiral Basta. Starved men in hot weather break quickly. The foragers generally brought in rye; the men had no mills to grind it, but dried as coffee would be, in any kind of utensil, being stirred all the time, it could be used like rice, and cooked with meat or other things. About a pound per man per day was considered sufficient. The beeves driven along for meat were often unfit to eat. The water was mostly from swamps, or much muddied by constant use, and brandy to cut the water was absent. The men had fallen by hundreds from dysentery, and the hospital train had not got forward. Yet the emperor would not face the facts, and on July 22 he wrote Berthier: —

"Answer General Jomini that it is absurd to say that there is no bread, when there are five hundred quintals" (cwts.) "of flour a day; that instead of complaining, he ought to get up at four o'clock in the morning, go himself to the mills, and to the administration, and have thirty thousand rations of bread made a day; but that if he sleeps and weeps, he will have nothing. That he ought to know that the emperor, who had many occupations, nevertheless went every day himself to visit the administration," etc.

The army needed rest; and as the first object of the campaign had been forfeited, Napoleon put it into cantonments, while Davout, Poniatowski and the Westphalians were coming up. "The fatigue of the army, want of artillery, uncertainty of the forces at his disposition, all concur to impose on Napoleon a necessary halt," says Coutanceau. The Guard was in Vitebsk ; Eugene was at Janovchi and Surash ; Nansouty and Montbrun were pushed out to Porechi and Rudnia ; Ney came on to Liosno ; St. Cyr remained at Bechenkovichi ; two of Davout's divisions were in Vitebsk, and one reaching out towards his main force, which, after the affair at Mohilev, had on August 2 reached Dubrovna, with Grouchy at Babinovichi keeping up touch with headquarters. Poniatowski came on to Mohilev July 28. Junot's corps took up position at Orsha. Latour-Maubourg, left at Rogachov, was to pay heed to the rear.

Polish Voltigeur.

The emperor would have liked to keep moving. On July 31 Murat wrote: "I think if it were possible to push our heads of column on Smolensk, Your Majesty would occupy this great town without obstacles. . . . Everybody thinks that the enemy can only fall back on Dorogobush with Bagration." But Napoleon did not know just what forces he could dispose of. He asked Davout, July 30, "the truth for myself alone;" and next day wrote: "Send me the situation of everything, so that I may decide on the part to take, which can only be the result of perfect knowledge of things." On August 8 Jermalov wrote the czar: "Davout could have in effect occupied Smolensk before us without much effort, because some of his troops were in Orsha. . . . Thus we have operated our junction in an unhoped-for manner, in the presence of considerable forces of the enemy. We are numerically more feeble than the enemy, but by zeal, the desire of fighting, fierceness even, we are as strong as he is."

From Vitebsk, July 29, 1812, Napoleon wrote Berthier : "That the situation of the cavalry, infantry and artillery is such that I am resolved, if the enemy does not force me to make contrary dispositions, to remain seven or eight days in refreshment quarters, to repose the army." That he is to notify Ney " to put his three divisions in good localities," near Mohilev, " to have good barracks made for his men where they can be sheltered from the rain, and to begin regular distributions and rationing." Like orders were given the others. And next day he wrote Berthier that " the junction of Bagration with the main army will be made at Smolensk ; that it might have been prevented, because it cannot take place for five or six days ; that the heat is so great and the army so tired that the emperor judged it essential to give it several days' repose." On July 30 Davout was notified : " My intention is to give seven or eight days' repose to the army, which is very tired ; that I have preferred this disadvantage to that of arriving at Smolensk before Bagration."

Only for the moment did Napoleon consider putting an end to the campaign as one of a number of alternatives. Here such a plan would have been faulty. He had announced his purpose to beat the enemy, or else march to Smolensk ; he must either abandon his work or go on with it, and to abandon it now would give the Russians time to arm the nation, and show Europe that the Great Captain was no longer invincible. Until Smolensk could be reached, or one battle could be fought, he must keep on ; and in a battle he hoped to set all things right. At the opening of the campaign he had had his choice of a slower and more methodical advance into Russia, by keeping the troops back until his means of victualing them could be perfected ; or of disregarding the question of food and moving rapidly upon the enemy, hoping to rectify every error by a battle. He had chosen the latter method, and must now abide by it. But the one thing required was greater speed.

Buturlin states that Barclay and Bagration, united at Smolensk in the early days of August, numbered one hundred and twenty thousand men — one hundred and fifteen would be nearer the truth; they had left twenty-five thousand with Wittgenstein, and five thousand had been disabled at Mohilev and Ostrovno. The two armies had started with one hundred and eighty thousand men. Taking out the above, we ought to have left one hundred and fifty thousand men, showing a loss of thirty-five thousand men on the road. This allowed but a reasonable number of absentees. The French corps, on the contrary, were dangerously reduced by sickness, or by wandering away in search of rations. Not only were there stragglers by thousands, but the provost-marshal parties to gather these up consumed an equal number of men. The overwhelming French forces on the Niemen had already been reduced to nearly the figure of the Russians.

Despite the details of the strategical movements of the Grand Army, we must remember that Napoleon never lost sight for a moment of all the questions of transportation, victual, hospital service, paymaster's duties, and the still more serious question of artillery and ordnance. He kept sight of his army everywhere.

On July 8 he wrote Clarke: "There are in Mantua, Peschiera and Legnano, which are unhealthy countries, many young conscripts. . . . These are so many lost men," and ordered them assembled in battalions in more healthful places. To Berthier: "The major-general will make General Bourcier understand that under whatever pretext it may be, I will not have horses which are not full five years old. That I prefer to receive none. That as to height, I leave him the master to do what he can, but that I will not have any modifications of age." On July 31 he wrote Maret: "I see with pain that the three thousand sick at Vilna are in distress, and even lack straw. . . . See that measures are taken to ameliorate this state of things." And on August 4: "I find it convenient to stop to give a little repose to the army and organize magazines. Make yourself busy organizing those at Vilna and along the route. See that the governor has the boats unloaded and their cargoes stored, so that they may return to Kovno."

The emperor's care in prescribing routes, ordering their repair and erecting magazines was constant, but for lack of means, the orders he gave could as a rule be carried out only in part, at times not at all.

The late marches had been disheartening, especially to the allies. The reports sent home by Deroy, the crown prince and Wrede are full of meaning : —

Deroy's report on August 11 says that there was not enough straw for the troops to lie on, and that the thatching of the roofs had been stripped to feed the beasts; that dysentery was so general that not three per cent. were free from it; that the number of stragglers and dying men was beyond description. "Often one met groups of ten to fifteen dead lying around a dead fire, leaning on their knapsacks, with their guns beside them. We passed beside them without according them the least pity, and yet less judging them worthy of attention." "Though the nature and cost of this war were strange and unknown to the Bavarian warrior, the will of his king sufficed. With full confidence in the genius of Napoleon, which impressed all things, and in his fortune, until now unlimited, the Bavarian courageously followed the battalions used to victory. . . . With each day courage and gayety disappeared. . . . Whoever remained behind was considered lost. The songs so much in use in the Bavarian army had long ago disappeared; for entire days you heard not a syllable, not even curses. . . . On the faces of the masses of corpses which lay along the route, each soldier thought to read the fate for which he was reserved : to die of hunger." On August 12 Wrede wrote the king : "The marches and countermarches, the want of food, the heat and the roads have thrown more soldiers into the hospitals, and have made us lose more men, than if we had delivered a most bloody battle."

All this was in summer. What would happen when bad weather came on ? In the Life of Brandt are a number of details of camp life in these cantonment days, and the scene is familiar to every old campaigner.

Encampments were assigned to the divisions, and the adjacent woods furnished material. In two days a regular permanent camp of huts was created, and was protected by throwing out cavalry, sustained by infantry posts, on the wide plain. " Pillage and theft were severely forbidden. Some French soldiers taken in the act were shot. . . . Troops of workmen were formed, composed of distillers, brewers, butchers and assistants ; to them were joined Russian prisoners and deserters, the last being in great numbers. They rendered excellent service. There were constructed at Dubrovna, and in neighboring villages, establishments where brandy and wine were made. The troops cut, harvested, threshed, ground and cooked. Our people ground the wheat in the mills. As a rule, this was ill done. The French had a species of hand-mill by which six or eight men could grind in a day 250 to 260 rations. That was not the case with us. At the same time we amassed much forage in the camp. From day to day things grew better, and the barracks were provided with benches and chairs. The place of arms in front of the camp was planted with trees. In truth these soon became dry, but they were replaced with others, while the first were burned. All this was obtained with great effort, but it was then a principle to keep the soldier busy all the time. . . . The Cossacks interrupted us in our occupations, they surprised the villages where we were working, but a well-organized service and the fire of the infantry, of which they were much afraid, generally kept them at a suitable distance."

As always, the emperor remained a reader. On the 7th of August he wrote Barbier in Paris that he " desires some amusing books. If there are some good new romances, or older ones which he does not know, or Memoirs agreeable to read, you would do well to send them to us, for we have moments of leisure that are not easy to fill here." In the trying days of earlier campaigns there had not been so many moments of leisure. The emperor's abnormal bodily activity filled them all.

Sword of the Period.

Chapter 3

SMOLENSK AND VALUTINO. AUGUST, 1812.

SWEDEN made a treaty with Russia; England helped both.' Poland was less helpful than expected. By threatening Warsaw, Tormasov contained Reynier and the Austrians, while the Russian right was reinforced opposite Macdonald and the Prussians; Wittgenstein outmatched Oudinot and St. Cyr at Polotsk, and Napoleon's plans so far had miscarried. Still he believed the Russians would soon stand for battle, and victory would cure all these evils. He was right: Barclay and Bagration had agreed to advance towards Vilna and fight. But Napoleon had conceived a scheme for a turning manœuvre by his right, to force battle at Smolensk, and although the Russians came on to Rudnia, from lack of information he did not seize the chance. He began his turning movement August 10, and on perceiving this the Russians retired to Smolensk. The Grand Army continued the manœuvre, and early August 16 stood in front of Smolensk. The city was defended and a first attack failed. On August 17 this was unsuccessfully renewed. What Napoleon wanted was battle, and to force this, he needed to cut off the Russian army. He had lost the Rudnia chance, and now should have crossed the river above Smolensk and seized the Moscow road, as there was every chance to do; but he wasted time in front of Smolensk, as if the Russians would come out and fight, backing on the town. Instead, they were intent on regaining the Moscow road, and had only held Smolensk for this purpose. During the night of August 17–18 they evacuated the city, the French followed them across the river, and a small French force went forward to pursue them. Murat and Ney attacked the enemy at Valutino, August 19, but, unsustained, accomplished naught. The Russians had again avoided battle, and were well on the way to Moscow. Napoleon had promised to stop at Smolensk, but as a Russian pause on the Moscow road looked like battle, he followed on. The army had dwindled to half its force, but was still faithful. Had Napoleon accurately gauged the manifest facts, he would have seen that he could not reach Moscow and hold himself there; but still he pushed on, expecting both that Barclay would fight and that Alexander would yield.

ALTHOUGH Napoleon did not immediately hear of them, several political changes happened during the early part of the Russian campaign which tended to upset the calculations on which he had predicated success. On March 24 Russia had signed a treaty with Sweden, which, as Bernadotte continued his negotiations with Napoleon, was kept secret ; peace with the Turks was ratified July 14 ; and on July 18 a treaty was made, by which England subsidized the czar, and afforded the Russian fleet in the Baltic certain harbor privileges. The military disappointments were more serious. In opening the campaign, Napoleon calculated that success in the centre would force back the enemy's wings ; but as Barclay and Bagration were now basing on Moscow, Wittgenstein on St. Petersburg, and Tormasov on the Army of Moldavia under Chichagov, which was advancing to its support, and each army could move independently, this calculation failed. Napoleon had also intended that the Poles, after joining the Grand Army, should make a diversion by way of Mozyr into Volhynia and cut Tormasov's communications on the Pripet, but other matters claimed precedence of this operation ; and instead of being neutralized by the retreat of the centre, the Russian right and left wings were becoming a distinct threat.

On the French right wing matters looked ill. On July 24 Reynier had met a detachment of Tormasov near Chomsk, and pushing it back, had reached Antopol ; Tormasov, having on the 27th captured the French brigade holding Kobrin, was raiding Poland with Cossacks and threatening Warsaw ; whereupon Reynier retired to Slonim, and Schwartzenberg, who had been ordered on to Minsk to sustain Davout, came back from Niesvish at his earnest solicitation. All this Napoleon approved, when informed of the facts, and placing Schwartzenberg in command, instructed him through Maret, August 2, " that my intention is that with the two corps assembled, which must make forty thousand men, he is to march on Tormasov . . . to deliver battle to them; that he is to enter

Volhynia, if necessary, and that he shall have a care to so act
that in no case can the one or the other come near me." But
the emperor was persuaded that Tormasov had not more than
ten thousand third-battalion men, for as this army would have
been more useful as a reinforcement to Bagration, he could
not see why it should be so faultily employed; and although
wont to take advantage of the enemy's errors, he was now
unwilling to credit them. No one thing attracts the attention
more than the passing of Napoleon's power to gauge the value
of events. Of old he used to found or alter plans on the information collected, from which he could with astonishing accuracy deduce the hard facts; now he seemed to disregard facts,
unless they fitted into his preconceived plans; and his under-
rating of the enemy's force and exaggeration of his own, not
only towards the enemy but towards his own marshals, in the
attempt to breed that confidence which numbers produce, was
by reaction becoming dangerous.

On August 10 Schwartzenberg drove out of Pruzhani a
detachment of Tormasov's, which retired to Gorodechno, and
when, two days later, the Russian army came to its aid from
Chomsk, he attacked that. Including Reynier's corps, he had
a distinct superiority; and although he did not win a decisive
or a brilliant victory, Tormasov retired during the succeeding
night on Kobrin. Later he withdrew to the Lutsk country;
Schwartzenberg followed, and took place in his front.

On the French left wing, though Oudinot had reached
Dissna, Macdonald had so far done nothing to coöperate with
him. From Ushach, July 23, Napoleon had written Oudinot
that it would be advantageous to make headquarters at Polotsk; that a manœuvre on Sebesh ought to compel Wittgenstein to yield up Drissa and Druia; and on July 30 that
he was to destroy the Drissa camp, so that it could not be
used for operation in his rear; in pursuance of which, Oudi-

not crossed the Dvina to Polotsk, July 26. Urged on by Napoleon, who estimated Wittgenstein at ten thousand instead of nearly thirty thousand men, Oudinot sallied out to meet the Russians, and reached Kliastizi July 30, with two divisions, less than twenty-five thousand men, leaving the third behind to hold the Drissa. Wittgenstein had been about to cross the Dvina at Druia and fall on the French rear, but when he heard of Oudinot's advance, and that Macdonald threatened to cross at Jakobstadt, he retired towards Sebesh; and when Oudinot still advanced, he determined on attack as the best defense. His van struck Oudinot's July 30, at Kliastizi: each commander held his own, and brought up his troops. Next day Wittgenstein's energetic onset forced Oudinot beyond the Drissa to Bojarchino. On August 1 Wittgenstein sent his van under Kulniev across the river, but Oudinot

Wittgenstein.

drove it back, and following it up heedlessly with Verdier's division, was in his turn forced back. As a result, Oudinot retired August 2 to Polotsk, and Wittgenstein took up a position behind the Drissa at Sokoliche. To enable Oudinot to resume the offensive, Napoleon sent St. Cyr and the Bavarians, twelve thousand strong, from Bechenkovichi to Polotsk, and on August 7 Berthier was ordered to write Oudinot : —

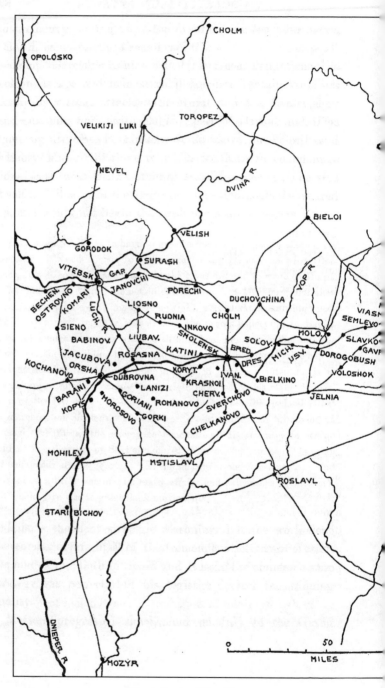

East Central Russia

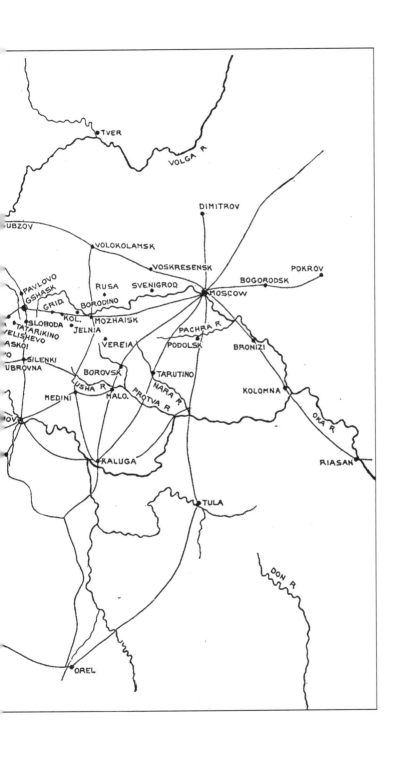

"That in no campaign have we followed the Russian corps with more attention, and we are perfectly familiar with their organization. That everything leads us to believe that he has not more than twenty thousand men before him. . . . This very light manner of doing things compromises the general operation, because it may lead the emperor to make false movements. If we were not very superior in forces to the enemy, the retrograde movement of the 2d Corps on Polotsk would be a veritable fault. After the fine victory he had obtained, it is astonishing that it should be the enemy who remained master of the battlefield. He fell back, the enemy advanced. The enemy knew that two divisions had crossed the Dvina, he advanced still more. War is a matter of opinion " (sentiment, or morale), "and the art was to keep for himself the opinion that he had got for himself after the great advantage he had won."

With St. Cyr coming up, Oudinot on August 7 again advanced from Polotsk; and when Wittgenstein, who had taken position at Rosiza, advanced on Svolna on August 11, Oudinot next day retreated, writing to the emperor that the enemy was trying to turn his right. He was hesitating and abandoned the initiative to the enemy, who again forced him back to Polotsk August 16. Here St. Cyr came up. Unaware that Oudinot had been so heavily reinforced, Wittgenstein attacked Polotsk August 17, but without success, though the fight was hearty. Oudinot being wounded, St. Cyr took command, and next day attacked Wittgenstein; and though the victory was not decisive, it was a success, and much needed to bolster up the serious position of the Grand Army. St. Cyr was created marshal. Oudinot got small comfort, his chief, on August 19, ordering Berthier to write him : —

"The emperor has seen with pain that you did not follow Wittgenstein, to whom you are opposed, and that you left this general master to move on Macdonald, or to cross the Dvina to make an incursion on our rear. You have the most exaggerated notions on the force of Wittgenstein. . . . You must not let yourself be imposed upon by such commonplace " (grossier) " traps. The Russians publish everywhere, and in the rear, the startling victory they have won over you, because without reason you let them sleep on the battlefield. Reputation in arms is everything in war, and equals real forces. His Majesty orders you to seek Wittgenstein, and to attack him wherever you shall find him, having a care to manœuvre him if he has a strong position. If he has no position, he cannot resist you. Macdonald, who is ordered to move with all his force on Riga to besiege this place, has been stopped, in consequence of your manœuvres, at Dünaburg." . . . He then tells him that all the Russian numbers are grossly exaggerated. "It is thus that Tormasov had at Volhynia the reputation of having sixty to eighty thousand men. Prince Schwartzenberg marched on him with twenty-five thousand Austrians. The phantom dissolved. Tormasov was found to have only two divisions of infantry and two of cavalry, forming four thousand men. They were dispersed, beaten and lost three thousand men."

Macdonald meanwhile had not crossed at Jakobstadt, but marched up the left bank to Dünaburg, the Russians retiring. The Prussian auxiliaries blockaded Riga.

According to the 9th Bulletin, on August 4 the army stood thus : Headquarters at Vitebsk, with four bridges ; Eugene at Surash, Murat at Rudnia, Davout at the confluence of the Beresina, a small stream near Dubrovna, and the Dnieper, with three bridges and bridge-heads ; Ney at Liosno ; Junot at Orsha, with two bridges and bridge-heads; Poniatowski at Mohilev, with two bridges and bridge-heads ; Oudinot in advance of Polotsk ; Schwartzenberg at Slonim ; Reynier at Roujana ; Latour-Maubourg near Bobruisk and Mozyr ; Macdonald at Dünaburg and Riga ; Victor at Tilsit ; Augereau at Stettin.

The outlook was clouding more and more. Alexander had retired to Moscow, where, by appealing to their religious and national fanaticism, he had excited the Russian people to rise against the invader; the Army of Moldavia, released by the Turkish treaty, was marching up to join Tormasov; the Army of Finland, no longer essential against Sweden, was soon to reach Riga, on the French left. Matters looked so grave that, contrary to his habit, Napoleon called in some of his marshals to a council of war. He had not done this since Essling, and now his peculiar assertiveness made the council fruitless. Some desired to remain *in situ*, based on the Dvina-Dnieper line, which plan Napoleon opposed, as these streams, when frozen, would no longer be a barrier; others advised to push the operation to the end, and with these Napoleon sided, for he could see no issue except to conquer a peace or fail ; and as his self-confidence led him to believe in success, he kept on with his preparations. On August 9 he wrote Berthier to order the communications from Smolensk to Vilna to be organized by way of Minsk, as being shorter than by Vitebsk, and more in the direction of Warsaw. In a letter to Maret of August 9 he says: " The army having passed, the country ought to settle itself, and with money one ought to be able to find all that," meaning transportation. But the country did not get settled, nor was transportation ever equal to more than a fraction of the demand. Berthier wrote the emperor August 12 that in Russian Poland " the peasants refused to make the harvest for their lords. The rye remained uncut. . . . It will deprive the army of this most precious resource ; " and suggests that the peasants be allowed to make the harvest for one third to them, one third to the army, and a third to the lords.

While the troops were resting from their serious hardships in this land of vast distances and scant supplies, and while on right and left the French fortunes were dwindling, Napoleon had been maturing a plan for moving across to the Dnieper towards Davout at Dubrovna, and turning the Russian left, so as to cut it off from Moscow. It was not until the 6th of August that he knew the force of the two Russian armies, and that they had retired on Smolensk, and had a vanguard near Krasnoi. He wrote Eugene: "My intention is to march on the enemy, probably by the left bank of the Borysthenes, to seize

Smolensk and deliver battle to the Russian army." The 9th
he sent a similar letter to Maret, to whom the day before
Berthier had written : " It is thought that the enemy will be
the other side of Smolensk. God grant it. The emperor continues to be satisfied with the situation of the army. These
ten days of rest have brought in many men." On the same
day the emperor wrote Davout asking for the nature of the
country and about the route to Krasnoi via Mstislavl. "This
march would be advantageous, and would permit us to arrive
in two columns so as to avoid a rather strong position that the
enemy has in front of Smolensk. This road would turn it."

Barclay anticipated him. He had written the czar from
Smolensk as early as August 3 : " While here, I have gathered
provisions, which, thanks to the zeal of the inhabitants, arrived
quickly, and I propose shortly to attack the enemy, in the con-
viction that his forces are not all assembled." But all was not
rose-color for Barclay. A chill between the Russian leaders
had begun with Barclay's complaining that Bagration was
slow in joining him. Bagration wrote : " I am not the servant
of Barclay. I have always thought until now that I served
the emperor and the country. . . . I now see that I serve alone.
In three days I shall be in Smolensk to turn the army over
to him." But on reaching Smolensk, Barclay's friendly attitude prevailed on Bagration to do duty under him, and he
wrote Alexander : " I consider at the moment no personality,
but only the general interest, the good of the country, and the
renown of your empire ; " and Alexander wrote Barclay :
" I am satisfied to have learned your good understanding
with Bagration. . . All personal consideration must disappear
before the good of the country." Bagration was, however,
only temporarily swallowing his griefs, for in a week the two
were again at odds. Barclay complained to the czar that he
was surrounded by officers who talked of his combinations in

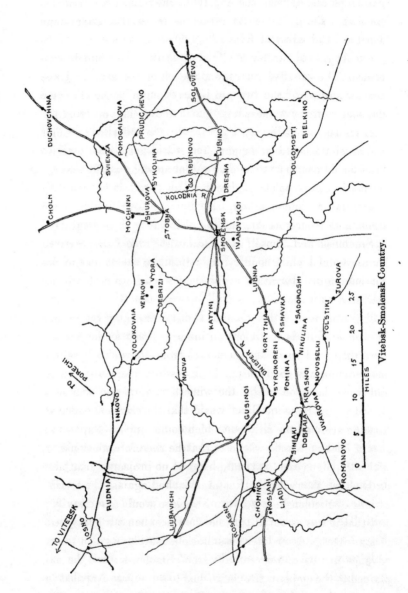

Vitebsk-Smolensk Country.

public places, so that the enemy learned them all; and his chief of staff wrote to Bagration as if on the latter alone depended the safety of Russia.

On August 6 Barclay held a council of war, at which were present Constantine, Bagration, the chiefs of staff and the quartermasters of the two armies, and this was unanimously for sharp offensive measures, and a movement on Rudnia. Toll's hope was to destroy the French left, and swing around and crush the centre and right. The risk seemed small because the wooded country to the east of Babinovichi would cover a retreat in case of mishap. Barclay was afraid, if he went too far, that the French would seize Smolensk, or else turn his right flank from Porechi; and his plan was to leave Bagration at Smolensk and himself move towards Porechi and Surash, having gained which country, and minimized the danger to the Russian right, Bagration could then advance and battle be delivered at Rudnia.

Toll won over to his opinion Constantine and Bagration. Wollzogen tells us that Constantine urged that as the French were dispersed on a vast semicircle from Velish to Mohilev, the occasion was good to march on Rudnia, pierce the centre and wheel back on one of the wings; this opinion was supported by the rest, but Barclay said that the czar had confided him the army as the only one which could oppose Napoleon; that if beaten, Russia was lost; that he therefore must use it with scrupulous care, and could listen to no project of an attack on Rudnia; that with the Russians backed against the fortifications of Smolensk, in a battle Napoleon would lose heavily; and that it was essential that he should exhaust a great part of his forces. After later consultations Barclay agreed to an advance not beyond three days from Smolensk; and he explained to the emperor that he wished to anticipate Napoleon's concentration, and by an attack to gain time for the perfection

new forces in the interior; that he would attack the
's left so as not to uncover the Smolensk road; that
...... would be gained; and that he would avoid disaster in
case of loss, by keeping open an easy retreat.

On the 7th, accordingly, Barclay moved towards Vitebsk,
sending Nevrovski with a division down the left bank of the
Dnieper. Well pushed, the manœuvre might have been a
serious annoyance, for the Grand Army was dispersed over
a large area, seeking rest and supplies; but it could not well
have had permanent success, because, though the Russians
reckoned on an equality, the French were still in superior
numbers. His plan was excellent, but it was not well executed:
from dread of Napoleon's bold manœuvres, he blundered. On
August 7, in three parallel columns, he started towards Rudnia, and next day the central van met and threw back some of
Montbrun's cavalry, at Inkovo; but from reports of the Cossacks he was again led to fear that at Inkovo the French might
fall on his right from Porechi, where indeed some French
horse stood in front of Eugene at Surash; and he obliqued to
the right towards Vydra and Stobna, Bagration being on his
left at Katini. The Cossacks kept on towards Rudnia. On
the 9th the two right columns reached Mochinki, Bagration
Vydra; and here they remained, as Barclay was uncertain
what manœuvre on Napoleon's part his advance might call
forth. He feared to carry his initiative too far.

Barclay's plan was to attack Murat and Ney at Rudnia, but
not follow them up if they retired, for he considered his hold
on Smolensk essential. As he wrote the czar, August 9: " In
debouching from my new position I can attack with superior
forces the enemy's left flank, cover my communications with
the upper Dvina, and protect the left wing of Wittgenstein.
Such a position procures advantages not doubtful, and gives
us entire liberty to act according to circumstances." And

again, after the event : " I would have attacked the enemy at
Rudnia if he had stayed there, when I could have hoped to
destroy a part of his forces before the rest could have assembled. A general battle beyond Rudnia in the vicinity of
Liubavichi and Babinovichi would have served nothing, even
had we achieved a glorious victory. It would have cost a
great loss in men which we could not have replaced, because
our reserves were yet partly behind, partly not yet organized.
On the contrary, the enemy had behind him and on his flanks
army corps which could easily have reinforced him." It would
seem that Barclay's strategic plan was not as strong as the
battle fervor of his lieutenants, but he showed his wisdom
in saying : " What signifies to create in imagination learned
marches and movements, when the destruction of an enemy,
who had subjugated Europe, could be attained only in drawing out the war ? "

The combat at Inkovo aroused Napoleon, who ascribed it
to careless cavalry work : " It seems that the enemy has retired," Berthier wrote to Ney, " and that it was a force of
cavalry, probably provoked by Sébastiani, who does not know
how to remain in cantonments to rest, and moves out to the
plains, where he thinks there is yet no enemy." Believing at
first that Barclay might be about to take the offensive in earnest, Napoleon purposed to concentrate on Ney. On the 9th
he wrote Eugene : " Assemble near Liosno. If it is an offensive movement of the enemy, arrive as near as you can ; " and
to Davout : " If the movement of the enemy is an offensive
movement, it will be necessary for you to reunite your army
at Rosasna." It would have been easy to bring on a battle
here, for the Russian leaders were for the moment keyed
up to just this. Clausewitz thinks Napoleon should have
marched straight on Smolensk and have fought the Russian
army, which by advancing towards him showed its disposition

to engage battle. Believing Barclay would stand, he had his choice between a battle and his strategical turning operation, and in a battle he might employ a tactical flank manœuvre. But Chambray says (as the documents tend to show) that he did not initiate his turning manœuvre until he believed Barclay's advance would not be followed up; and as he had already matured his sweeping manœuvre around the Russian left on Smolensk, and as a partial reconnoissance developed no Russian troops, he concluded that the Inkovo combat had been a mere attack of Platov's on the outposts, as Ney had reported, and he acted accordingly. Each commander was curiously ignorant of the other's movements, which speaks ill for the French, and much worse for the Russian scouting — in their own land with large bodies of light horse. That Napoleon did not seize the chance offered him by Barclay was a pity. His own operation was perfectly conceived, but its sole object was to bring the Russians to battle, as with their constant retreat he had not yet been able to do; and now Barclay, feeling that he was as strong as Napoleon, was in fact affording him the very chance so long desired, although he may have doubted it. Under the influence of the council of war, the enemy was ready to stand and fight; here was the best opportunity since the French entered Russia; and who can doubt, with the forces each could put in line, that Napoleon would have utterly crushed Barclay? As it was, the emperor did not know the Russian battle fervor. Had he advanced, Barclay would have taken up a defensive position and waited; but when the French began a movement around his left, to seize Smolensk in his rear, he felt compelled to retire, and the battle offered Napoleon here could not be brought on under favorable conditions at Smolensk. This was, however, less a mistake of the emperor than a misfortune. Had Napoleon been sure of the purpose of the Russians, he might have marched straight against them; as it was, he did not believe that, after sufficient rest, he could force them to battle except along the left bank; and once the troops were afoot, he went on with his turning operation: "I intend to march on Smolensk to see if the enemy will wait for us, which seems quite probable, because his reunion with Bagration is made, and he can scarcely expect much more," he wrote Maret, August 9, and proceeded to assemble on his right.

This was the third and last grand manœuvre in this campaign; it was planned to be made in close order, the front of march on Smolensk being only fifteen miles, not much more than battle front for two hundred thousand men. Moreover, he saw that, once on the march, if the Russians continued their advance against him, " the French army would," by the direction it was then taking, " have attacked the Russian army in the rear."

Having made his plan, the emperor acted.

To Berthier, August 10, he wrote : "Give orders to General Eblé to make big day's marches with two corps of pontoniers, so as to be on hand the 13th early at Rosasna, and to set to work at once to throw at that place four bridges." And to Davout : " It is probable that I shall march on Smolensk with two hundred thousand men. As you are in the country, study a little the roads to know if one might not march in three columns, one along the great road, one on the slope of the waters of the little torrents that pour into the Dnieper, and the third on the right, but without being distanced farther than two or three leagues one from the other." And again on the same date : "I should have made all my Guard leave this morning, but it rains so much that I retard its movement one day to let the bad weather pass. I also retain Friant's division, which, being well off in barracks, is sheltered from the rain ; but everything is ready to leave. . . . Have all the means at hand, without, however, throwing the bridge, but in such fashion that your sappers and pontoniers shall have in advance all that is necessary, and may be able to throw the bridge as quickly as the head of the left shall appear, without sooner unmasking the movements."

It appears odd to see the great soldier arresting the march of a corps on the score of rain, but it fits into the combination of numerous little lapses to which failure is traceable. We shall find it again in 1813.

Seeing no further sign of the Russians, Napoleon wrote Davout, August 10, that they had probably retired; that " he was justified in believing that the enemy would hold in Smolensk, and that it would be a decisive battle;" and he ordered afoot the Guard, Ney, Davout's full corps and Eugene, preceded by Nansouty and Montbrun, so as to reach Rosasna the 13th. Grouchy was also to come up, Poniatowski and Junot to advance on Romanovo, and Latour-Maubourg to cover the right at Mohilev and Mstislavl. The Russian leaders were puzzled at finding no enemy on whom they could utilize their battle fervor; Bagration was still at Katini; and Barclay, after awaiting a French onset from Porechi until the 13th, again started towards Rudnia.

On the same day Napoleon left Vitebsk for the front, where the Grand Army was passing the Dnieper. "Everything leads us to believe that there will be a great battle at Smolensk; we must have hospitals," he had written Davout the day before. "They must be at Orsha, Dubrovna, Mohilev, Kochanovo, Bobr, Borisov and Kiev. Have the location of those of Orsha and Dubrovna chosen." Reaching Rosasna, he found two bridges thrown, and Grouchy, followed by Friant, Gudin and Morand, was put over; a third bridge, thrown at Chomino, accommodated Murat, with Nansouty and Montbrun, followed by Ney; the Guard and Eugene crossed next day. Junot and Poniatowski came on to Romanovo, the latter having left six thousand men in Minsk; and Latour-Maubourg reached the Dnieper. Under cover of the extensive morasses and woods of this region, aided by the cavalry divisions near Rudnia, Napoleon had secretly concentrated

the Grand Army on its own right, assembling on the Dnieper
left bank, along the Smolensk road, a force of one hundred
and eighty-five thousand men, wherewith to seize Smolensk
in Barclay's rear, cut him off from Moscow, beat him in
battle, and throw him off to the north, thus repeating the
simple manœuvre so often before successful in destroying the
enemy — just what he had done in the campaigns of Marengo,
Ulm, Jena. At St. Helena he spoke of this operation as one
of his finest.

"The junction made, Barclay marched with one hundred and eighty
thousand men on Vitebsk to deliver battle to the French army, but Napoleon executed that beautiful manœuvre, which is the pendant of that
of Landshut, in 1809; he covered himself with the forest of Bieski"
(? Babinovichi), "turned the left flank of the Russian army, crossed the
Borysthenes, and advanced on Smolensk, where he arrived twenty-four
hours before the Russian army, which retired in great haste."

It has the hallmark of the Napoleonic manœuvres, in that
before he crossed the river and threw himself on the new
line, he concentrated on the hither side, and then debouched
from his bridges in one mass. The inception of this manœuvre was as perfect as its predecessors: would it be carried
on with the same vigor, that vigor which alone insures complete success? August 9 Davout had written that, "in directing the major part of the troops by way of Babinovichi, the
movement would be masked by the forests and the country,
and in establishing at the head of the woods some troops,
one would be easily protected from the enemy's parties, to
which on the march the flank would be exposed." As a
fact, Napoleon did not cover his movement by the forest
of Babinovichi, for his cavalry went out of it on the line
Liosno-Luibavichi. But this is unimportant.

On August 14 Murat, with Nansouty, Montbrun and
Grouchy, set out along the Smolensk road, followed by Ney,

Davout, the Guard and Eugene, and flanked on the right
by Poniatowski and Junot, marching toward Tolstiki. In
the afternoon, at Krasnoi, Murat reached Nevrovski's division, ten thousand strong; Ney's van soon came up, and
Nevrovski ably defended the road by utilizing the ravines
and woods, and by forming square at intervals to resist the
French cavalry, but at a loss of quarter his force. Ney took
Krasnoi, and Nevrovski retired to Korytnia, pursued by
Murat, whose continued attacks he threw back with true
Russian constancy. "Never have we seen greater courage
on the part of the enemy," said Murat. And although he
and Ney had long been at odds, he continued: "Marshal
Ney and his staff have constantly marched with me. It is
not for me to praise this marshal, whose bravery and talents
Your Majesty has so often had occasion to appreciate." From
his night's bivouac, Napoleon wrote Maret, August 15: "I
am at Krasnoi. I am marching on Smolensk. It is possible
that to-morrow or the day after there may be a great battle."
He added that reports from prisoners were divided as to
whether a part or the whole of the Russian army was at
Smolensk, and Maret was to send the news in various directions. On August 15 the van, near which Napoleon remained, got to Lubnia, driving Nevrovski before it; the rear
of column reached Krasnoi, and Napoleon heard that the
Russians had abandoned Smolensk — probably belated news
of their march towards Rudnia. The manœuvring force was
concentrated: if only the Russian army could be blinded for
a day or two, its fate would be sealed.

Meanwhile, unaware of the impending danger, Barclay,
on the 14th, was at Volokovaia. On the 15th Bagration,
beyond Katini, on his way to Nadva, received news of the
Krasnoi fight and, guessing its purport, dispatched one of
his corps to Smolensk and himself retired to Katini, where

he learned the facts; then, breaking the bridge he had thrown over the Dnieper, he started early next day towards Smolensk; and Barclay, informed of the danger, did the like.

Just after midnight of August 15-16, Napoleon wrote Eugene that he should in all probability be in Smolensk towards 8 or 9 A. M.; Murat was ordered, if he found only Russian cavalry in front of the town, to seize it, but if he found infantry, to stop and report; and Ney was ordered to move at 3 A. M., to enter the city, and in connection with Murat to keep good order there. Starting about five o'clock in the morning, at eight he came in sight of Smolensk. Nothing practically was done that day except to reconnoitre the place. There is much dispute as to hours. The emperor arrived before Smolensk at some time after noon. Berthier, already there, we are told in the journal of a Wurtemberg captain, advanced with a staff officer and viewed the fortress with his glass. Shortly after, the emperor came up and talked in a lively manner with Berthier. Then the emperor advanced alone to within a short distance of the fortress, Berthier following in the rear, and when, by this reconnoissance, he saw that the town was occupied, he gained the impression that Barclay was assembling for battle, and ordered an attack to be opened.

Smolensk lies on the south bank of the Dnieper, in a beautiful amphitheatre, the Petersburg suburb on the north bank. Although low, the heights about it command the town, and make it quite unsuitable for a strong place. It was an old sacred city, had sixteen churches and several convents, a palace or two, and was full of gardens. In the suburbs the houses were nearly all of wood. Built for eighty thousand inhabitants, it had barely a quarter as many. Toll tells us that Smolensk proper was fortified in the ancient sixteenth

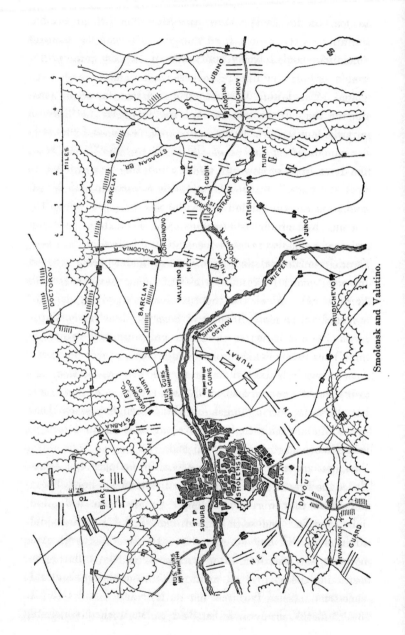

Smolensk and Valutino.

century method, with an irregular brick wall of three miles circuit, twenty-five feet high and ten feet thick, with seventeen little bastions formed of round and square stone towers, and a useless dry ditch, a covered way and a fairly good glacis. The towers looked strong, but were in effect weak, and on the southwest corner the wall was protected by a big earthwork citadel, a regular pentagon, erected by Peter the Great, but really the poorest part of the enceinte. Along the river were no towers. On the right bank was a crownwork of earth. The walls would easily resist field-guns, and could scarcely be escaladed; the towers were less thick than the wall, and might be battered down with twelve-pounders; but the French were not aware of this. Outside the town were a number of ravines, some sharp ones running down to the river, and all affording excellent opportunity for defense by infantry. A wooden bridge crossed the Dnieper, and several boat or raft bridges had been, or were later, thrown by the Russians. From the north bank ran many roads, the main ones to St. Petersburg and Moscow.

Smolensk was already held by twenty thousand men,— a division of Bagration and the Nevrovski division, which had been driven from the ravines and suburbs back into the town, —the whole force being under Raevski and Paskievich. The first French assault was against the citadel, by Ney, in his usual gallant style, and was received in perfect cold blood. Twice the French soldiers reached the top of the counterscarp, and twice they were hurled back by the Russian reserve, timely put in. The initial attack thus failed. All accounts differ as to this day — August 16. Davout says in his Memoirs: " The emperor, after having reconnoitred the whole position of the enemy, determined to throw himself into the place, and to seize it out of hand if it were possible." The 13th Bulletin merely says that " during the 16th we remained

in observation." Raevski's report says that he got no reinforcements till evening; Bagration claims that he entered the
town at 10 A. M. Raevski speaks of a battle, and says that
a captured French officer could see Napoleon examining his
position through a glass, and that Murat, Ney and Davout
were all in his front. But as Davout only arrived at four
o'clock, and Poniatowski at five o'clock, until then the emperor had but Ney's eighteen thousand men, and Murat with
Grouchy and Nansouty. Would he have been justified in
trying to seize Smolensk out of hand? Bogdanovich says
the whole affair was narrowed down to a cannonade, and the
enemy undertook only feeble attacks. Raevski also states that
Napoleon's attacks were feeble; that he saw a decisive point
without profiting by it; that if he had displayed as much
vigor as next day, the Russians would have been destroyed.
Bagration made a great boast of his defense of Smolensk.
" The fifteen thousand men of the army confided to me held
during twenty-four hours against all the forces of the enemy,
and one may say almost disputed the victory in overturning
the assailants, not letting the enemy approach to within two
versts of the town, and in laying low up to ten thousand men."
This savors of exaggeration.

Before dark Barclay came up, and stationed his divisions
on the right bank heights near the St. Petersburg road.
The French corps gradually arrived, and by night one hundred and fifty thousand men were in line, drawn-up in a semicircle around Smolensk, Ney on the left, Ledru and Razout
in second line, Davout in the centre, Compans and Dessaix
in support, then Poniatowski, and Murat leaning on the
river. The Guard was in reserve at Ivanovskoi. Ideville
wrote Maret that the emperor had been in the saddle from
9 A. M. to 7 P. M., which speaks well for his activity that day.

Early August 17 the marshaling was completed. Junot was

still guarding the line to the rear at Tolstiki; and Eugene was kept at Liadi to forestall a Russian attempt to cross below and cut the French communications. Not having surprised Smolensk, Napoleon sent Guilleminot to discover a crossing up river, by which to make a further manœuvre to turn the Russian left and seize the Moscow road, for which duty Junot was selected. This was in manifest and natural sequence to the design of the entire operation; and it should have been pushed home at any cost; but Junot was far in the rear, and before the battle at the walls of Smolensk had been decided, a turning manœuvre was deemed by the emperor too late.

Assuming Smolensk to be the objective, the manœuvre had been skillfully conducted; yet Bagration's quick reinforcement of Smolensk, and the repulse of a first attack, had prevented its seizure. What could be done to repair this initial failure, so that the operation might yet succeed? The capture of Smolensk town was but an incident; the real purpose was to seize the Moscow road, cut off the Russian army, and oblige it to fight at a disadvantage. Coutanceau, in summing up the record evidence, says: "Napoleon desired to march on the enemy by the left bank of the Dnieper, seize Smolensk, then meet the enemy and beat him, *after* debouching from this town." Having failed in this, why not throw bridges at Dresna, and put the nearest corps over to seize the Moscow road? This was what Barclay dreaded. Smolensk was of as much importance to the Russians as to Napoleon. Alexander desired that battle should be delivered here: "The ardor of the soldier would have been extreme, for it was the entrance of the first really Russian town which he would have defended against the enemy." But Barclay said, Napoleon's "intention by this unexpected movement was clearly to cut us from the army of General Tormasov, from the governments of the south and even from Moscow. If we had hesitated the least in the world to take from him this advantage, he would not have missed extending himself as far as Dorogobush, and to get ahead of us at this point of the passage of the Dnieper." Though Napoleon's eye was as rapid and his planning as sound as ever in his tent, we shall see him here hesitate in his decision on the field, until too late to secure the real fruit of his turning manœuvre. In capturing a worthless town, he will forget the essence of the operation — to seize the communications of the enemy on the Moscow road, and force him to disastrous battle.

If Napoleon was too slow in his decision, so was not Barclay. He had no idea of fighting a decisive battle until he could choose his own place and time, and in front of Smolensk was not a suitable position. How could he debouch from two gates and attack a superior enemy? He was aware that to hold the road to Moscow was his only means of withdrawing to a better field; and in order to secure this, he decided to hold on to Smolensk, and at the same time forestall Napoleon's sending a force to occupy the road in his rear. As only a part of the Russians could be used for the defense of Smolensk, there being but few and unsuitable guns mounted on the walls, in the night of August 16–17 he relieved the troops in the town by a fresh thirty thousand men under Doctorov and Konovnitsin, and at early dawn on the 17th, while he himself remained near Smolensk, Bagration, having left a post opposite Shein Ostrov, where there was a ford, was started eastward, and took up a position astride the Moscow road behind the Kolodnia brook. This promptness was proof that Napoleon had had no time to lose; and on reaching Smolensk, he can scarcely have failed to see the danger of delay. The Russians had been constantly escaping him, and he had never yet been able to check their rearward movement. It was not wise to rely solely on their late enthusiasm for battle. Here was another chance. By extending his right across the river, and establishing a corps suitably supported upon the Moscow road, the longed-for battle could be forced, or the enemy thrown back on the St. Petersburg road, eccentrically to his true line of retreat. But during Bagration's movement of the 17th, which was about to destroy all the results of his manœuvre, Napoleon stood still in front of Smolensk, as if hoping that the Russians would debouch and accept battle in front of the town. He mounted his horse at 8 A. M., but scant reliable evidence exists as to what he did this day.

During the morning of the 17th, little of importance occurred. Doctorov had begun his work of defense by driving the French out of the southern suburbs, and this may have led Napoleon to think that the Russians were still ready for battle; but how he could persuade himself that they would fight, backing on Smolensk and the river, is hard to understand. They had had enough of that at Friedland. If the constant Russian retreat had made him despise them more than ever, as is so frequently alleged, one would think he would have run the risk of sending even a single corps to seize the road in their rear and oblige them to stand for battle. Here the emperor's judgment was as much at fault as his lack of speed.

When, between 1 and 2 P. M., Napoleon saw that he was in error, and that the Russians in Smolensk purposed only defense, he himself opened the attack. First the suburbs were recaptured, including the cemetery, by Ney and Davout, the ravines playing a marked rôle in the defense; whereupon Ney went in again opposite the citadel; Poniatowski on the up-river side; Davout on the Roslavl suburb. The centre batteries opened the battle; sixty guns on the right covered the bridges and the enemy beyond. To this fire the Rus-

sians suitably replied from batteries on the hills which en-
filaded the French right and left, but these continued their
work. The suburbs were gradually taken, the ravines crossed,
and by 5 P. M. the fighting was pushed fiercely to gain the
covered way, or a footing on the wall, especially near the
Malakovka gate, but in vain. Poniatowski all but forced
his way into a breach made by his field-guns in the walls,
and Ney came close to capturing the citadel, while Davout
drove Doctorov out of the south suburbs. But still the town
held out. Napoleon assembled all his guns to make a
breach in the curtain, but the thickness of the walls re-
sisted the light batteries; and it was not then known that
the towers were weaker. The guns set fire to many wooden
houses; but though the conflagration prevented wheeling up
ammunition, it did not spread rapidly, as each dwelling
stood in its own little garden. Fabry thinks this fighting
does not look like an attack pushed home; and Barclay
reported to the emperor that, as the enemy had concentrated
all his forces on Smolensk, he merely defended it long
enough to stop the enemy's march on Jelnia and Dorogobush,
so that Bagration might get there in time to prevent the
army being turned.

At 9 P. M. the French withdrew from the attack. Barclay
had reinforced the place by an extra division, and got the
rest of his forces on the road; and during the night of
August 17–18, he vacated Smolensk. " The town was afire,"
says the 13th Bulletin. " In the middle of a beautiful night
of August, Smolensk offered to the French the spectacle
which is offered to the inhabitants of Naples by the eruption
of Vesuvius." "At 2 o'clock " (A. M., August 18) "the first
grenadiers who mounted to the assault found no more resistance, the place was evacuated . . . and one of the most
beautiful towns of Russia was in our power, and all this in

the sight of the whole army of the enemy." Breaking the
bridges, Barclay retired to the heights on the north, as if to
protect the St. Petersburg road. Why he did not at once
join Bagration is hard to say, for Napoleon would scarcely
have ventured to march on St. Petersburg with the whole
Russian army on his flank. A division well handled would
have been enough to make Napoleon uncertain as to his
movements, if it kept up a slight demonstration from this
direction, especially as woods hid the troops. But to forestall a French turning operation, Barclay and Bagration " decided together that the First Army should occupy Smolensk,
and should remain on the right bank of the Dnieper, covering the march of the Second Army on Dorogobush." "If
the route to Moscow were lost, the Russians would have to
fall back on St. Petersburg, deprived of their reinforcements,
and besides, the coöperation of Tormasov and Chichagov,
from which Barclay expected the greatest results, would be
torn from them." "The First Army was to arrest the enemy
until the moment when the Second Army had reached the
crossing of the Dnieper at Solovievo ; " then it was to follow.

When, towards midnight of August 16–17, Barclay gave
the order to retreat, there was great indignation among the
defenders of the town. Bagration had begged Barclay to
continue the defense and then take the offensive, and many
generals joined him, as they felt they had won a great
victory. Constantine was at the head of the opposition, and
it would have been a happy day for Napoleon had they tried
to do this. There was a protest to the order, and Bagration
formally accused Barclay. Even the czar was discontented
when he heard of it, and it may have been part of what led to
Barclay's removal. In the rear discontent was great. Barclay's reason for giving up Smolensk remains a plain fact —
that he could be turned out of it by a crossing of the river

above. He also said in his report: "Let us admit that I had
held on to Smolensk the 16th. The enemy, who needed only
to cross the Dnieper above the town, would have forced me
to withdraw my troops. The Dnieper in the month of
August was not difficult to
cross in many places."

Grand Duke Constantine.

Out of some thirty thou-
sand Russians in the town
and sixty thousand French
actually in contact, the losses
had been about twelve thousand French to ten thousand
Russians. Davout gave his
as six thousand men, Gudin's
alone being seventeen hundred : forty per cent.

The emperor did not
change his position, but Junot came up and went into
line behind Poniatowski.
During the forenoon of the
18th the French occupied Smolensk proper, and as the city
was a necessary depot, at once set about extinguishing the
fires. Ney was ordered across the Dnieper, and Morand put
over in boats to protect the repair of the permanent bridge
and the throwing of pontoons ; but Barclay sent enough
troops under Korv to force the few French back across the
river, and then to maintain the St. Petersburg suburb until
4 P. M., when, as Ney could be held back no longer, the troops
set fire to it and retired on Barclay. For three days the
strategically worthless town had arrested the Grand Army,
when time was of the essence.

The entry into Smolensk was not a triumphal one. The

men had looked forward to this city as the term of their serious hardships; they had expected to defeat the Russians and earn some repose, amidst smiling fields and in pleasant quarters; but instead of a fine city full of wine and bread, there was a semi-civilized, half-burned town, whose inhabitants had fled, and had either hidden, destroyed, or hauled away all provision. To look back on the long stretch which separated them from their homes, and foresee a further pursuit of a still fleeing enemy, gave rise to no small disquiet.

To Maret, from Smolensk, the emperor reassuringly wrote, August 18 : —

"I have just come in. The heat is excessive and there is much dust, which tires us a little. We have had here the entire army of the enemy. It had orders to deliver battle here, but did not dare to. We have taken Smolensk with the strong hand. It is a big city, having a respectable wall and fortifications. We have killed three or four thousand men of the enemy, wounded treble, and found here many guns. Several of his division generals have been killed, from what they say here. The Russian army is marching, very discontented and very much discouraged, in the direction of Moscow. Schwartzenberg and Reynier together have beaten the Russians." There is a note on the original letter: "His Majesty having thrown himself on his bed immediately after having dictated this letter, and the courier having left without waiting, this letter is sent . . . without being signed."

Although natural enough, this again is one of the countless items which show that Napoleon was no longer in the heyday of his strength.

Indeed, Smolensk must have been a keen disappointment. The crop of 1811 had largely failed; that of 1812, yet growing, had been destroyed by this war, and to feed two hundred thousand men required cantonments so distributed as to be dangerous. To march back through Lithuania almost meant starvation; to retire via Mohilev and Mozyr was to traverse a marshy country unfit for an army; to withdraw to Poland via Lutsk and Brest Litovsk was easier, but any retreat might raise all Europe against him, and Napoleon could see nothing but further advance on the Russian army, which he must beat before he could dictate peace in Moscow. To be sure, Wittgenstein on the left and Tormasov and Chichagov on the right were threatening factors, but Napoleon counted on St. Cyr and Macdonald, on Schwartzenberg and Reynier, to fend them off, while Victor, with over thirty thousand men, was on the Niemen, and could be sent to support either the right on the Bug or the left on the Dvina. Loison and Durutte had fine divisions in Königsberg and Warsaw; others were organizing on the Oder; the new conscription (*premier ban*) was assembling on the Elbe. There were fifty thousand men in Prussia, and as many more coming on as reinforcements. All Europe was contributing its quotas to fill up the gaps.

By past successes Napoleon had learned that a decisive victory would dissipate all collateral dangers. Could he but reach the Russian army, he would put an end to all his difficulties. He had agreed to stop at Smolensk; but how, he argued, could he arrest his operations now? What were his promises to his officers and men compared with his and their eventual success?

Barclay remained on the heights north of Smolensk until the evening of the 18th; and as the main Moscow road was along the river bank and covered by the French batteries, he then sent Doctorov by a long circuit via Sykolina and Prudichevo towards Solovievo. The rest he led, part to the north of Gorbunovo and part through this village towards Lubino, by a bad country road, on which he covered scarcely a mile an hour. In the darkness, Eugene of Wurtemberg, with the rearguard, made a big circuit, lost his way, and reached Gedeonovo only after many hours' march. Korv for a moment took position on the heights behind Gedeonovo to sustain him, and the two were to fend off the French advance. Bagration, under orders to head for Moscow, had already retired many miles along the main road; but the French pressed Barclay so stoutly that he had to instruct his lieutenant to stop. Bagration had left some Cossacks under Karpov, and these Barclay reinforced with foot and artillery.

The Russian commander had not conducted his operations skillfully; and had Napoleon with his usual rapidity manœuvred to turn the Russian left, passed the river at Dresna with a mass, leaving what was essential to contain the Russians for some hours at Smolensk, he could have reached the rear of Barclay's column on the Moscow road, even if Bagration had got away. There was no danger of Barclay manœuvring against the French communications; for Napoleon with his superior numbers could have turned and crushed him. The same lack of decisiveness which at Vitebsk gave Barclay time to retire, was still more apparent; and without pushing to the end his handsome strategical operation, but accepting as a fact that he could not bring the Russians to battle near Smolensk, when they had just refused battle at the town, and that they had already retired too far to catch up with, he merely sent a small force on in direct pursuit. Although partly concealed by woods, he had seen Barclay's forces on the St. Petersburg road, and he should have gauged them as a large part of the Russian army, which he might cut off and beat in detail. During the 18th Napoleon personally paid little heed to anything outside Smolensk. He had sufficient opportunity to send Junot across the river to anticipate the Russians on the Moscow road; he had abundant chance for action; but he wasted the precious hours in trivial work which a staff officer could have accomplished.

All this may sound hypercritical; but we must try Napo-

leon by his own standard; our question is how far his own
decrease of energy affected his power to wage war; and here
he was quite behind his better days. It were absurd to
blame his shortcomings; but his failure must be explained.
There is no desire to make too much of small lapses; yet
each tells its story. Something like mental weariness based
on a physique no longer equal to the strain of his gigantic
conceptions seems to have been at fault.

Early on August 19 Murat forded the Dnieper and Ney
crossed on pontoon bridges at Smolensk, whilst Junot marched
up to Dresna and Prudichevo to throw a bridge where Napoleon had reconnoitred; and it was even at this late moment
a mistake that the bulk of the army was not put over here,
in natural prosecution of the original plan. But Napoleon
ordered Grouchy in the direction of Duchovchina, and Murat
with Nansouty and Montbrun along the Moscow road, to
hold the Russians by a smart attack, and to explore the
roads; and by the time the French army had crossed into
the burned St. Petersburg suburb, Barclay had marched off,
leaving only his trailing rearguard.

Karpov's Cossacks had been reinforced by troops under
Tuchkov, who first took up a position two miles east of
Valutino, and Eugene of Wurtemberg held Gedeonovo long
enough for Korv's rearguard to retire to Gorbunovo, and enable the first column of Barclay's main army, under Baggavut,
to reach Lubino. Ney moved out behind Murat to follow
the Russian retreat, the direction of which was yet unknown;
Eugene's column was found standing along the Stabna brook,
and attacking it, Ney lost some time, whereas he might have
contained it and marched around its flank on Lubino. Eugene, backed by Korv, fought in retreat to Gorbunovo, and
held Ney fully three hours. No orders to push the fighting
had been given to Ney, nor dispositions to that end made;

and Murat, on meeting Karpov's Cossacks, paused instead of driving them away.

Meanwhile, Tuchkov had reached the heights east of Valutino. Ney's combat against Eugene had carried him away from the Moscow road, and on Napoleon's arrival at the front he was ordered towards the right and to attack. Drawn up behind the Kolodnia brook he found Tuchkov, and fell upon him fiercely. Here was still a chance to redeem the operation, but it needed the eye of the master; yet instead of remaining with Ney, Napoleon, as if satiated with effort, returned to Smolensk. Tuchkov defended the ground, step by step, until he reached the Stragan brook, where he received reinforcements, and took up a position

Eugene of Wurtemberg.

astride the Moscow road, extending two miles or more to the north and south, with Lubino in his rear and the Stragan brook in his front. Had Napoleon remained and pressed the fighting by ordering Davout up to Ney's succor, the Russian resistance might have been broken and the bulk of Barclay's column got cut off. But as Ney alone could not break down the Russian guard, Barclay, who realized that he must check the French to effect his escape, had time to complete his long circuit. The fighting on both sides was severe and costly.

On his first arrival Murat had failed to push home against the Cossacks, and now on Ney's right had been prevented from manœuvring by the woods, ravines and marshes; each time he essayed to push in on the Russians by way of Latishino, he was checked by the charges of Orlov Denisov. That his lack of vigor was due to want of good-will towards Ney, existing since Ulm, has been alleged; but this is doubtful; the prime fault clearly lay with the emperor for his absence at this critical moment; he alone could direct in a case like this. His marshals were never equal to the extreme test; and wonderful as they were as lieutenants, few of them rose to conditions such as Napoleon was wont to create. The Peninsular campaign was proving this every year. Junot, who had crossed the river at Dresna, was supposed to advance about the Russian left to reach the Moscow road in their rear; yet, though Murat made a number of demands on him to go forward, one at least in person, Junot clung to his position near the river, and, though usually hasty and impetuous, utterly failed to coöperate. He was afraid to exceed his orders. A year later he died insane. Finally, to the aid of Ney, Napoleon sent the division of Gudin, who, at 5 P. M., renewed the assault on Kosina heights; the Russian line was all but broken; but being reinforced by Konovnitsin, the French were finally checked, and Gudin was killed. By nightfall Bagration's mass had come up, including Baggavut and Korv. Unaware of this, Ney persisted in attacks on the Russian right; but despite magnificent gallantry, he could make no impression; and falling night stopped the slaughter, in which between five thousand and six thousand men fell on each side. The French had had more men ready to put in line; but owing to the absence of Napoleon this had not been done, and no good had been won by the sacrifice; indeed, until midnight the emperor remained ignorant of the fierceness of the struggle which was going on within ten miles of him. On learning the facts, he rode out to the battlefield. Arriving by 3 A. M. of the 20th, he found that the enemy was at a safe distance, marching along the road to Moscow.

The trouble with the fighting of the 19th was that Napoleon assumed that no result was to be gained by pushing the Russians, whom he deemed to have escaped. With the facts as we have them, however, and which Napoleon with his old activity would have ascertained, he could probably have arrested the enemy by actively ordering forward the troops from Smolensk; or he might at least have inflicted a heavy blow on Barclay — perhaps have brought on the decisive battle he craved, or even have beaten him in detail.

The French claim the battle of Valutino (among Russians the battle of Lubino) as a victory; but the Russians had succeeded in what they attempted; the French had not. Tuchkov had held back the French until Barclay could get his whole column on the Moscow road : Napoleon had not brought the Russians to a general battle. The early accounts of this battle are hard to decipher, for as the French knew the country ill, and the Russians destroyed the sign-posts, the names in the several accounts are much mixed.

With reference to the battle at Smolensk, Barclay wrote the czar : " The splendid combats that the First Army sustained at Smolensk are known to Your Majesty by my report. The enemy was stopped, and the Second Army so gloriously covered that it lost not a man; after having attained the veritable end of these combats, we left to the enemy the débris of Smolensk. The army continued its march in two columns on Dorogobush," and on the 20th crossed the Dnieper at Solovievo.

Napoleon had reached Smolensk early August 16 ; and by neglecting to carry forward his turning manœuvre so as to seize the Moscow road in Barclay's rear, the 16th, 17th, 18th and 19th were practically wasted. That he did not sufficiently heed the severity or importance of the recent fighting is shown by his letter of August 20 to Berthier: "Write to the Intendant-General that the service of the ambulance is badly done; that it is astonishing that since yesterday, when there were engagements of the vanguard" (this was the bloody battle of Valutino), "the surgeons of headquarters, some ambulances and empty wagons . . . should not have been sent to the vanguard to pick up the wounded; and that the administration has no head."

Despite abundant cause for it, the French archives seem to show small signs of discouragement, even at Smolensk. Ney was still full of energy, and assuming the enemy to be much demoralized on the retreat, and that the French morale had "mounted to the highest degree of enthusiasm," on August 20 he proposed to take, each night, as the moon was generally shining, a fresh brigade of infantry and harass the enemy's rear, "so as to keep all the Russian army under arms, and thus tire them out, while the French were comfortably sleeping." This was a gallant proposition, but one can scarcely think that the " whole Russian army " would be kept under arms more than one or two nights by whatever even Ney might do with a French brigade.

Despite his recent lapse from energy, the emperor kept an eye on matters in the rear. He was fearful of Cossack raids on the road back to Vitebsk, and on August 20 he sent to Inkovo and towards Vitebsk to see that the communications were not disturbed. And on the same day he wrote Eugene: " My Son, I send you a report of the commandant of Krasnoi. You did not then give orders to the cavalry as I told you to do, to protect my rear and cover it from the Cossacks." Eugene had meanwhile put his division over in Smolensk and taken position on the Petersburg road; the Guard occupied the city, and Poniatowski remained on the left bank.

When, on August 21, Barclay crossed the Usha at Usviati and found his army was still in a mood for battle, he determined to make a stand, and drawing up behind the stream, ordered Bagration, who had retired to Dorogobush, to come back to the chosen line. The advantage of the position was not marked: Clausewitz says it was as good as any other, if the Russians were at that time to fight a great battle. On the 23d Murat came up to the Usha and found the Russians in line; next him came Davout, then Ney, put in the rear on account of his heavy losses; Junot still stood near the place where he had crossed the Dnieper; Grouchy had reached Duchovchina, and Eugene, in his rear, was on the road thither, having sent a division to Surash to hold head against a Russian threat on Vitebsk. Poniatowski had started, south of the Dnieper, via Bielkino and Jelnia, towards Dorogobush; Latour-Maubourg was guarding the communications at Mstislavl. Napoleon with the Guard still occupied Smolensk, but kept his attention fixed on the vanguard column. He was still waiting for them to turn and fight. On August 22 he sent word to Davout: " My Cousin, you do not write me. I desire you to write me every day. . . . I recommend Murat not to tire the troops too much in this extreme heat, to engage only in affairs of the rearguard, and to take position as soon as there shall be reason to think that the enemy has assumed one to receive battle."

So soon as the Usha was reached, word was sent to headquarters that Barclay was standing, and on its receipt, during the night of August 23–24, Napoleon reiterated orders to Eugene and Poniatowski to speed their march forward, and sent Latour-Maubourg instructions to come on rapidly. On August 23, in the evening, he wrote Davout: " In twenty-four

hours the whole army can assemble. I await your news this
evening to set the Guard in march, so that if the enemy desires to wait for us, we can deliver battle." And as the army
needed further reserves, on August 23 orders were dispatched
to Victor to move on Kovno in four columns with the utmost
speed. Junot and the Young Guard were sent on the 24th
along the Moscow road, followed next morning by the Old
Guard, the emperor leaving Smolensk at midnight, after writing to Maret: "I leave to-night to go to Dorogobush, where
it seems the armies are in presence, the enemy having come
to a halt. They assure me that there is a position there
of which they desire to profit, to deliver battle and cover
Moscow."

Murat had been anxious to attack without waiting for
Napoleon, and had thrown Montbrun against the left of
Barclay's position; but as Davout judged his foot too weak
to open a fight against the whole Russian army, no more was
done. Made uneasy by Montbrun's attack, and unaware that
the French had no great force in his front, Barclay did not
await battle on the Usha; but breaking up during the night of
August 23–24, he marched to Dorogobush, whence he reached
Viasma the 27th. Nor did he find ground here for a good
battlefield; and, burning the town, he kept up his retreat
until August 29, and then came to a front at Zarevo-Saimichi.
Although he had been full of fight when he advanced towards
Vitebsk, Napoleon's outmanœuvring him for the moment
drew his temper, and he did not get worked up to the true
fighting-pitch again until he got to Viasma. Here Miloradovich came up with fifteen thousand men, and, on the road
towards Gshask, Barclay turned to meet the Grand Army.
But he had delayed too long. Kutusov reached the army from
Moldavia, with the reputation of having conquered a peace
from the Turks, and with orders to take supreme command.

With regard to this failure to bring about a battle, on August 26 the emperor wrote Maret : "The enemy having constructed fortifications, set up batteries and redoubts, and having announced the intention to hold a position here, has as usual lacked resolution. We have entered the town, which is quite considerable, because there are eight or ten

Kutusov.

steeples. The country is good, and they assure me that it remains very fine to Moscow. The heat we are having is excessive. The weather continues to be very fine. They say the enemy is resolved to await us at Viasma."

The Russians had retired in excellent order, the rearguard under Rosen easily holding back Murat and Davout ; indeed, these two marshals failed to work amicably together ; and, the horses being so ill nourished on rye straw that they were

unserviceable, the French could not match the yet well-con-
served Russian cavalry. The French column made slow progress. The squadrons in the van, crowded on the post-road,
were stopped at each brook, at each wood, at each bridge, by
well-located batteries, and here had to await the foot, which
usually arrived to find the enemy gone. Moreover, after
passing Smolensk, the signs of a national war increased.
In Lithuania, the inhabitants had cared little who was the
winner; in Russia proper, the entire population deserted fire-
sides and farms at the approach of the French. Villages were
found abandoned or burned, and all provisions disappeared;
Viasma's rich magazines were destroyed; Gshask was half
in ruins, and but a part of it was saved by the French van in
hunting for food. The farther the Grand Army advanced,
the more hopeless the prospect looked. The leader alone
seemed to be buoyed up by what many call his blind belief
in his destiny, but what was really the dread of turning back
defeated, and by the confidence that he still should win.

Had not Napoleon, on leaving Smolensk, expected to
deliver battle at Usviati, he might have debated the question
of further advance; but on reaching this town, August 25,
and finding his hope again deferred, the cost of the first step
being paid, he decided to keep on in pursuit: "It is probable
that the army of the enemy will await us at Viasma. We
should reach that place numerous and in order," he wrote
Eugene, and so Smolensk and rest were forgotten. Murat,
Davout, Ney, the Guard and Junot marched along the great
Moscow road; Eugene and Grouchy on parallel country roads
to the left, so as to cross the Dnieper at Molodilova; Poniatowski on the right via Voloshok, the emperor accompanying
one or other column, and spending the nights in castles near
the route; and on the 29th the army was near Viasma.

Along the road, the emperor busied himself not only with

the smaller tactical details, but with the broad strategic scheme. Some of his orders have much importance.

On August 26 he had written to Davout : " My Cousin, form a vanguard of infantry, which shall march with the cavalry an hour in front of your army corps, and always take position a league in advance of you. This vanguard should itself be preceded by two battalions of voltigeurs. The rest of your corps, place it always in line of battle an hour in the rear. . . . You must make little day's marches and with order. If the plain is as believed, and the cavalry can pass on the right and on the left, the march can be so directed as not to be tiring for the foot. It ought to be finished early " (each day). " All the probabilities are that the enemy will await us at Viasma. We must then arrive there in order. Have the bridges all well prepared, and have double bridges made." On the same day he ordered Berthier to arrange with Victor to protect the French communications, even to the point of marching on Smolensk. " I suppose that St. Cyr has sufficient with the 2d and 6th Corps to hold Wittgenstein in check, and to have nothing to fear from him, and that Macdonald can move on Riga to invest the place." Then he directs reinforcements to move on Kovno : " That thus it would be only in case St. Cyr were beaten by Wittgenstein and forced to recross the Dvina, that Victor would first have to march to his aid ; that, this case excepted, he is to follow the direction of Smolensk." And on August 27, to Augereau in Berlin, he wrote : " My Cousin, I have calculated on the arrival of all the reinforcements which are to rejoin my army, so as to form successive reserves in my rear. It is therefore proper that everything that is not destined, by dispositions determined by me, to make a part of your army corps, should continue its route to rejoin me. You are not to retain a single hussar, a single chasseur, a single artillery wagon. Make everything march. I should be very much annoyed if, at the distance where I am, the reinforcements which should come to me were stopped and turned away from the destination I have given them."

The Cossacks gave no little trouble to the column on the march and in its rear, and to check them, little blockhouses were built, or houses were fortified with palisades and ditches, " in such a manner that one hundred men of infantry and fifteen of cavalry may be protected from all attack ; " each intermediate post was thus defended, and the commandant of Smolensk was ordered to see to their safety.

There were no military difficulties to be encountered in the march from Smolensk to Moscow except those of battle and victual. Strategy there was none. It was an advance on the heels of a retiring foe along a single road, and with flanking columns: but the Russians were well supplied, and what they could not use as they fell back they destroyed, and the French, horse and man, were on short commons. Along the road proper, nearly the entire population decamped. At a little distance from it, the population did not desert the farms so generally, and this was an invitation to the French soldiers to straggle and pillage, with the result that the Grand Army lost between Smolensk and Borodino a full third of its numbers. Thousands of stragglers were caught by the Cossacks: death was their easiest fate.

As to the destruction of the Russian villages there is much conflicting testimony. It was manifestly to the advantage of the Russians to let nothing fall into the hands of the French; it was equally to the advantage of the French to conserve everything. Yet so careless are pillagers, indeed so careless is any army on the march, that the chances are that the French did as much damage as the Russians.

In the midst of work Napoleon found time to do a kindly act. General Deroy, commanding a Bavarian division, was wounded at Polotsk. Before knowing of his death from his wounds, Napoleon wrote, August 27: "Monsieur le Général de Division, Comte Deroy, I write you this letter to testify my entire satisfaction at the fine conduct you held at the combat of Polotsk, and the regret that I have to know you are wounded. I wish myself to let you know that I have named you Count of the Empire, and have accorded to you a dotation of thirty thousand francs, transmissible to your children; and wishing to reassure you on the subject of your family, I have sent you a brevet of six thousand francs pension for Countess Deroy."

Eugene was marching on the French left and Poniatowski on the right, and now rather anticipating the continued retreat of the Russians, Napoleon wrote Berthier, August 30 : —

"It is proper that, in case anything happens, the viceroy should be able to turn the right of the enemy, and Poniatowski his left, and that the three vanguards should be so near each other that they may attack in unison. This will necessarily spare blood and put the enemy out of condition of resisting. . . . Notify the viceroy that it is essential that with all his cavalry and a good vanguard of infantry and artillery, he should be able to turn the right of the enemy and take part in the action " (*aux coups de canon*), "if there is one. That it is the only means of sparing blood and accelerating the retreat of the enemy. Give the same order to Poniatowski for the right. He is to turn the left of the enemy."

Little was known on the Continent about the progress of the Grand Army, and what Napoleon wrote home was one-sided. The charge of lying is constantly made against the emperor for what he wrote in these evil days ; but as a matter of fact, mendacity was indulged in, not only by him in Russia, but by every one, everywhere in Europe, and certainly on the other side of the Channel. In what war to the knife is the truth ever told at the time ? Napoleon wrote for effect upon the French public, and what he wrote had this effect. He neither expected to convince nor succeeded in convincing England. The British clenched their teeth and played their own game. The "London Times" seems to have been able to publish in London both the French and the Russian statements with a promptness which argues wonderful enterprise for those days, and much of the Continent was hoping for Russian success.

Smolensk was the natural terminus of the 1812 campaign. When Napoleon was unable to bring the Russian army to battle there, the campaign — not the war — was definitely ended. He started with the belief that a sharp advance into Russia, and one or two decisive victories, would bring this nation to his feet, like the other European peoples. This belief was the natural sequence of Friedland; but it was an error. As Spain could not be subdued by military success alone, so with Russia, the backward civilization of which made its faith and patriotism strong. As the Spanish mountain regions enabled irregulars to hold their own against well-disciplined armies, so the Russian steppes enabled armies to withdraw at will from contact with the invader, and thus thwart his efforts. The Spanish guerrilla warfare was in Russia matched by constant retreat across the plains; nor were there mountain ranges, or seacoasts, or frontiers to limit operations. Napoleon had found the task in the Peninsula difficult; and the Austrian imbroglio having compelled him to leave it to his marshals, he could not be reproached with failure; here he had put into the scale his individual strength and ability, as well as all the power of France and her allied peoples, and he could not withdraw from the contest. And yet at Smolensk he was called on to decide whether or not he would advance farther into the bowels of the land; and he decided from mistaken premises. The power of truly gauging the facts had passed from him.

From a military point of view he could stop at Smolensk, put the Grand Army into quarters from which assembly was easy, and by holding the Dvina and the Dnieper would be in a somewhat similar situation to those he held in 1805 in Moravia before Austerlitz, and in 1807 in Poland before Eylau. As he would be draining a large section of the empire, the Russian army would sooner or later come forward and attack him. Making Smolensk a secondary base, and there accumulating material for a further campaign in 1813, was the only safety offered him, if he was unwilling to retreat. But Napoleon had built up his entire structure, military and political, on sharp, brilliant successes; and while the defensive basis of action would be proper for the soldier, it might be the ruin of

the statesman. Nor indeed can we be certain that the Russians
would not have kept up their waiting policy. Napoleon was
not accustomed to make safety his guiding star; and he could
not believe that Russia would not yield: could he but reach
her ancient capital, Moscow, he now argued, he could surely
dictate terms to St. Petersburg. In a way Napoleon's belief
was justified, for he thought he had fathomed the character of
Alexander. His confidence was founded only on the moral
standpoint; from a military standpoint, while it was possible
to reach Moscow, he clearly could not hold himself there. He
was farther away from his base than any conqueror, other than
the head of a migratory invasion, had been in modern times.
So long a line of operations demanded either friendly nations,
or heavy forces on right and left to protect it from being interrupted; or else the main army must be so superior in force
that in case the enemy moved towards this line, it might turn
upon him, cut him off and destroy him. In 1805 and 1806
Napoleon relied on his speed and superiority to neutralize
the danger of his line being cut; but when in 1805 he reached
Moravia, we have seen how he put out flank armies to protect
his four-hundred-mile long line of operations, and have
admired the skill with which these were so located as to be
nearer for the purpose of rallying on the main body than were
those of the enemy. In 1807 he was equally careful to protect
his line, which, from the Elbe, was over three hundred and
fifty miles long.

But the conditions were not such here. Arguing, as
Wartenburg ably does, on the situation as it will be when the
Grand Army shall have reached Moscow, — and the emperor
could do this at Smolensk, — we find that Napoleon crossed
the Niemen with three hundred and sixty thousand men; he
reached Vitebsk with two hundred and forty thousand men; he
started for Smolensk with one hundred and eighty thou-

sand men ; he left Smolensk with one hundred and fifty thousand men ; he met the Russians at Borodino (the battle he must fight) with one hundred and thirty-five thousand men ; he reached Moscow with ninety-five thousand, at the end of a line of communications five hundred and thirty miles long. These figures demonstrate that superiority in numbers could not be relied on to protect his communications. Neither were there flank detachments in sufficient force. On the right, Tormasov's and Chichagov's joint army of over sixty thousand men, in the Lutsk-Ostrog country, could hardly be held in check by Schwartzenberg and Reynier with thirty-five thousand men; and this army threatened a point in the main communications four hundred miles to the rear from Moscow, while itself was less than two hundred miles distant from that point. On the left, Wittgenstein on the Drissa was soon to have forty thousand men, and was faced by St. Cyr in front of Polotsk with but seventeen thousand ; and this force threatened Borisov on Napoleon's communications only one hundred miles distant from Polotsk and three hundred and fifty from Moscow. In other words, neither by superiority nor by flank armies was Napoleon's line of communications protected. At Smolensk the military situation was within control; at Moscow it was beyond the control of any man. At so distant a point Napoleon could rely only on the moral force of his position : his military situation would be utterly untenable.

Thus there was in reality offered the emperor but a slender chance of safety. If he stopped at Smolensk, he ran a certain risk of political damage ; if he advanced to Moscow, all military chances were against him. But with an army at Smolensk, he could personally return to France and bid defiance to his political enemies, organize a fresh campaign for 1813, and by suitable concessions, or good luck, retire, or win with honor. His personal power in Europe was by no means exhausted; it was yet a distinct factor in the calculation. And in 1813 he would be better equipped logistically for an advance from Smolensk, for he would have time to provide proper transportation. This plan offered him a show of success, political and military. The advance on Moscow now could succeed only if Alexander and Russia were content to be browbeaten by a show of military power Napoleon no longer possessed. Yet Jomini and Clausewitz both approve Napoleon's decision to advance from Smolensk on Moscow, as his only proper course. It is difficult to agree with these eminent authorities.

Russian Infantry
Officer.

CHAPTER 4

BORODINO. SEPTEMBER 1 TO 7, 1812.

WHEN the army reached Gshask September 1, within eight days of Moscow, it seemed natural to keep on, though the Grand Army was almost a wreck and the rear looked doubtful. Barclay was superseded by Kutusov, who stayed at Borodino to fight. Napoleon reached his front September 4, and prepared for a decisive struggle. The Russian army stood across the Moscow roads behind a brook and the Kolotsa River, with one big and three small redoubts in its front. Napoleon would not try too marked a turning manœuvre lest it should again retreat, but prepared to break down its centre. There was a vast array of guns; Kutusov had one hundred and twenty thousand men, Barclay on the right, Bagration on the left; Napoleon somewhat less, with Eugene on the left, Davout, Ney and Murat in the centre, and Poniatowski on the right. The Russians were well fed, the French had scant rations. Napoleon opened the battle early September 7 with the guns, and by advancing the centre to take the redoubts, and Eugene to capture Borodino and the big fort, while Poniatowski was to turn the Russian left. The first assault failed, but later the redoubts were taken, Eugene captured Borodino, and Poniatowski advanced slowly. The Russians retired somewhat, and Ney, feeling sure he could drive them into rout, called for reinforcements. But at this moment a Cossack attack on Eugene's left arrested the emperor's attention, and he delayed sending Ney help. The Cossack attack proved trivial, but an hour had been lost. The infantry fighting died down, but into the heavy masses on either side eight hundred guns poured constant fire. Eugene by a final effort captured the big fort, and this was the end of the battle. The Russians had used every man; Napoleon still had the Guard. He believed the Russians must have reserves, and declined to put the Guard in. Had he done so, we know to-day that he would have destroyed the Russian army. As it was, the French had not won the decisive victory needed. They had lost thirty thousand men, the Russians probably forty thousand, but Kutusov's army retired during the night in fairly good order, and the French bivouacked on the battlefield. Borodino was a battle fought in parallel order all along the line without grand-tactics. In it the French army showed wonderful gallantry, and the Russians equal devotion. The percentage of losses was, for such large bodies, the greatest of modern times. Otherwise the battle had no unusual features.

ARRIVED at Gshask September 1, within eight days' march
of the sacred city of Moscow, the ancient capital of Russia,
which was full of food and material and a fit resting-place
for the foot-weary troops, and especially when the Russians
again speeded their retreat, it seemed to Napoleon more natural to proceed. Having sent orders to Victor to come on
to Vitebsk or Smolensk with his corps, and to Augereau to
bring half his force to Königsberg and Warsaw, to protect
his line of advance, the emperor confidently set out to follow
the Russian forces. If he had any misgivings, we are not
permitted to know them.

The rear of the Grand Army was ill cared for. As a general rule, orders given by the emperor were supposed to be
executed apart from any difficulties in the way, but he was
now too far distant to know the facts or punish laxity or dis-
honesty. The able administrators could not, and the lazy
ones would not, carry out instructions; and many an em-
ployee, divining the future, lined his own pocket. Repairs on
bridges and roads were neglected, and the collection of victual
was so ill attended to, that the convalescents following the
army had issued to them only half-rations. Habituated to
exact obedience, few officers dared act on their own initiative, and the well-provided line of communications it was
Napoleon's purpose to create became a road of starvation,
because the impossible was ordered and the possible was not
done. Napoleon had also found out that his staff was ill-
trained. He had written Berthier, July 2, that "the general
staff is organized in a fashion that one can see nothing
ahead by its means," and now, on September 2, he wrote:
"My Cousin, the general staff is of no use to me. Neither
the grand provost of the gendarmes, nor the wagon-master,
nor the staff officers, not one of them serves as he ought to
do." But he none the less made skillful preparations for

what was in his front, believing he should yet win a decisive battle, and that this would cure the difficulties in his rear, which he was keen enough to suspect, at least in part, but practically never mentioned.

Meanwhile, battle never left the emperor's mind. On August 30 he wrote Berthier: "Give orders to General Eblé to leave at five o'clock in the morning to rejoin the vanguard. He will have all the bridges in the rear repaired. He will march with all his personnel," and all his tools, but no pontoons. "You will make this general understand that as we are nearly in the presence of the enemy, and as it is probable that in three or four marches there will be a general battle, success may depend on the rapidity with which are established the debouches, and the bridges over the torrents and the ravines. That it is indispensable for him to be there, so that, as soon as shall be possible, he may construct these debouches. For an army like this one, there are needed always at least six. For this purpose he is to work with the engineers, and not await any new order to see to the erection of bridges over the ravines and little streams." Chasseloup was also given similar orders to coöperate with Eblé. And then, as he had been riding with the van, he added: "Let me know where is to be found the 'Little Headquarters,' of what it consists, and when it can leave." Next day he wrote Berthier "to have the caissons which are empty loaded with brandy, to be used on a day of battle;" and on September 1, to Maret: "It is probable that in a few days I shall have a battle. If the enemy loses it, he will lose Moscow. My communications from Vilna to Smolensk are not difficult, but from Smolensk here they may become so. We need more troops, some national guards. They need not be good, because they are opposed only to peasants."

Grave abuses had grown up under the trying conditions of

the march. One has only to read between the lines of the following Order (of which only the substance can be given) to see how much there was to cure. In effect, the abuses did not, could not, get cured; scarcely palliated.

ORDER OF THE DAY.

GSHASK, September 1, 1812.

"His Majesty the Emperor and King has ordered as follows : " 1st. All wagons to move after the artillery and the ambulances. 2d. Private wagons found in the way of the artillery or ambulances to be burned. 3d. Only the artillery wagons and ambulances to follow the vanguard ; other wagons to be two leagues in the rear, and any such found nearer to be burned. 4th. At the end of the day no wagons to rejoin the vanguard until after it has taken position, and fighting has ceased ; any wagons transgressing this rule to be burned. 5th. In the morning such wagons to be parked outside the road ; those found on the road to be burned. 6th. These dispositions to apply to the whole army. 7th. The chiefs of staff of each division and corps to see that the baggage wagons march in the rear and separate, and in command of a good wagon-master. 8th. General Belliard, chief of staff of the vanguard, to see that these orders are obeyed at the vanguard, and that the wagons do not pass the defiles without his knowledge. 9th. This order to be read September 2 to all the corps, and " His Majesty gives notice that on September 3 he will see himself to the burning in his presence of the wagons found in contravention of this order." But next day he wrote Berthier : " See to it that the first baggage wagons that I order burned shall not be those of the general staff. If you have no wagon-master, name one and let all the " (staff) " baggage march under his directions. It is impossible to see a worse order than now reigns."

Davout came in again for his share of scolding. On September 2 Napoleon wrote : —

" My Cousin, I was ill satisfied yesterday with the manner your corps was marching. All your companies of sappers, instead of mending the bridges and the debouches, did nothing, excepting those of Compans' division. No direction had been given to the troops and the baggage to pass the defile, so that all found themselves on one another's heels. Finally, instead of being a league behind the vanguard, you were close upon it. All the baggage wagons, etc., were in front of your corps, in front even of the vanguard, so that your wagons were in the town before the light cavalry had debouched.   Take measures to remedy such a bad condition, which might seriously compromise all the army." And on the same day, to Berthier : "My Cousin, for two days I have not seen a report of the position of Davout. I do not know where his corps is. Let me understand why this is. It is his duty to make a report every day."

Inasmuch as Davout was always noted as a strict disciplinarian, we may assume that equal criticism was applicable to the other corps.

From the enemy's signs of readiness to defend the road to Moscow the emperor now guessed that the long anticipated battle would within a few days be delivered, and he began his preparations. At Gshask, September 2, he wrote Berthier to give orders to Murat, Davout, Eugene, Poniatowski and Ney to repose and rally the troops, "to have roll-call at three o'clock in the afternoon, and to let him know positively the number of men who will be present in the battle; to have an inspection made of arms, cartridges, artillery and ambulances; to make the soldiers understand that we are approaching the moment of a general battle, and that they are to prepare for it." He demands, by ten o'clock in the evening, a statement of the number of troops, of guns, their calibre, the rounds they have, the number of cartridges per man, the number in the caissons, the state of the ambulances, the number of surgeons and their material.   Also the detached men who are not present, who will not be present the next day, but who can be up in two or three days, the number of horses without shoes, and the time necessary to shoe them. "These reports are to be made with the greatest attention, because on their result will depend my resolve." Murat, Poniatowski and Eugene were to advance slightly and rectify their position.

The Russian nation, or at least the nobles, for the serfs had no part in the matter, had undertaken the campaign with great enthusiasm, especially in the Moscow district, where ten per cent. of the male population was allotted to the field. The nobles did not understand the wisdom of retreat: invariably assured that the Russian armies were successful, they asked why such constant retreat, and who was at fault? The blame was cast upon Barclay, who was not of Russian blood; and Kutusov, the victor of Rudshuk, became the hero of the nation. Despite his autocratic power, the czar had assembled a commission to select a new commander, and Kutusov proved to be the choice. The Chancellor, Rumantzov, who had been in favor of the French alliance, was also suspected of playing into the enemy's hands; and Sir Robert Wilson, the English envoy, conveyed to the czar, from the army officers in St. Petersburg, what was really a mutinous message, based on the fear that Rumantzov might make peace. Alexander received the message sensibly, and assured Wilson that " he would sooner let his beard grow to the waist, and eat potatoes in Siberia, than permit any negotiations with Napoleon so long as an armed Frenchman remained in the territories of Russia." As to the suspicion expressed, the czar not only retained his confidence in Rumantzov, but he would not submit to dictation: his course at this time shows him to have had unusual balance.

We remember Kutusov in the Austerlitz campaign. He was a good average soldier, perhaps no better than Barclay. He was now seventy, too portly to ride, and not active. Although he had failed in 1805, he yet represented the fighting quality of Suwarrov, and having won the peace in Turkey, he was trusted. Had Barclay fought at Dorogobush, or at Gshask, the nation would have demanded a brilliant victory; but when Kutusov withdrew from Borodino, it was felt that the best possible had been done, — as indeed was true. Had any soldier weighed the conditions at Gshask, as present facts enable one to do, he might have predicted just what happened: the French must march to Moscow; there must be a battle to dispute their advance; and once in Moscow, they could not hold themselves. The advance beyond Smolensk had been a fatal error.

That Kutusov would not fight in Barclay's chosen position, because he might lose part of the credit of a victory, is less probable than that he delayed battle so as to get acquainted with the army. As Clausewitz says, one position was about as good as another. On an open plain, hundreds of miles wide, without marked hills, no stone-built villages to act as redoubts, and few unfordable streams, any position might be turned, and no enemy would attack earthworks if he could turn them. Had not Napoleon ardently longed for a pitched battle, he never would have attacked at Borodino. The new commander had orders to fight the battle which the czar and the nation demanded for the safety of Moscow; and not deeming the position of Zarevo-Saimichi a good one, he had fallen back August 31, on which day Napoleon and the French van reached Vilichevo, with Junot at Viasma, Eugene on the left at Pokrov, and Poniatowski on the right at Sloboda. On September 1 and 2 Kutusov continued his retreat towards Mozhaisk, and on the 3d reached the chosen place on the heights back of the Kolotsa, opposite Borodino. Here he stopped, resolved to receive a battle.

At Gshask, September 1, news of Kutusov's appointment fully convinced Napoleon that the Russians would fight, and here he concentrated the arriving corps, so as to advance well massed. Murat marched through Gshask, and took position, September 2, a few miles beyond; Davout and Ney remained nearby the town, Eugene at Pavlovo, and Poniatowski in the Sloboda country, Junot still being back at Tieplucha.

At Gshask, September 3, another attempt was made to stop the evil of straggling, and Berthier was instructed to write to the corps commanders that " many men are lost by the disorder in which foraging is done ; that they must arrange measures to put a term to a set of things which menaces the army with destruction ; that the number of prisoners which the enemy makes mounts every day to several hundred ; that under the severest penalties soldiers must be forbidden to straggle."

The reports called for by the order of the 2d showed one hundred and twenty-eight thousand men in line, with six thousand more to arrive within five days ; and during September 3 Junot came up. It had been raining for three days, but on September 4 it cleared, and the army moved under pleasant skies forward from Gshask toward the fateful field of Borodino. By afternoon Murat, at Gridnieva, ran into the Russian rearguard, which after a defense until nightfall retired to Kolotsi. Personally, Napoleon was at the front, bivouacking at Gridnieva. Next day Murat again attacked the Russian rearguard at Kolotsi, while Eugene turned their flank at Lusosi, and the body fell back on the main army at Borodino, which Murat drew near by 2 P. M., Eugene advancing by way of Bolshi Sadi and Poniatowski by way of Jelnia.

Two post-roads ran from Smolensk to Moscow, an old one and a new. The village of Borodino lay on the new road, where it crossed the Kolotsa, an affluent of the Moskwa ; the old one being here two miles and a half to the south. The country is rolling rather than strongly accentuated, but the many brooks run in ravines more or less deep. The country was full of woods, and where these had been cut down were left what we call slashings, alternating with open fields. For a couple of miles the Kolotsa, fordable in places, but needing bridges for quick passage, meanders along parallel to and

Battle of Borodino.

south of the new road, until near Borodino it crosses and leaves it to flow northerly towards the Moskwa; and just above Borodino a little brook runs from the south in a marked ravine, and falls into it. East of the brook, the land rises into a plateau a mile wide; then comes another ravine and another plateau. Near the head of this brook, a mile southerly from Borodino, lay the village of Semenovskoi, on a sloping hill with the brook in its front. It had been razed, for a wooden village, easily set afire, is more of a danger in the line of battle than a defense. On the west side of the brook-ravine are three hillocks, each of which had been crowned by a simple arrowhead field-work, open in the rear — a redan. Between Semenovskoi and Borodino was a hill crowned by a good bastioned redoubt, and in front of all these works the slope was gentle and favorable to artillery fire. Several small works covered the right wing. On the old road, due south of Borodino, is the village of Utiza. North of Borodino lies fairly open country, and between the two roads are a number of hamlets and villages. The position was liable to be turned; but it was also one easy to defend, for in its front assaulting troops could not manœuvre and preserve their formation, and a column forcing its way forward in a ragged mass would be apt to be decimated by well-placed guns.

After a reconnoissance Napoleon first ordered the capture of the intrenched villages of Fomkina, Alexinki, Doronino and Shivardino, which would threaten the French right as the columns marched along the new post-road. Fomkina was easily taken by Murat, who there crossed the Kolotsa, followed by Davout; and while both took Alexinki and deployed in front of the Russian centre, Poniatowski debouched from Jelnia, captured Doronino and threatened the enemy's left flank. Shivardino was valiantly defended, and when lost, retaken;

but by 10 P. M. this position also was yielded to Compans, the Russians falling back on their line of battle. For the night Napoleon's bivouac was near Valevieva on the new road, the Guard with Eugene's corps in its front. Ney came up in Davout's rear; Junot still lay at Gshask. With battle to face, the emperor took short rest. By 2 A. M. he was in the saddle, and with Caulaincourt and Rapp set out to reconnoitre the Russian position.

Kutusov probably had one hundred and twenty thousand men in line, of whom seventeen thousand were irregulars and militia, wherewith to meet Napoleon's somewhat less number. He had leaned his right on the Moskwa near Maslova, whence the line ran behind the Kolotsa to Gorki, and the left wing stretched out through Semenovskoi to Utiza. The line was slightly convex, and troops could be easily moved to and fro back of the Russian front. That the left wing was not protected by the Kolotsa and might be turned from Jelnia, was the origin of the field-works erected; but the sandy soil did not pack well and time had been short; and Kutusov knew that impregnable works would be turned and not assaulted.

Barclay was in general command in the right wing from the big redoubt to the Moskwa, his line being broken by a ravine at Gorki. Bagration commanded the left wing, from the big redoubt to a large wood slashing between Semenovskoi and Utiza. Baggavut, with Ostermann on his left, lay north of the new road, with Ouvarov's Cossacks out on the right as far as the Moskwa; Doctorov extended from the new road to the great redoubt, which he was chosen to protect; Raevski stood on his left to Semenovskoi; and holding the small redoubts were Borozdin and Nevrovski. At first Tuchkov was on the right. The Russian cavalry was four hundred paces to the rear, and the Imperial Guard in reserve one thousand paces behind that: this was much too near, and they lost heavily from the French guns. The Russian right wing, although strong, was in a way lost. Clausewitz suggests that it might have been assembled in closer order so as to fall upon the flank of the French should they drive back the centre, but Kutusov was there to fight and not manœuvre, and he was well aware that he was no match for the emperor in manœuvring, should he try.

This position, drawn up by Bennigsen, was tactically strongest on the right. The left was less strong, for, held by but a small body, this flank was open to be turned by the old Moscow road. Late on the evening of the 6th, after Napoleon's reconnoissances of the left, Kutusov recognized this weakness, and part of the corps of Tuchkov, with ten thousand Moscow militia, was transferred thither to strengthen this wing near Utiza.

Kutusov issued no proclamation, but he paraded the Smolensk statue of the Holy Virgin, which had been borne by the priests from that city, and told the soldiers that they were fighting for her and for God, against the enemy of all God's laws. During the 6th the Russian soldiers attended divine service, and the men received absolution, with the order from their priests to die, if need be, for the conservation of their sacred city of Moscow.

Napoleon issued his usual

PROCLAMATION.

IMPERIAL CAMP on the heights of Borodino,
September 7, 1812, 2 A. M.

Soldiers! Here is the battle that you have so much desired. From now on victory depends on you: it is necessary to us. It will give you abundance, good winter quarters, and a prompt return to the fatherland. Conduct yourselves as at Austerlitz, at Friedland, at Vitebsk, at Smolensk, and let the most distant posterity point with pride to your conduct on this day. Let it be said of you, "He was in that great battle under the walls of Moscow."

In gauging Napoleon's short proclamation, which every company commander read to his men, one must not consider it from the standpoint of the highest intelligence, but adapt it to the limited understanding of the men in the ranks. In any event, whether it was this, or the knowledge that they must win, which produced the effect, the French fighting was perfect so far as the courage of the men is concerned. Never in modern times have two armies of this size stood to their work under such decimation as these did during the few hours of the most stubborn fighting at Borodino.

The French were busy in bringing up detachments, perfecting details of position, and placing batteries. The emperor again rode the Russian line during the afternoon of the 6th, rejoiced that the enemy was finally to stand for battle. His plan was rapidly matured. On the left Eugene was to contain Kutusov's right, Davout and Ney in the centre were to break down his left wing, while Poniatowski on the right should turn his left flank to aid Davout and Ney. This Napoleon believed would throw the Russian army back on the Moskwa, where he could fight them to a finish. The plan was simple ; the emperor merely busied the Russian right to crush the centre and to turn the left.

As we can see it now, a plan more in accordance with Napoleon's battle habit would have been to let Eugene with less troops contain the Russian centre and right, and to have Davout with all his divisions attack between the Utiza wood and the left Russian redoubt, with Ney on his left advancing on Semenovskoi, the Young Guard between the two, and the whole followed up by Murat, while Poniatowski, supported by Junot, turned Tuchkov's left. This heavy mass would have broken the Russians' left before it was reinforced, and have compelled them to form a new front, as the Austrians did at Leuthen. Backing as they did on the Moskwa, it would

have given much greater chance of a decisive result. Or had
Davout moved with Poniatowski's column to turn the Russian
left, a similar result might have been obtained. Davout suggested that he might break through at the southerly redoubt
and at the same time turn the Russian left ; and knowing his
marked capacity for fighting against odds, the suggestion was
good ; but the emperor feared that Davout might run across
obstacles which he could not readily overcome, and thus get
stalled at a distance from the main body. Still, the Russian
left was the weak spot, as Napoleon had discovered. His plan
was in effect an echeloned attack by his right, and fearing
that too evident a turning manœuvre would persuade the
Russian army to retire, and thus again defer the battle he had
long anticipated, he decided to exhibit nothing of the kind
until the whole army was afoot and advancing.

As in all great battles, there is disagreement as to detail :
no two accounts agree as to minor manœuvres, but all are
alike in the larger factors. One thing was marked : the Russian soldiers had rest and good rations the day before the
battle ; the French had little bread and were busy moving
into place. Yet their fighting was as staunch as the foemen's.

At early dawn next day the French army was marshaled,
with Poniatowski on the Jelnia-Utiza road ; on his left Friant, Dessaix and Compans, of Davout's corps, stood in the
right front of Shivardino, with the Guard in their rear, its
artillery sent to the front line. Ney came next, to the left rear
of Davout in front of Alexinki, and Junot shortly marched
up in their rear. Much against Davout's grain, his divisions
under Morand and Gérard (late Gudin), and Grouchy's cavalry, had been added to Eugene's force, which stood north
of the Kolotsa, between Valevieva and Borodino ; and if
Eugene was merely to contain the Russian centre and right,
this was taking a valuable force from the active French

wing.　In the rear of Davout and Ney stood Nansouty, Mont-brun and Latour-Maubourg, the latter having just come up from Mstislavl via Jelnia.　A great body was thus massed opposite the three redoubts, to break down the Russian defense.　Some of the German accounts place Davout with two divisions, and Ney in first line, Murat and Junot in second line, and the entire Guard in third line, in reserve.　The positions of the divisions are so variously stated in all the reports — even the French official ones — as to be uncertain.　This is in no wise strange.　Set two intelligent staff officers to describe the position of troops in a line of battle already marshaled, and the difference of their reports would be in every case marked.

In the evening was issued the order of attack for early morning of September 7.

" Camp, two leagues from Mozhaisk, September 6, 1812.　The Order for Battle."　After indicating the assembly of guns for the initial cannonade, the Order goes on : " During this cannonade Poniatowski will move from the village " (Jelnia) " towards the forest, and will turn the position of the enemy.　Compans will move along the forest to capture the first redoubt. The combat being thus engaged, orders will be given according to the dispositions of the enemy."　Then is ordered a cannonade on the left, to begin at the same time, and the skirmishers of the left to advance as soon as they see the right move forward.　" The viceroy will capture the village " (Borodino), " will debouch over his three bridges " (which he was to throw early in the morning) " on the heights, at the moment when Mo-rand and Gérard shall debouch, under the orders of the viceroy, to seize the redoubt of the enemy, and form the line of the army.　All this is to be done with order and method, and having a care to keep always a great quantity of reserves."

Sixty-two guns in Davout's corps and the Guard, and forty in Ney's were selected to engage the Russian artillery in front of Semenovskoi ; the rest of the Guard artillery was to be held ready.　Compans, to whom Napoleon personally gave his

orders, was to assault the most southerly of the redans at
Semenovskoi, Dessaix was to second him, and Friant to advance
in reserve. At the same moment Poniatowski was to begin
his march about the Russian left flank. So soon as Davout
had won the works, Ney was to advance on Semenovskoi, and
as his corps was barely fifteen thousand strong, ten thousand
Westphalians were later added to it as a second line. When
the attack of the French right began, Eugene was to advance
on and capture Borodino, cross the river, and fall on the
Russian right wing with his own divisions, while Morand and
Gérard were to assault the big redoubt south of Borodino.
The French line was not over two miles and a half long, and
the force made it very deep. The Russians extended over a
wider front, but during the battle they successively moved
troops down to their centre and left, into even greater depth
than the French. This massing of men and the tremendous
array of guns opened the way for frightful losses.

Having issued his orders, Napoleon lay down for rest; but
as he could not sleep, he called in Berthier, and after working over all the plans of the battle until after five, he mounted
and rode to the work at Schivardino, captured the day before;
and in front and somewhat to the east of this work he took up
his stand, and here remained all day. He was suffering from
a severe cold, and could hardly speak. From this position he
could see the Russian centre and left in their intrenchments,
and here he intended his main attack to fall. Borodino was
hidden by the woods, as was also Utiza. Had Napoleon chosen
a manœuvring battle, he would have changed his position from
time to time; but having made up his mind to break down
the Russian centre before he actually turned its left, he was
wise to remain where his subordinates could find him.

At 6 A. M. of September 7 the guns opened along the whole
line, and Compans, followed on the right by Dessaix, Friant

in reserve, as well as Poniatowski's corps, started on their several tasks. From the outset, it did not look as if the attack on the big redoubt was going to be made in sufficient force. Compans and Dessaix advanced lustily on the works, while on their left Ney led up his divisions; shortly the French were hand to hand with the Russian foot, and before eight o'clock they forced an entrance into the works; but, open in the rear, these had no value. Compans, being wounded, left Dessaix in command, who also fell; Rapp succeeded him, and Davout's horse was shot under him, giving the marshal a serious contusion. But he kept the saddle, and his plucky divisions maintained their holding. Voronzov, in one of the redoubts, was killed; but the defenders, advancing fresh batteries, and with the second line under Nevrovski hurrying up, hurled the French out with mutual heavy losses. Bagration now made haste to defend the works with a fresh division of Tuchkov's corps under Konovnitsin, a division of cuirassiers and a brigade of the Young Guard. Kutusov, who had taken post at Gorki, on the new road, from which he could see the French army better than the emperor could see his lines, early recognized that his left was the threatened wing, and when Barclay sent from the right the corps of Baggavut, which arrived towards 9 A. M., Bagration had already reëstablished the matter, and one division went to Utiza, while another was thrown into the slashing south of the three redans. Observing, somewhat prior to this time, that the Russians might find a gap between Davout and Poniatowski, as the latter had moved to the right of the slashing on his turning manoeuvre, and that only some of Murat's cavalry divisions were there, Napoleon ordered Junot, from his post behind Ney, to oblique forward to Davout's right so as to hold it. Junot had, about 8 A. M., barely started, when the Russian countercharge threw back the French assault; and he was halted and ordered into

action between Ney and Davout, to fill a still more threatening gap. The narrow space compelled him to mass his corps,
but the Russian charge did not then reach his line. About
9 A. M. Davout and Ney advanced afresh on the Semenovskoi
redans, and Murat led up Latour-Maubourg on Davout's
right and Montbrun behind Ney. Ney headed Ledru and,
in company with Compans' division, after a brilliant charge,
once more forced a way into two of the coveted works ; while
Razout's division went forward on the third redan, and had
almost captured it, when
the Russian cuirassiers
rode down upon it; but the
French foot held its own
until Bruyère's heavy horse
came up to the rescue.
Between them all the works
fell. But Bagration was in
his element. Even Ney was
no better fighter. The
Mecklenburg grenadiers in
the Russian service, with
some guards and cuiras-
siers, what remained of
Voronzov and Nevrovski,

Baggavut.

and some light cavalry were sent in to recapture the Semenovskoi works; and after a fierce struggle one was wrested
from the French, and Murat came near capture, the report of
which was circulated in the Russian army, much to the
elation of the troops. The fighting around the redans was
so fierce that Kutusov drew in Ostermann to the centre,
massing his troops more and more ; and in the heat of battle
he so huddled his divisions that their organization was almost
lost.

During this time Junot's Westphalians moved on towards the right and forward to occupy the slashing, but the delay had enabled Eugene of Wurtemberg, backed by Galitzin's

Galitzin.

cavalry, to occupy it, and they drove the Westphalians back. Encouraged by this success, Galitzin rode out against the French right, and seized a reserve battery; but taken in reverse by one of Dessaix's regiments, was compelled to release his hold.

While this was going on, Eugene and Poniatowski were intent on their own work, the latter having taken Utiza, and the former Borodino. But, from late hardships, Poniatowski's corps had dwindled to ten thousand men, and he made no progress through the marshy woods in his front against the Russians who were fending off his onset. Still, when the Westphalians came into action in the slashing, he seized the hillock which dominated the Russian left; but Tuchkov drove him out with part of Baggavut's troops, losing his life in the charge, and Poniatowski was forced to a pause, having accomplished practically nothing. It was becoming evident that the fighting would have been better pushed farther on the Russian left.

Nor was Eugene more fortunate. Upon seizing Borodino, within an hour after the opening of the battle, Plausonne had driven the enemy across the Kolotsa; but Doctorov met him firmly and threw him back to the left bank. Leaving Delzons to hold Borodino, Eugene, under cover of his guns massed in the village, again advanced, about 8 A. M., against the big redoubt, Morand in the lead, one regiment in line in front, sustained by the others in column. With a splendid rush he drove out the defenders under Paskievich, and was making preparations to hold the work, when Doctorov brought up his second line of foot, and hurling it on the redoubt, sustained it by a guard brigade under Iermolov. Morand had suffered heavily from the Russian artillery, and, also attacked on the right by Vasilchikov, was driven out and forced down into the ravine, leaving Bonami's brigade in the redoubt, where it was captured. What was left of Morand was received by Broussier and Gérard, who advanced on his left and right respectively. Shortly Eugene was back at the Kolotsa, and his guns alone were shelling the big redoubt.

Thus what at eight o'clock had seemed like success at the great redoubt, at the redans, and at Utiza, had gone lost, and by nine all the French assaults, delivered too much in detail, had broken against the wonderful Russian defense. But Ney and Davout were far from discouraged. Friant, hitherto in reserve, was brought into line on the left of Razout, and the two corps again advanced on the Semenovskoi redans. The onset was made with vigor and well together, and in another hour the French had captured them, and crossing the ravine in its front, Friant seized even the site of the village itself. They were aided by Latour-Maubourg, who rode up on their right, and fell on the left of Konovnitsin, whose regiments received him in square; this enabled the Russian cuirassiers to come to the rescue, but after a long struggle the French foot and horse drove the enemy's line back. Still the Russian infantry was equal to the test, and the right held the big redoubt with determination. The French centre was not able to force its way farther than the captured redans and the village; but it held the works; and by one more joint effort, sustained by the artillery, Ney and Davout — though opposed by Bagration in person, who, desperately wounded, was later succeeded by Konovnitsin — were able to drive the enemy behind the ravine. Here the Russians stood, and the French rushes forward on the tired but still cheerful line were uniformly thrown back. Though the French had won the redans for which they had fought so fiercely, they had not broken the enemy, and from shortly after noon artillery fire was the predominant sound of the battle in the centre, as also on the right : this never ceased.

On the French left, after being thrown back, Eugene was about to renew his assault on the main redoubt, when, hearing that Russian cavalry was appearing on the left bank of the Kolotsa, he deferred the advance, and led back Lecchi to Delzons' aid at Borodino. Ney, holding Semenovskoi under the fire of two hundred guns, was calling loudly for reinforcements to give the *coup de grace*, and Napoleon was about to send in the Young Guard to his support, when an exaggerated rumor of the attack on Eugene's left came in; and as such an attack might compromise the French rear, Napoleon delayed putting in these *élite* troops to sustain Ney, and instead, sent Claparède to succor Eugene, should he be pressed. But the Russian cavalry — it was Ouvarov, with Platov's Cossacks in support, five thousand men in all — found the ground unsuited to a sharp diversion, and beyond throwing back Ornano's weak French cavalry corps which opposed its advance, it accomplished nothing. It could not indeed have had any great result; yet although Clausewitz, who was on Ouvarov's staff, condemns the diversion, it had stayed Napoleon's hand for a critical hour. Delzons' division in square could now hold its own, and Eugene returned to the assault on the big redoubt.

Throwing Gérard, Morand and Broussier forward on this work, and Montbrun's cavalry into the gap between Ney's left and his own corps, Eugene once more started out. In anticipation of a fresh onset, the Russian commander had drawn Ostermann from the right to relieve Raevski's decimated regiments, and his foot came into line with his right on the Moscow road and his left out towards Semenovskoi. Assuming this to be an offensive manœuvre, all the batteries that could be assembled were trained on Ostermann's corps, to which the Russian guns replied heartily, and from Borodino to Semenovskoi, on a front of a mile and a half, over eight hundred guns vomited death into the contending masses. Ostermann advanced in fine style, but Montbrun's squadrons outdid themselves. Montbrun was killed by a cannon-ball before starting, and Caulaincourt took the lead. Riding up against Ostermann's line, backed by the Russian Old Guard on the left of the works, these fine troopers drove it back, rode around the big redoubt, and actually forced their way into the rear outlet. Caulaincourt was also wounded. Such work by horsemen against unbroken foot could not of course succeed, and, attacked by the cavalry of Korv and Pahlen, the French squadrons were thrown back with heavy losses ; but the gallant ride enabled the foot divisions to reach the redoubt, surround and escalade it, and put the Russian defenders under Lichachev to the sword. Eugene was about to launch Grouchy on the retiring battalions, but the Russian horseguards held him back, and with Korv and Pahlen, compelled him to retire. It was nearly 3 P. M. The French had won the great redoubt and the three redans on the Russian front, and kept their hold on Semenovskoi, but the Russian troops could neither be forced out of the ravines in the rear, to which they had retired, nor driven into panic.

Some time before this, as Junot was accomplishing no good

at the slashing, he was moved to Davout's right, to give countenance to Poniatowski, who at 1 P. M. was still at Utiza.
Slow progress was made by Junot against Baggavut, but by
steady pushing he gradually worked to the front, by 5 P. M.
was on a line with Poniatowski, and the two corps advanced
together. Why the emperor had paid no greater heed to this
part of the field during the day can be explained only by the
desperate nature of the fighting in his front. Once started,
the onset of Poniatowski and Junot was vigorous, the Russian
left was driven in, and the hillock beyond Utiza recovered;
the Westphalians came forward, and the Russians fell back
to reform on the heights southeast of Semenovskoi. It was
6 P. M. In the centre, since three o'clock, cannonading alone
had gone on, but this had been murderous. Cavalry and
infantry had both essayed to advance, seeking to escape the
hail of shells, but only for a brief moment could they do
so. The losses had been unparalleled, and the mutual exhaustion was such that neither did the French advance beyond the
works, nor the Russians attempt to recapture them. Not long
after 6 P. M. even the artillery fire died out.

The capture of the great redoubt was the end of the battle.
The Russians had lost their first position, but they were
in no more disorder than the French, and could not be
driven farther back. When Ostermann was ordered to make
a counter-attack, and started out, ployed into column, the
attempt was futile; he was stopped by the French artillery;
and although with him Kutusov used his last fresh man, the
conclusion drawn by Napoleon from Ostermann's advance was
that no commander would so utilize his only reserves, and that
more must be at hand. He himself still had intact his own
reserve, the Guard, which had not been put in. Nor did the
emperor order it in now. There was no further fighting after
Ostermann's advance was driven back.

Though the serious problem of Eugene and the heavy fighting of Davout and Ney had during the day needed his personal supervision, Napoleon remained constantly at his post near the Shivardino redoubt, leaving each of his lieutenants to work out his task. At 4 P. M., when the battle was practically over, he rode over to Ney and Murat; but for an hour, from the dying down of the artillery fire, he had seen that nothing more could be accomplished. Towards 7 P. M. he rode back, and as Bousset says, " against his usual habit he had a heated color, with his hair in disorder, and wore a tired expression." He was convinced that the Russians would decamp during the night and yield up Moscow without further pressure, and he preferred a half success to risking what he had already gained. In effect, Kutusov did retire during the night, in remarkably good order considering his losses, and started towards Moscow in two columns, by the old and the new roads. After the battle the Russian troops were well fed; the French had scarcely any rations. The Russians chanted *Te Deums,* but technically Borodino was for them a defeat, because they gave up the battlefield. Borodino was certainly won by the French, but it was a Pyrrhic victory. It enabled Napoleon to reach Moscow. But as the losses made it certain that he could not hold himself there, unless Alexander would treat for peace, the strategic gain was naught. The indecisive victory meant for the French certain failure of the Russian campaign: had Napoleon put in the Guard and destroyed the Russian army, Alexander might have treated; with the Russian army still intact, he had ample means of defense left.

The battle of Borodino, or of the Moskwa, was one fought in parallel order, " all along the line," a mere push of masses, without grand-tactics of any kind. Except that the cavalry did some work unusual for that arm, and that the percentage of losses was greater than in any battle of the nineteenth century, it has nothing to distinguish it. The casualties are variously given. Probably thirty thousand men killed and wounded for the French, and forty thousand men for the Russian army, is somewhere near the truth. The French practically took no trophies, despite Napoleon's claim in a letter to the Emperor Francis. Nearly all the ammunition had been used up, some sixty thousand rounds having been fired by the French artillery, and nearly a million and a half infantry cartridges.

The battle was not the decisive one Napoleon must win to accomplish his object. A decisive victory can be won only by breaking the centre, or by manœuvring against. the flanks or communications of the enemy, or by hurling fresh troops upon him at the moment when he is retiring exhausted. As at Smolensk, there was no attempt to do any of these things. Twice during the battle Napoleon acted on the side of caution: when he delayed sustaining Ney, because the Cossacks had attacked his left, and when he decided not to put in his reserves. That the execution of the battle was not as good as its plan has to do with the conditions as much as with Napoleon's own act. When the weakness of the Russian line had been demonstrated by its lack of effective fire, say at 3 P. M., the emperor did not throw his Guard, still twenty thousand strong, upon it. Up to Borodino, in a doubtful victory, he had always dealt such a blow at the supreme moment, so as to hasten the beaten enemy into flight. Why he did not here do so will never be known, and whether he was right or wrong will continue to be a subject for discussion. It seems that if, about 3 P. M., the Guard had been put in, the effect, at no excessive additional loss, would have been to make Borodino a crushing Russian defeat. But Napoleon did not know the facts now plain. Had he put in his reserves without success,

his army must have become a fleeing mob in half an hour.
It may have been the fear of reaching Moscow with a force
too much depleted that stayed his hand; and yet it was
far better to do this, if he had destroyed Kutusov, than to
reach Moscow with twenty thousand men more, when Kutusov was still afield. Moreover, he had shown no especial
care to save his troops in the late advance; he had pushed on
regardless of the constantly increasing numbers who fell out
of the ranks, and without any uncommon measures to keep
the army intact. It is the manifest duty of the captain to be
careful of an army on the march; and equally his duty to
sacrifice so much of the army in battle as may be necessary
to win the kind of victory needed. What Napoleon had so
far shown us of the art of battles is, first, the way to reach
the weak side of the enemy, the flank or rear, with least danger to ourselves; and second, the secret of selecting the in-
stant for putting in the reserves so as to turn a simple victory
into a decisive one. At Borodino there is no trace of either of
these arts. At the important moment Napoleon had been too
far away from the critical points of the battle to gauge the
necessities of the case. Was it his health which dominated
his powers?

As Jomini has pointed out, there are battles where victory
should be early sought; others in which victory should be
delayed until the end of the day. If one side needs the
victory early, the other side needs to defer it. At Waterloo
the decisive moment for Wellington was when Blucher could
put in his appearance; at Marengo the decisive moment for
Bonaparte was when Desaix was to arrive from Rivalta. On
the other hand, Napoleon should have striven to win the field
of Waterloo early, and the Austrians should have kept up
their attack on Bonaparte at Marengo so as to crush him ir-
retrievably before noon. Now at Borodino, Napoleon was in

force in front of the Russian left wing by 6 A. M., and he had rightly guessed that their main body was in the other wing. It should have been his main effort to break down the left wing before it could be aided. His troops were well in hand. By not massing his attack in the early hours, he permitted reinforcements to reach the left in season to protect it. The big redoubt and the three redans were carried by the French after Kutusov had had time to bring up forty thousand men and over one hundred guns to support the troops first there: it cannot, therefore, be doubted that the redans would have fallen at the first rush, if Ney and the Westphalians united had assailed them; and meanwhile Davout with his full corps might have backed up Poniatowski in the turning manœuvre against the Russian left. Eugene was quite equal to containing the enemy's right and thus protecting the new Moscow road; and there seems no reasonable question, had the turning manœuvre been made in force by 6 A. M., that the Russian left would have been rolled up like a scroll, that Kutusov would have had to form a fresh line backing on the Moskwa, and that the emperor could have threatened the Russian communications to such good effect as to win the decisive battle he needed in order to bring about a peace.

As to refusing Ney the Young Guard when this marshal begged for reinforcements at some time before noon, it should be said that Napoleon was actually about to send in Mortier and the Young Guard to sustain Ney, when the Cossack diversion on the left attracted his attention and arrested his hand. As to his neglect to put in the Guard, we must remember that, from what Napoleon knew of the Russians, from history and his own experience, he was aware of their exceptional power of defense under any normal conditions. He could not know that the Russians had put in their last man and, as at Eylau, had no reserve left. He believed they still must have fresh troops on the right, and that the Russian Guard was intact. Had he guessed the truth, there is no doubt as to what he would have done, and the Russian army would have been practically annihilated.

The assaults were not delivered by Napoleon in his usual masses. The hand of the giant was not seen at Borodino. They were delivered by masses too small, though they were repeated until all but the Guard had been put in. Partial assaults are the usual stamp of the lesser leaders. The big redoubt should not have been attacked at 10 A. M. by Morand alone. If it was to be taken, as a means of containing the Russian right wing, Eugene should have thrown the bulk of his force, save reserves, upon it. Had this been done, and had Ney been sustained at Semenovskoi by the Young Guard, the Russian centre would have been pierced, and victory sure by noon. Even at 3 P. M., after the redoubt had been taken by Eugene, Ney should have been supported. Bagration had been succeeded by Doctorov, and his divisions were almost destroyed; Baggavut, with the relics of Tuchkov's corps, was much broken; Ostermann alone was in any kind of order. Had the whole Guard been put in, on the right of Semenovskoi, the Russians would have been forced into retreat during daylight; and by a pursuit as vigorous as that at Austerlitz, the Russian army would have been put beyond use, and Alexander would have been left without resources. But on the other hand, the French army was itself in bad order; neither foot nor horse had kept any organization; Napoleon believed that there was still an untouched Russian reserve, and the chance of a decisive victory went lost. It is perhaps hypercritical to-day to say that Napoleon should have done this or that. It is all an academic question. But it remains true that the splendid vigor of mind and body which we have seen and admired at Rivoli, Austerlitz, Jena, Friedland, that alertness that kept the master mind on every point, was not apparent at Borodino.

Napoleon's unusual prudence was in a way traceable to the situation. His enemy had a homogeneous army, well disciplined, well fed and full of religious enthusiasm, fighting at the gates of its sacred capital. His own army was made up of twenty different peoples, in ill state, not all loyal to the man or his cause; it was in a way dispirited by the long advance and all its sad privations, and had practically no magazines to fall back upon. Napoleon dared not run the risks he had at other times so lightly assumed. He needed rest, food. Moscow would give his army these; and a half victory would open its gates, and, as he reasoned, would assure peace. To look at the other side, even a partial defeat might demoralize the army; a *sauve qui peut* might be started, and would a single man of them all escape? This is an additional argument for stopping the 1812 campaign at Smolensk.

The huge number of wounded on both sides were later, so far as was possible, got to Moscow, where many of them perished in the conflagration. Those of the French wounded who escaped the fire succumbed on the retreat. Among the French general officers killed were Montbrun, Plausonne, Romeuf, Bonami, Marion, Compère, Huart; among the wounded were Caulaincourt, Nansouty, Grouchy, Latour-Maubourg, Rapp, Compans, Friant, Morand, Lahoussaye. The superior officers suffered equally. The Russian list of general officers killed and wounded was even greater, among them Bagration, Tuchkov and Kaiserov killed, and Galitzin, Gorchakov and a score of others wounded.

From Mozhaisk, September 4, Napoleon wrote the Emperor Francis " to announce the happy issue of the battle of the

Moskova, which took place September 7, at the village of Borodino. . . . I assume the losses of the enemy to be forty or fifty thousand men. He had one hundred and twenty to one hundred and thirty thousand men in line of battle. I lost eight or ten thousand killed or wounded. I took sixty guns and made a great number of prisoners."

French Mounted Rifleman.

CHAPTER 5

MOSCOW. SEPTEMBER 8 TO OCTOBER 19, 1812.

THERE was no pursuit after Borodino. Napoleon simply followed the Russians, who occasionally turned to arrest him. He knew that with his few remaining troops he could not hold himself in Moscow, but he believed that its capture would bring Alexander to terms. The Russians marched through Moscow and beyond, and the French took the city September 14. Here they expected to find everything necessary for the army, but the city was half deserted, and a conflagration consumed eight thousand houses. Napoleon failed to divine that he could not bring Russia to terms, and stayed on, hoping for advances, meanwhile considering four operations: to winter in Moscow, to retire by the south, to retire on Smolensk, to march on St. Petersburg. But he did nothing. Meanwhile, Kutusov moved to the south of Moscow, Murat was sent out to meet him, and thus matters remained some weeks, Napoleon striving to bring order out of chaos in the rear, and hoping daily to hear from Alexander, to whom he himself made weak advances, which were not noticed. Meanwhile Macdonald was blockading Riga, Wittgenstein much outnumbered St. Cyr near Polotsk, Chichagov and Tormasov had forced back Schwartzenberg and Reynier at Brest Litovsk. On this immense theatre Napoleon had little over two hundred thousand men, and was vulnerable at many points. He saw the facts clearly, as a Note early in October shows, but he drew from them wrong conclusions. Finally, on October 18, Kutusov defeated Murat near Tarutino, and next day Napoleon began the retreat from Moscow, already determined on.

LEAVING a rearguard on the field on the morning of September 8, Kutusov led his defeated but not disheartened army back on Mozhaisk. Napoleon got together the available cavalry under Murat, supported by Dufour's (late Friant's) division, and sent him forward to take this town; but the Russian party at its entrance held him back. The emperor remained all day at his bivouac near Schivardino. He appeared "overcome with lassitude," says Constant, but at 1 P. M. he rode over the battlefield. The wounded were given such care as was possible in and about a large convent nearby; but three days elapsed before all had even their first dressing. To the uninitiated this sounds lamentable; but whoso remembers the battle of Gettysburg with its thirty-odd thousand wounded men, in the midst of a thick and intelligent population, with hosts of doctors and surgeons hurrying up by rail and road from all the adjoining towns and cities, and recalls how scant attention and how long deferred a wounded man might then expect, can understand the difficulties in a sparsely settled country like Russia.

Davout and the Guard had followed Murat; the rest of the army was still near the battlefield, hardly in the mood of victors. No army losing a quarter of its effective strength in one day's fighting can escape a similar shock; and the enormous distance from home was not reassuring. On the 9th the Russians retired to Semnia, the emperor reaching Mozhaisk with Murat, the Guard and Davout, Ney coming up. As flankers Eugene marched on Rusa, Poniatowski on Vereia; Junot remained on the battlefield, to care for the wounded. The retreat and following towards Moscow was continued, the French reorganizing on the way, and searching for food in all directions.

This movement little resembled the tremendous pursuit after former victories. The Russian rearguard was under Miloradovich, and Clausewitz, who was with him, states that the French van struck it only once with any force. It is true that whenever the enemy can flee, the victor can pursue; but this assumes a less exhausted army than the French after Borodino, and more push than Napoleon exhibited. Moreover, the arm for pursuit is cavalry, and Murat's regiments were in sorry plight; and as resistance at Moscow was to be anticipated, the army must be saved for fighting there. It has been suggested that Kutusov should have moved south to Kaluga to threaten the flank of the Grand Army as it moved on the sacred city; but had he done so, Napoleon could have contained him with a detachment, entered Moscow without fighting, and inflicted on the Russians a more serious moral blow than he did.

Personally, Napoleon remained in Mozhaisk until September 12. Recognizing that he could not long hold himself in Moscow without peace, he wrote Berthier, September 11, to hurry all available forces on to Smolensk, and there, as an additional security and threat, form a strong reserve; but he still expected that his occupation of Moscow would result in peace, or at least he so acted.

Leaving Mozhaisk September 12, Napoleon drove forward to Petelina, and next day to Borisovka. Kutusov, standing in front of Moscow, from Fili to Troizkoi, called a council of war to decide whether another battle should be fought, and the vote was cast in favor of fighting to the death; but Kutusov knew that the army was more important to Russia than Moscow could be, and did not choose to be bound by the council. On the 14th he marched through the city, and by late afternoon had vacated it, retiring as far as Panki; whereupon the bulk of the population deserted it, and even on that day a few fires were discovered in the suburbs. When the French drew near, Miloradovich strove to approach Murat, but though declining to receive him, Murat did not check Sébastiani, commanding his van, from stipulating with the Russian general, in order to save the city from a conflagration, which a battle within walls might start among its wooden structures, not to interfere with his transit, and not to enter the city until two hours after he had left it. Murat did not ride into the Dorogomilov suburb until 2 P. M., September 14; but his squadrons then crossed the Moskwa and entered the city proper.

When Napoleon first came in view of this goal of his ambition, — from the top of the nearby Hill of Salute, — "one could not mistake joy and contentment in his features," narrates an officer of the Prussian lancers, who was able to note his looks. The Guard was sent in to occupy the Kremlin; as they came along, Davout and Ney took up a position west of the city, Poniatowski, who had been the right wing, on the south, Eugene coming from Svenigrod towards the north. Murat's van was on the road southeast at Karocharovo. Temporary imperial headquarters were set up in the west suburb.

No sooner established in Moscow than the emperor began working to protect as well as to strengthen his holding.

On the 10th he wrote to Maret: "It is believed that Wittgenstein has left the Drissa to move between St. Petersburg and Moscow. If this is verified, write to St. Cyr to pursue him, and to arrive at the same time as he does, to cover my flank. In this case also write to Macdonald that he has *carte blanche* to commence the siege of Riga, or to do what he thinks will be most useful to my service. Write to Schwartzenberg that the enemy has done everything to prevent our reaching Moscow, that he will do everything to drive us from it; that I am certain that everything that was at Mozyr and at Kiev is moving on Moscow. That he is to follow sharply the movements of the enemy and not let himself be deceived. That if the enemy, who is in his front, falls upon him, he is to follow and fall upon him. That is well understood. Explain this fully. Henceforth the enemy, struck at the heart, will think only of the heart, and think no more of the extremities."

And next day, with a view of creating a strong reserve at a point not too far in the rear, he instructed Berthier to write in similar vein to Victor, whose corps had crossed the Niemen September 4, and could reach Smolensk by the 27th, that certain specified troops were to be directed on Smolensk.

"It is then from Smolensk to Moscow that he should move. The numerous troops which arrive in the rear and those of Lithuania are

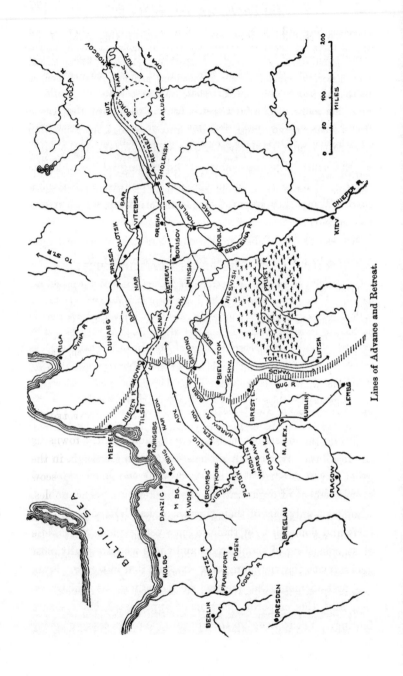

Lines of Advance and Retreat.

sufficient to guard the rear. . . . Vitebsk needs nothing. However few troops there are there, the enemy will leave it alone. I should myself keep nobody there, so soon as the hospital is cleared. Victor should then direct everything, battalions, squadrons, artillery, isolated men, on Smolensk, so as from there to be able to come on here."

On September 10 he wrote Maret, ordering clothing and other equipments to be sent to Smolensk. And to Berthier: "We much need French guns . . . to arm the stragglers, and naturally the wounded who have lost theirs. We need twenty thousand." Moreover, with his now settled habit, he ordered Berthier to "tell St. Cyr that the corps of Wittgenstein has not twenty thousand men all told; that he himself is much superior in force, and that if he arranged with Macdonald, he could attack him and beat him by turning his flank." And for effect on the people of France he issued a

CIRCULAR TO THE BISHOPS OF THE EMPIRE.

From our Imperial Quarters at Mozhaisk, September 10, 1812. To the Bishop of X. . . . The passage of the Niemen, of the Dvina, of the Borysthenes, the combats of Mohilev, of Drissa, of Polotsk, of Ostrovno, of Smolensk, finally the battle of the Moskwa, are so many motives to address thanks to the God of armies. Our intention is, then, that on the receipt of these presents you should consult with those in authority. Assemble my people in the churches to sing prayers, in conformity to the usage and the rules of the church in similar circumstances.

NAPOLEON.

While the desertion of the country and country towns by the local authorities in Spain had been trying enough, in the great city of Madrid this had not occurred; but in Moscow every element of organization was broken up. The nobles, who spent only part of their time there, had left, with all their serfs and domestics, for their country estates, and the middle class, consisting of shopkeepers and those who are really most necessary to the victualing of a city, had fled in terror. From the first moment, the question of victualing was embarrassing, and the emperor must have appreciated his insecure footing. Yet to keep up the appearance of success, an empty ceremonial of delivering up the keys of the city was gone through.

Like Rome, Moscow lies upon seven hills. Both European and Oriental in characteristics, having two hundred churches with colored domes and belfries, its aspect was most picturesque. Napoleon had been told that the better classes favored a change in the Russian administration; he had talked idly about rousing the people against their rulers; but far from this being true, the French found bitter enemies in every class, and officials and people alike turned from them as from the pestilence. Hitherto, in all captured capitals public order had been preserved, but here the famished soldiery exceeded all bounds, each one seizing what first came to hand. Although the magazines were guarded, the shops could not be, and all were gutted.

During the night of September 14-15, fires began to break out, the first one noticed in a large storehouse. This was extinguished. Then the great bazaar near the Kremlin was found afire, and the shifty winds fed it. The fires continued, and by the morning of the 16th the whole city was aflame. The emperor, already housed in the Kremlin, was driven out, and went to Castle Petrovski outside the walls. As the equinoxial rains came on, the winds grew less violent. The Kremlin had been injured, but not destroyed, and on the 18th, after the conflagration had consumed some eight thousand houses, it was controlled, and Napoleon reoccupied the palace.

Who set Moscow afire has ever since been a question. The Russian nation professed rage at the act, of which they accused the French; but the French could not have deliberately fired Moscow, the place being essential to save them from disaster. It is easy to understand that careless French pillagers may have continued their habit of destroying what they could not use, sometimes by the torch; or that among the fleeing

Russians many preferred to burn their household gods rather than to have them fall into foreign hands; or that many miscreants or marauders, often soldiers, may have set fire to houses to cover up their crimes; but all these acts are incident to the military occupation and show no deliberate intent. People at that day stated and believed that Rostopchin, the governor, set fire to the city in a fit of patriotic fervor: indeed, he confessed to the act at the time, although later he formally denied it. He burned down some of his own country houses to prevent their use by the French; and there is suggestion that Kutusov was aware of his intention, and strove to prevent it. It was generally believed by the French that the governor had employed incendiaries. The whole story is a mass of contradictions. Unless we believe that Rostopchin fired the city, we can only ascribe the tragedy to accidental fires started by pillagers of both nations. Probably all three causes existed, and the elements did the rest, for a very few fires in a city built of wood, and aided by the equinox, would soon produce a conflagration.

It was now that Napoleon made his most fatal error. Had he as of old reasoned correctly from the facts, — especially from the act of Rostopchin, — he would have recognized in the destruction of their sacred city proof positive that the Russian nation would never treat with the invader, and that he must retire at once if he would reach his magazines and reserves before winter set in. But he continued to hug the delusion that Russia must treat; and instead of withdrawing towards Kaluga and Smolensk, — or into the rich provinces of the south, which would have given a fresh offensive aspect to the war, — he remained in ruined Moscow, where he knew he could not long subsist; for although any well-peopled city can feed an army, a burned city whose inhabitants have fled affords no asylum; and the very machinery of victualing had

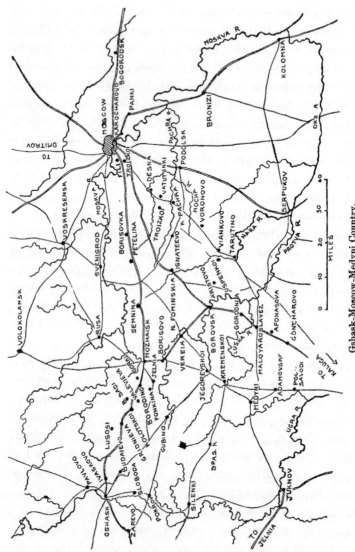

Gshask-Moscow-Medyni Country.

disappeared in Moscow. One of the most valuable qualities in any department of life is the ability to recognize the moment when it is wise to retire from an operation; but the emperor could not give up his plan — could not acknowledge failure. Even if the soldier Napoleon gauged it as essential, the man Napoleon could not face the idea of retreat; the word had been spoken but twice since Castiglione: at Eylau it was barely whispered, and at Essling it was acknowledged and explained, but merely to take a fresh start. He had never yet faced failure, and could not believe in it now. Moreover, retreat was no easy matter. The route to Smolensk was eaten out, though it could still be reached via Kaluga and Jelnia. The route by way of Kiev on the Dnieper was through a better country, not yet ravaged; and it led towards Schwartzenberg's army and a fresh base on the line Zamosc-Lublin-Warsaw; but should Austria not prove loyal, this would bring about trouble; and not only did the Tormasov-Chichagov army lie athwart his path, but the French magazines were at Kovno, Vilna and Minsk, in the other direction. Had Moscow been completely burned, Napoleon would have retired at once; as it was, enough of the city was left to warrant delay, in the hope that the Russians would ask for a truce. Many supplies were left, enough to suffice for awhile, or perhaps to feed the army back to Smolensk. There were more luxuries than necessaries: wines were in plenty; preserved fruits and sugar were found in sickening quantities; but of flour there was little, and of meat only what had come along with the army. The troops were kept on scant rations. At least two thirds of the provision on which Napoleon depended to bring the war to a successful issue had been burned; and such of the Russian authorities as had not fled were worse than useless in collecting victual. Some speedy action must be taken to bring matters to a focus, or the Grand Army would die as in a trap.

Looking over the entire field, the emperor considered four operations : to winter in Moscow ; to retire on the southern provinces ; to retire via Kaluga on Smolensk ; to march on St. Petersburg. The first was not feasible, as it would mean that for six months he would be separated from western Europe ; and that was time enough for all his enemies to rise against him, and change the whole political status. The last, had the men and material been at hand, was the most Napoleonic ; it would take Wittgenstein in reverse, and force him into Ingria ; and Victor, St. Cyr and Macdonald could join Napoleon's army via Pskov. This plan most strongly appealed to the great soldier ; but then, he reasoned, Kutusov would follow as if he were in retreat, and might cut him off in the Vitebsk region ; he would be marching into a country of marshes and excessive cold, into a strategical *cul-de-sac*, from which was no issue except along the Baltic coast, and where were no victual or forage. Kutusov and Wittgenstein had as large a force as Napoleon and his lieutenants, and with irregulars could make small war on his flanks and rear, and cut off convoys and foragers. To be sure, a march on St. Petersburg could at any time be turned into a mere demonstration to bring Alexander to terms ; and if this failed, the Grand Army could file off to the left at Waldai or Novgorod towards the Dvina near Sebesh. But in this plan the difficulties exceeded the chances. There remained open the route to the south, where the troops could winter, and resume operations in the spring ; and if this were adopted, a few weeks' delay to hear from Alexander would matter little. But all this planning was in mere subservience to Napoleon's belief that the Russians must yield ; for the safest operation was either to march on and beat Kutusov, sending a detachment to destroy the Tula arsenal, and then to retire on Smolensk by way of Kaluga and Roslavl ; or else to retire at once by way of Volokolamsk and

the upper Dvina on Vitebsk. As a matter of fact, Alexander
had made up his mind to defend the Russian throne at any
risk : he would not have yielded had Napoleon stood before
St. Petersburg ; and the Russians knew that the French could
never march across the desolate waste from the old capital to
the new one. They themselves would scarcely have faced the
hazard. Moreover, the French army was in ill case, the Russian
army fairly sound, and instinct with one purpose ; the French
soldier was in want, the Russian soldier had not abundance,
but did have what sufficed ; the French horses were perishing

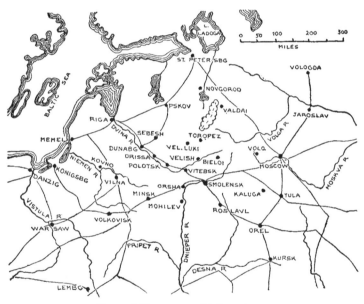

Proposed Manœuvre on St. Petersburg.

daily, the Russian were used, like our American broncos, to
subsist on even bark and twigs when hay or straw was wanting.
Indeed, Napoleon could not meet the enemy on an equal footing : his cavalry was half dismounted, and most of the guns
had no teams. Whatever plan excluded another battle was

the safer. And yet, as an immediate sequence to the indecisive victory of Borodino, as a mere measure of safety, Kutusov should have been followed up and beaten again.

From the moment Moscow was burned, the loss of each day was irremediable ; still, Napoleon, misled by his belief that Alexander would yield to his proposals, continued to delay. Everything appeared to go wrong. After his victory at Salamanca, Wellington had entered Madrid, and the war in the Peninsula had taken on fresh vigor. Schwartzenberg had retired behind the Bug, and Warsaw was in alarm. Wittgenstein was being reinforced. To be sure, Victor was at Smolensk, with ten thousand men coming on under Baraguey d'Hilliers, and Durutte's division was at Warsaw ; but this accession was far too small to change the status.

From Panki, September 16, Kutusov had retired along the Kolomna road ; but to approach the richer southwestern provinces, and annoy Napoleon by threatening his communications, he followed up the Pachra, and on the 18th was at Podolsk. This was a handsome strategic performance, for it covered the arsenal at Tula and the south, and was a distinct threat to Smolensk and Napoleon's communications. Russian cavalry scouted all the routes diverging from Moscow, and busied the French detachments. Murat believed the enemy had retired to Kolomna, and after a few days' rest, with Poniatowski and the divisions of Dufour and of Claparède, he advanced, September 22, to Bronizi in the trail of a few Cossacks; but when Napoleon heard of Russian movements on the road to Tula, he sent Bessières out in that direction with Lahoussaye and Friedrich, to form a corps of observation, gather news and cover the road until Murat had got in touch with the enemy. Poniatowski was ordered to Podolsk, which he reached September 24, and Murat was to reconnoitre out towards Kolomna, to make sure of the enemy's whereabouts, and then to follow, which he did a day later; and Bessières moved to Desna. Kutusov had continued his movement around the city to Krasnia-Pachra, and from here he sent Dorkov out to reconnoitre towards Mozhaisk.

Meanwhile, as no overtures came from Alexander, Napoleon recognized that the Grand Army was lapsing into a desperate strait; and on September 20 he so far overcame his conqueror's attitude as to write him a letter, which cannot be said to be a successful effort : —

"To Alexander, Emperor of Russia, Moscow, September 20, 1812. Monsieur my Brother, having been instructed that the brother of the minister of your Imperial Majesty at Cassel was in Moscow, I bade him come to me, and talked with him some time. I advised him to go to Your Majesty and make you understand my sentiments. The fine and superb city of Moscow no longer exists. Rostopchin had it burned. Four hundred incendiaries were arrested in the act. All declared that they set the fire by the orders of the governor and of the director of police. They were shot. The fire appears to have finally ceased. Three quarters of the houses have been burned, a quarter remain. This conduct is atrocious and without aim. Had it for object to rob me of some resources ? But these resources were in the cellars which the fire could not reach. Moreover, why destroy one of the most beautiful towns in the world and the work of centuries, to reach so feeble a goal ? This is the conduct which has been held since Smolensk, which has thrust six hundred thousand families into beggary. The fire engines of the town of Moscow had been broken or carried away, and a part of the arms of the arsenal had been given to miscreants, who obliged me to fire upon them with the guns of the Kremlin to drive them away. Humanity, the interest of Your Majesty and of this great city, demanded that it should be left with me in trust, because the Russian army uncovered it. They should have left the administration, magistrates and civil courts. It was thus they did in Vienna twice, in Berlin, in Madrid. It is thus we ourselves acted in Milan when Suwarrov entered it. Conflagrations authorize pillage, to which the soldier resorts to save the débris from the flames. If I believed that such things were done by the orders of Your Majesty, I should not write you this letter ; but I hold it for impossible that with your principles, your heart, the justice of your ideas, you have authorized such excesses, unworthy of a great sov-

ereign and of a great nation. At the time they carried off the engines
of Moscow, they left one hundred and fifty pieces of field artillery, sixty
thousand new guns, one hundred and sixty thousand infantry cartridges,
more than four hundred thousand " (pounds) " of powder, three hundred
thousand of saltpetre and as much sulphur, etc."

"I have made war against Your Majesty without animosity. A note
from you before or after the last battle would have stopped my march,
and I would even have been willing to sacrifice to you the advantage of entering Moscow. If Your Majesty still conserves for me some remains of
your ancient sentiment, you will take this letter in good part. In any case,
you can only thank me for having rendered an account to you of what has
taken place in Moscow.   NAPOLEON."

This letter the emperor confided for delivery to one Jacob-
lev, of the Russian civil service; and receiving no reply, on
October 5 he sent his aide-de-camp, Lauriston, to Russian
headquarters, with a proposal for an armistice leading up to
peace negotiations; and this Kutusov agreed to forward to his
master, alleging his want of authority to act upon it himself.
These proposals were much the same as others Napoleon made
at various times, when he saw that he had reached a point
beyond which lay extreme hazard.   In March, 1797, he thus
wrote Archduke Charles from Klagenfurt, because he saw that
every step farther would weaken his strategical position,
though he yet had much offensive power, or in case of necessity, having freed Italy, could retire without loss of repute.
Again, in June, 1807, at Tilsit, he made similar proposals, because he saw that farther advance would weaken his offensive
power, though he might have maintained a defensive attitude,
and had accomplished his task in subjugating Prussia.   But
in 1812, Napoleon neither had accomplished nor could accomplish his task of bringing the Russians to terms; nor did he
have the power to hold himself defensively in Moscow, not to
speak of further offensive operations. At Smolensk it would
have been different. In view of these facts, the czar was right

in ignoring Napoleon's proposals. They were a real confession of weakness, as the czar's had not been in his Vilna letter.

With regard to the missive intrusted to Lauriston, there was much suspicion among some of the Russian officers that Kutusov favored peace and intended to meet Lauriston secretly. Sir Robert Wilson was consulted, and after an interview Kutusov received Lauriston publicly, and agreed to convey Napoleon's letter (of which no copy exists) to the czar. No notice was taken of the letter, and the czar reprimanded Kutusov for receiving Lauriston, his orders forbidding any treating whatsoever with the enemy.

From the outpost reports the emperor was convinced that Kutusov had left the Kolomna for the Kaluga road; and as Chichagov, released by the peace from the lower Danube, had marched up to join in the campaign now centring in Moscow, he had new and awkward conditions to face. Although Kutusov had asked for Chichagov's army as a reinforcement, this had left Bucharest July 31, and by September 20 had joined Tormasov in the Ostrog-Lutsk country, making over sixty thousand men. Napoleon's idea that Kutusov's retreat was towards reinforcements was not the fact; the Russians were playing a heroic game, and were preparing at the proper moment to deal him some lusty blows. The emperor must have regretted his error in not making Prussia a loyal ally, so as now to draw on her for reserves on which to fall back.

At one moment Napoleon proposed himself to turn in force on Kutusov; but finally he detailed Murat, and upon his advance, Kutusov retired September 26, Murat having by Napoleon's orders striven to turn his right flank; and on October 4 he was behind the Nara, in a previously intrenched position, holding the Tarutino crossing; here Murat kept touch with him at Viankovo, Bessières in support at the Pachra. The main army was in quarters all around Moscow,

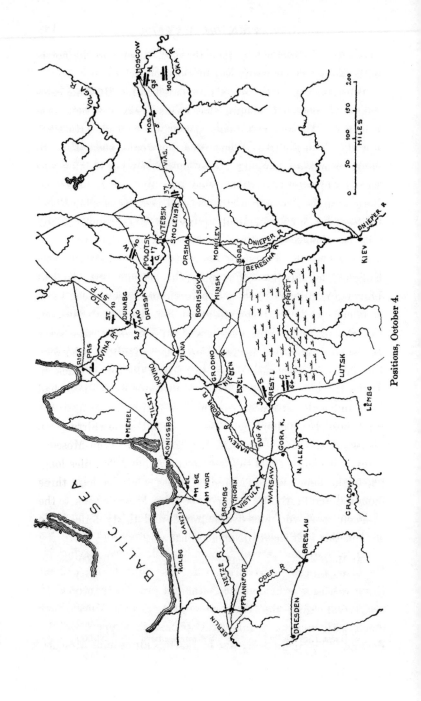

Positions, October 4.

Davout in the southern part of the city, Eugene in the north, with van out at Dmitrov, Ney at Bogorodsk.

Because Napoleon had miscalculated in his Russian campaign, we must not imagine that he had ceased to weigh the evidence. He was fast being persuaded that the Russians would not make peace, and that he would soon have to retreat; and on gauging the situation October 4, this was what he found. On the extreme left, Macdonald, at Dünaburg, with the Prussian auxiliaries, had been blockading Riga; on September 22 Steinheil arrived at Riga from Finland with ten thousand men, and the Russians undertook the offensive; but as the Prussians forced them back into the city, Steinheil led his men off to join Wittgenstein. St. Cyr had been reduced by sickness and poor victual to seventeen thousand men, while Wittgenstein, at this date, had forty thousand. On the extreme right, Chichagov and Tormasov, over sixty thousand strong, had advanced on Schwartzenberg, who with his thirty-four thousand men was gradually forced back to Brest Litovsk. Between the two French wings, Victor had been in Smolensk since September 27, with his own troops and those left behind by Napoleon, in all some thirty-seven thousand effective. Thus, of the triangle of Riga-Moscow-Brest Litovsk, the left side was over five hundred miles long, the right side over six hundred miles, and the base three hundred and fifty miles long; while from Moscow back to the Niemen at Kovno was five hundred and thirty miles. To defend this vast theatre Napoleon had —

At Moscow	under himself	95,000	men.
" Mozhaisk	" "	5,000	"
" Smolensk	" Victor	37,000	"
" Riga and Dünaburg	" Macdonald	25,000	"
" Polotsk	" St. Cyr	17,000	"
" Brest Litovsk	" Schwartzenberg	34,000	"
A total of		213,000	"

As Wartenburg points out, Napoleon had taught the world a new system of strategy, but he had not followed this up by as excellent an organization; and the Grand Army was not equal to so severe a test of his strategy. The modern world has been taught by Prussia what perfect organization and logistics can do. This perfection depends on: universal service; preparations for mobilization; preparations for feeding and moving armies, making use of all modern scientific and material advance; a general staff made up on the modern plan. In Napoleon's military economy these essentials are indicated, not perfected. He had opened his campaign with four hundred and fifty thousand men, and in three and one half months his army had dwindled to little over two hundred thousand all told. As compared with this, in 1870, the Prussians opened the campaign with three hundred and seventy thousand men, and in three and one half months they had placed on a theatre of about one third the extent of that in Russia four hundred and twenty-five thousand men, with nearly as many troops in the rear from which to draw. In other words, the perfection of the Prussian organization and mobilization enabled them to keep on increasing their power; Napoleon's kept on decreasing; and as a result, the Prussians could remain in Paris until they forced a peace on France, while Napoleon was compelled to leave Moscow because he had not force enough to hold himself. These are not parallel cases — the conditions were quite different; but the one illustrates the other.

On the uprising of the people in the French Revolution Napoleon had built up his wonderful system of war; but of itself this required many improvements to uphold and maintain it, and these Napoleon did not add. "In peace prepare for war," is no idle phrase. You cannot get ready to mobilize a large army without many years of preparation.

Napoleon prepared in a marvelous manner, considering his short years of peace. But he retained in his own hand all power, all knowledge, all mechanism of the Grand Army; he was his own general staff; and, with such large armies as he eventually commanded, it is not possible for one man to do this, even if he be a Napoleon; for military work on a large scale must be divided and specialized, as all other modern work is done. Napoleon's step forward was from mercenary armies controlled by the central political authorities to a people's war of masses; but he never worked out the idea to its legitimate conclusion and subdivision. Had he lived and wrought longer, he would no doubt have done so.

The first news of Borodino which reached St. Petersburg had been that of a Russian victory. Kutusov's later report described the battle as drawn, but this was not generally published, and as people could not see why, if they had won a victory, Moscow had been abandoned and burned, there was much discouragement. Some of the imperial family were in favor of peace, some anticipated a march on St. Petersburg, and made ready to evacuate the city. Alexander would not yield to further French dictation. Count Lieven, sent to London as ambassador, testifies that the czar had said : —

"I have chosen just this moment to send you to London, so as better to enforce by so doing my firm intention not to make peace until I shall have thrust the enemy out of our frontiers, even should I, before I succeed in this, have to retire beyond Cazan. So long as I shall have to defend the Russian territory, I shall ask from London only munition and arms. When, with the aid of Providence, I shall have driven the enemy beyond our frontiers, I will not stop there, and it will be only then that I shall have an understanding with England on the more efficacious assistance that I shall then claim of her, so as to arrive at delivering Europe from the French yoke."

He had notified other countries of his purpose in similar fashion, and with such a spirit in the monarch, Napoleon could expect no approaches from the Russian people for a truce. But he long misconceived this spirit. Alexander may not have been a great soldier, but he came close to being a great man.

Meanwhile everything went on as usual, and the emperor made his inspections and issued his orders daily, some with regard to the larger affairs, some relating to details.

On October 1 was issued an order for arming the Kremlin. On October 2 he wrote to Eugene : " My Son, you have left at the Abbey in rear of Mozhaisk two howitzers. . . . I do not know why you weaken your artillery. Take the horses of the officers who ought not to have any, and carry with you all your artillery. Convey my discontent to General X. for having left his pieces behind. It is contrary to military honor. One should leave everything behind except his guns."

On October 3 he wrote Lariboisière : " I have to-day visited the work-shops. I have found there little activity and little order. All the facts we know are that the enemy had one hundred thousand " (cannon) " balls in this park, and it is believed that he threw them into the water, which, being a pond, is easy to dry. You should work with activity to make a little ditch necessary for that purpose, and recover these balls. There have been made during the fifteen days we have been here but ten thousand " (cannon) " ball cartridges. I desire that, beginning with day after to-morrow, you should have this workshop arranged so as to make six thousand gun cartridges a day, which are to be stored in the Kremlin as fast as made."

On October 6 he wrote Maret about the portable mills which had been sent from Paris : " My intention is that you should take one of these mills to serve as model, have it worked under your own eye, and let me know how much it has ground in twenty-four hours, and how many men were needed to work it." He then orders fifty to be made like it at Vilna, and a sample to be sent to Warsaw and one to Königsberg, as models to produce others.

On October 8 he ordered Berthier to " write to the viceroy, to Davout, to Ney, to Mortier, that it is essential they should take measures each in his district to procure enough flour for two months, and biscuit for a month, so that they should always have at least three months' subsistence before them, and three months of wheat."

Much of this was not as easy to accomplish as to order. And all the activity of the great soldier could not correct the evil conditions which, day by day, were weaving tighter about him a net, from which he did not seem capable of making an effort to escape before it was too late.

The emperor has left a Note, made at Moscow, but undated, which probably expressed his views of the situation early in October, and suggested a plan for dealing with the adverse conditions. Those parts of the Note that best exhibit the emperor's trend of thought are quoted verbatim: —

" As the enemy is moving on the road to Kiev, his aim is evident. It is that he is awaiting reinforcements from the army of Moldavia. To march on him is to act in his favor and find ourselves without a place to lean on during winter quarters, having our right and left in the air, while the enemy would have his flanks and rear assured. Moscow, being abandoned by its inhabitants and burned, does not remain for us of any consideration."

To move on Kaluga is reasonable only as a means of moving on Smolensk.

If the army is to retire to Smolensk, is it wise to move upon the enemy? The emperor decides this in the negative, as every little fight of the rearguard would be a species of defeat.

To fall back on Poland for winter quarters, is it better to return by the route we came? " We should not have the enemy upon us ; we know the road, and it is the shortest by five marches ; we can go as quickly as we wish ; we may even receive at half distance our convoys coming from Smolensk, etc."

" We are victors, we are well organized, and if we have affairs and wounded, we shall be in the same position that we were in coming, with regard to the wounded of the vanguard. Truly, one may foresee difficulties in foraging, but forage can be got at three or four leagues distance, so that this would not be a difficulty of the first order."

" There is no species of doubt that if Smolensk and Vitebsk were countries like Königsberg and Elbing, the wise project would be the one already spoken of, to move into a fine country for winter quarters, and to make over the army. In the present circumstances, we cannot dissimulate that the war would drag itself along, but it would drag itself out much longer in bad countries such as Smolensk and Vitebsk, which offer so few resources, and where one would be so ill established to pass eight months in winter quarters."

"What aim have we to fill? To place the emperor the nearest to France, and give the empire the confidence that the emperor is in the midst of a friendly people during his winter cantonments. To canton the army in a friendly country, to approach our resources of clothing and equipments. To put ourselves in a position which strengthens the negotiations of peace which the emperor is making while menacing St. Petersburg. To sustain the honor of arms at the height where this glorious campaign has placed it. Without contradiction, a manœuvre which would fulfill these four conditions would be perfect."

But after this clear exposition of what should be done, the emperor enters into the discussion of a manœuvre which is quite impossible. In this project, Victor would march towards Velikiji Luki, reinforced by St. Cyr and Macdonald, and to coöperate, the emperor would march from Moscow on the same town via Volokolamsk and Bieloi, which would give over one hundred thousand men in one body; and at the same time Ney would march via Smolensk as a flanking column. With St. Petersburg thus threatened, Napoleon thought the enemy would make peace. The whole plan is magnificent, but it savors more of Kriegspiel than of actuality. It was a last intellectual effort of the great soldier to work success out of manifest failure. As a fact, only retreat on the magazines and reserves was now possible for the French army, and the plan assumes certain manœuvres on the enemy's part which might not be made. Nor was the threat against St. Petersburg so real as to have any probable effect on the Russian authorities. Napoleon's Note states the conditions well, but the campaign plan he suggests is impracticable, with nothing in its favor except an offensive attitude.

Later, Napoleon gave up this plan and considered a thrust against Kaluga, to deceive Kutusov, and resume the appearance of the offensive while retiring on Smolensk. On October 9 he wrote Maret that towards November he might take up winter quarters between the Borysthenes and the Dvina, to be near reinforcements, rest the army and more easily dispatch business. On October 16 he instructed Maret to persuade the King of Prussia to send him more troops: —

"It will be easy for you to make him understand that it is to his interest that everything should promptly finish, because by waiting he finds himself tired out and cramped ; that there is only one good way of finishing this struggle, which is to let Russia see the impossibility that exists of undermining the army, as it hopes to do by its great means of recruiting, which the czar not only is using in his states, but also by the aid of his allies. The same reasoning is to be made in Saxony. The same is to be made in Bavaria, at Stuttgart and everywhere. Not only do I desire that they shall send me reinforcements, but I desire also that they shall exaggerate those being sent ; and that the sovereigns shall put in their gazettes the great number of troops which leave, by doubling their numbers. It is well understood that the Prussian corps which is at Memel is not to be included in these reinforcements."

This dispatch, asking the various allies to exaggerate the number of troops they sent, is said to have fallen into the enemy's hands, and to have been sent to Austria with suitable comment. It was indeed a weak conceit.

It appears also that a cipher letter was written by the emperor to Maret on the same day. No translation of this letter has yet been made, but it is thought that its contents were those quoted in a letter by Maret to Count Otto, the French ambassador at Vienna.

The quotation is, "That it might happen that towards the month of November His Majesty would take winter quarters between the Borysthenes and the Dvina, so as to be nearer aid, to let the army rest, and more easily to attend to other affairs." Maret says : "The execution of this will produce a sensation, in those countries especially which are distant from the theatre of war. New combinations may result therefrom, whose existence would become manifest near you. It is therefore useful that you should be notified in advance, both of the fact itself and of the aspect under which it would be well to present it. I therefore communicate to you the text itself of my correspondence: ' His Majesty has had the wounded and sick evacuated on Smolensk to the number of two or three thousand, and proposes to leave Moscow the 19th, to move on Kaluga, to beat the enemy's army, if, as is announced, it intends to cover this great place, and according to the season move on Tula or Briansk, or return at once on Smolensk if the weather becomes rigorous. The emperor counts on taking winter quarters between Smolensk, Minsk and Mohilev, in the first week of November. He decided on this movement because Moscow, which has ceased to exist, is not a military position for his future operations.'" Then follows a statement of distances between the principal places, as far as they affect future manœuvres. "The army will find itself at Smolensk, leaning on a friendly country which will furnish all its needs, and the emperor will be ready to prepare his men for the Petersburg campaign, and to go himself where he may be needed." To this letter of Maret's is added a postscript, dated Vilna, October 26: " At the moment my courier is about to leave, I receive from Moscow, dated October 19, the following : ' The army is on the march. We shall decide to-morrow to blow up the Kremlin, and to move either by way of Kaluga or Viasma, to arrive before the great cold, and take winter quarters. Meanwhile everything goes well.' "

During the lull in hostilities following the capture of Moscow, there was the usual amount of intercourse between the outposts, and Bennigsen is said to have met Murat, who expressed himself in favor of peace, a fact that would naturally have strengthened the Russians in their idea of continued resistance. Kutusov meanwhile, behind the Nara with Murat still at Viankovo, had grown by accessions to one hundred and ten thousand men. He was deceiving Napoleon as to hearing from St. Petersburg, for every week scored a gain for the Russians; but when, a fortnight after Lauriston's message, he saw that he could no longer play this game, and that the

French must speedily retreat, Kutusov determined on taking the initiative. He did not move on Mozhaisk, because Napoleon, pushed to extremities, would have been far more dangerous than he was in Moscow, and he had no ambition to fight another pitched battle, when starvation and winter would soon compel the French retreat. A battle might have destroyed the French, or it might have destroyed this particular Russian army. The Russians had been wise in playing the Fabian game: all they needed was to force the French from the country. That was victory enough, for cold and hunger would do more damage than bullet and shell.

Kutusov lay behind the Nara opposite Tarutino, where the river, after running south, turns at a right angle nearly east. Murat, with twenty thousand men, was five miles north, behind a little stream that runs into the Nara near Viankovo, his left in the air, while the Russians had occupied some woods near its front. In rear of Murat's position was a defile through the woods at Spas Upila. Bennigsen, with Kutusov's consent, planned to turn Murat's left with two army corps and a large body of cavalry, seize the defile and thus surround Murat. Early October 18 the Russian cavalry under Orlov Denisov rode down on Murat's left, held by Sébastiani, drove him in, and actually occupied the defile, while Baggavut attacked the French in front. Had Kutusov smartly put in his entire force, he could have captured the army ; but Murat was quicker than he. Before the Russian cavalry could be supported, he drove Denisov out of the defile and recovered his communications. Russian laxness had saved him. Murat lost three thousand men, mostly cavalry which he could ill spare, and a number of guns. Lulled into security by the knowledge that Napoleon had sent a message to the Emperor Alexander, he had been careless in his outpost service. Kutusov's main force now remained at Tarutino, with van at

Viankovo. The Russians were manifestly ready to renew the conflict.

Up to this moment the weather had remained pleasant, and Napoleon asked facetiously where was the threatened cold. This very fact was one of the reasons for his delay, and even Kutusov's establishment at Tarutino seemed not to awaken him from his false security. In the Kremlin things apparently went on as in Paris : mails and couriers came in ; the emperor settled French measures of economy and state ; there was no outward sign of an impending disaster. But Russian horse under Davidov, Slavin, Fiquener, was hovering closer around the army ; a convoy had been seized on the Mozhaisk road ; the country population was more hostile ; even near Moscow raids were made and French foragers captured. Yet while he must have recognized that he could not remain in Moscow, Napoleon seemed unable to take the first step to abandon it, although after a fashion he was paving the way for doing so. On reaching Smolensk he had opened communications through Minsk, and established depots there, like those at Vilna and Smolensk. The whole line was garrisoned, but the Cossacks were giving more trouble. The chief difficulty in a retreat would be bread. For two days' march on either side of the road to Smolensk there was scarcely a grain of corn left ; but beyond was a fairly unspoiled country, and to the south, beginning with Kaluga and Tula, the country was still comparatively rich. Had Napoleon started his retreat early enough, or by the proper routes, he could have coped with the Russian army. It was not the burning of Moscow that drove the French out of Russia : the failure of the campaign was due, first, to the advance beyond Smolensk ; and second, to delay in Moscow, waiting to hear from the czar. It was to Napoleon, not adverse conditions, that the fault must be traced.

The bulk of the wounded at Borodino had after a· fashion been cared for. On October 5 Berthier was ordered to see to their dispatch to the rear, and next day to seize all the wagons in the vicinity to move them, and to have all army wagons coming up with rations carry back wounded men. On October 13 a light fall of snow hurried the emperor's action, and two days later, all patients who could be transferred to Smolensk were sent off.

Although the emperor gave no public intimation of it, he no doubt had matured his plans, for on October 17 he told Berthier to order Baraguey d'Hilliers from Smolensk to Jelnia, on the road to Kaluga, and to have the route kept open by parties of one hundred men every six leagues. Under the existing conditions, although not generally so regarded, the following has the appearance of a *ruse de guerre:* "To General-in-Chief Kutusov, Moscow, October 18, 1812. General Lauriston had been charged to propose to Your Highness to make arrangements to give to the war a character which conforms to established rules, and take measures not to have the country endure more than the indispensable evils which result from a state of war. In effect, the devastation of this country is harmful to Russia as much as it painfully affects the emperor. Your Highness will easily feel the interest that I have in knowing on the subject the definite determination of your government. By order of the Emperor, Alexander, Prince of Neuchatel and of Wagram." (Berthier.)

Napoleon was holding a review of Ney's corps, which with a view to the retreat had been drawn in to Moscow, when, about noon of October 18, preceded by the sound of battle, the news of the defeat of Murat ran in. This made action imperative. Orders were at once issued to the Grand Army to assemble without the city: Davout to move outside the Kaluga gate so as to begin a heavy march at the point of day; Ney to do the same; Eugene to move a league in advance so as to be able to march first; the Little and General Headquarters and the Guard to bivouac in square around the lodging of the emperor; Ney to leave a rearguard at the Kolomna Gate, Eugene to leave one at the St. Petersburg Gate.

So much for the marching divisions. To hold the city as long as necessary to keep the rear safe and to prevent interference on the road to Smolensk, Berthier was instructed to —

"Give notice to Mortier that I leave to-morrow morning with the army to pursue the enemy, and that my intention is that he should hold the Kremlin " with the Young Guard and Delaborde's division, to police the town and keep everything in order. " He is to have shot any Russian soldier found in the street," and to strive to gather as much food as possible. On the same day Napoleon gave personal instructions to Mortier how to fortify the Kremlin and hold it. " Should the whole enemy's army be against you, you must hold the Kremlin a number of days." " A chief of battalion of artillery has been charged to set fire to the Kremlin in case he is ordered to do so. Let him study the subject well." " After the army leaves, have the Intendant issue a proclamation to reassure the inhabitants, and to make them understand that you do not propose to evacuate their town." On the same day the emperor wrote to Lariboisière: " To-morrow, during the day, I shall start to move towards the enemy. Mortier with ten thousand men remains in town, and will defend the Kremlin in all events. It is necessary, then, that to-morrow morning all caissons and wagons whatsoever shall be assembled in the Kremlin. It is possible that I may come back to Moscow. There must therefore be nothing destroyed which is precious, such as powder, infantry cartridges, gun cartridges, lead to make balls ; but saltpetre and sulphur may be burned. I have powder enough. . . . The storehouses round the city can be burned. The Russian caissons and other material which cannot be transported to the Kremlin will be burned to-morrow at eight o'clock, with the sulphur and saltpetre."

The emperor notified Maret of the defeat of Murat, and of his intended march, on October 19: " Sébastiani, placed a league on the left of Murat in the vanguard, allowed himself to be surprised by a horde of Cossacks, the 18th, at five o'clock in the morning. . . . Losses were equal, except the guns which he lost. The army is on the march. We shall decide to-morrow to blow up the Kremlin and to move by way of Kaluga or Viasma, to arrive before the great cold and take winter quarters. For the rest all goes well." This last paragraph was in cipher not to be understood, and has been replaced like the one above.

In the 26th Bulletin, of December 23, we find: "Our outposts and those of the enemy agreed among themselves not to attack without giving three hours' notice. But the 18th, at seven o'clock in the morning, four thousand Cossacks debouched from a wood a half-cannon-length from Sébastiani, forming the extreme left of the vanguard, which had not been occupied nor reconnoitred that day. They charged in with a hurrah on our light cavalry at a moment when it was afoot at the distribution of flour. This light cavalry was unable to form short of a quarter-league to the rear. However, the enemy moving into this gap captured in a ravine a park of twelve guns and twenty caissons of Sébastiani's, with thirty baggage wagons. . . . At the same time the regular cavalry of the enemy and two columns of infantry made their way into the gap, hoping to win the wood and defile of Voronovo before us ; but Murat was there, he was in the saddle, he marched and broke the Russian line cavalry in ten or twelve different charges. He saw the division of six battalions of the enemy, . . . charged it and broke it in. This division was massacred. . . . Murat in this day showed what can be accomplished by presence of mind, valor and the habit of war. In general, throughout the campaign, this prince has shown himself worthy of the supreme rank where he is."

Mortier.

With regard to the wounded not yet carried off, Napoleon did all that was possible. But the transportation of many of these entailed grievous suffering, and of others, death. On October 19 he wrote to Berthier ordering that of all vehicles, belonging to whomsoever it may be, in the army, "to wit: caissons, wagons, coaches, barouches, cabriolets, britskas, carts," each was to carry one or two wounded, "any such wagons found without any wounded to be burned." On October 20, from Troizkoi, outside the walls at Moscow, Berthier was instructed to order Mortier to send forward towards Mozhaisk on the 21st, all who could march. On the 22d and 23d he was to fire the brandy storehouse, the barracks and the public establishments, all excepting the Foundling Hospital, where there were sick and wounded.

"He will set fire to the palace of the Kremlin. He will have a care that all the muskets are broken in pieces, that powder shall be placed under the towers of the Kremlin, that all the gun carriages shall be broken, as well as the wheels of the caissons. When these matters are finished, and the fire has started in several places in the Kremlin, Mortier will quit the Kremlin and will march on the road to Mozhaisk. At four o'clock the officer of artillery charged with the business will blow up the Kremlin as has been ordered. On the road Mortier will burn all the carriages which have remained behind, will bury all the corpses as far as possible, and break all the guns that he may find. . . . He will have fire put to the caissons and to everything which cannot be transported. He will take up all the small posts and draw in the garrisons."

The destruction of the fortifications of the Kremlin was justifiable as a military measure; but to apply the torch to the palaces of the czars and to the ancient churches was an act unworthy of any captain, in either success or failure.

On October 21, from Krasnia-Pachra, Napoleon reiterated to Mortier his order about the wounded : —

"I cannot too highly recommend to you to place upon the carriages of the Young Guard, on those of the cavalry or foot, and on all those which can be found, the men who still remain in the hospitals. The Romans gave civic crowns to those who saved citizens. Marshal Mortier will merit as many as he saves soldiers. Tell him that he is to have them placed on his horses and on those of all his people. It is thus the emperor did at Acre. . . . Let him assemble all the generals and officers under his orders, to make them feel the importance of this measure and how much they will merit from the emperor if they save five hundred men."

During the forenoon of the 19th the emperor left Moscow, the route given being towards Tarutino, to deceive Kutusov; but near Troizkoi the army was to file to the right on Borovsk and Maloyaroslavez, so as to seize the road to Juknov and get ahead of Kutusov on the route to Jelnia. This would save the retreat on Smolensk. The movement by way of Kaluga was probably intended to keep up in the Grand Army and among the Russians the idea of the offensive intention of the emperor. It is clear that he purposed actually to retire by way of Smolensk, for although the country was eaten out, yet the amount of supplies which had been accumulated on this road, and were still being wheeled up, would be the equivalent of all that they could get on any, except a route much farther south.

Sword of the Period.

CHAPTER 6

MALOYAROSLAVEZ. OCTOBER 19 TO NOVEMBER 14, 1812.

THE French had grown weaker, the Russians stronger, and the Grand Army, despite good weather, started from Moscow ill-supplied for its terrible march. To deceive Kutusov, Napoleon headed towards Kaluga, purposing to file to the right towards Smolensk, but Kutusov heard of his start, and marched towards Maloyaroslavez. Here was fought a bloody battle, October 24, to hold the road through Jelnia to Smolensk, which the French won, and could have absolutely headed off Kutusov; but for some reason unexplained, instead of utilizing this manifest advantage, Napoleon retired by way of Borovsk and Viasma, by which he lost four days, and permitted Kutusov to reach a point of danger on the French flank. Davout first acted as rearguard, and the army, strung over fifty miles of road, pursued its terrible way, Kutusov on a parallel line to the south, and the Cossacks harassing its flanks and rear. To pass Viasma, a battle had to be fought, and from this place on, Ney had the rearguard. The army was breaking up, the Guard, with which Napoleon marched on foot, alone remained in condition. On November 5 snow came. The underfed horses could not stand; guns had to be hauled up every slope by the men, or abandoned. Provisions had given out, and the men lived on horse and dog meat, stripping the dead for extra clothing. Bad news from right and left and from Paris reached Napoleon, but he could only order his lieutenants to hold on, and keep the Guard together for his own safety. He paid small heed to his marshals, leaving the rescue of his corps to each one. Eugene had attempted a circuit, via Duchovchina, but lost nearly all his men. Smolensk was reached November 9, the Grand Army here numbering but a third of its force seven weeks before. The expected rest could not be taken. Napoleon might have paused to concentrate the army, but he believed that Kutusov would not seriously attack.

SINCE crossing the Niemen the conditions had quite changed. Not only had the Grand Army grown daily weaker and the enemy stronger, but more Russian reinforcements had already come in than the Grand Army received during the whole campaign. Of these part were fresh levies, but the treaties with Turkey and Sweden increased the regular forces opposite Napoleon's wings to the danger limit. As we have seen, from Bucharest, Chichagov had joined Tormasov on the French right; and when Sweden secured the connivance of Russia and England in her scheme to acquire Norway, the czar was enabled to increase his forces under Wittgenstein on the French left. Ill-used Prussia was prepared to rise, but Austria, suffering less, was not yet ready to lend a hand. News from the Russian headquarters claimed that Napoleon would fail; yet little faith was placed in these predictions, and Napoleon's assurances of success were constant. When Moscow fell, Hardenburg believed that Napoleon had won.

The plans for the administration of the provinces along the line of communications had been but scantily carried out. The country was full of wandering peasants driven from their homesteads, and of army stragglers stealing to eat. Communication with the rear was much interrupted; the various towns were ill-garrisoned; only Smolensk had sufficient troops. Augereau's 11th Corps, gauged at fifty thousand men, was the next large reserve behind Victor, but, largely made up of " refractories," its quality was bad, and it had no cavalry. Part of it crossed the border to participate in the final rout, but as every man was needed to hold Germany in hand, when fresh accessions alone could prevent disaster, none were to be had.

In his previous wars the emperor had seen to it that his orders were carried out, and he now assumed as accomplished too much of what he could not inspect. It is said that Berthier smoothed things over in his reports, but although, as Major-General, he toned down the manner of Napoleon's orders to his marshals (as by altering " *il est ridicule* " to " *il est facheux*," etc.), the matter was always there; and at this critical period he no doubt told his master the whole truth.

Neither did everything move smoothly on the other side. The St. Petersburg authorities intended that the Russian wings should coöperate to inclose the Grand Army, but they were worse at calculating distances than, in the orders issued at this time, Napoleon occasionally appeared to be. The wings were too far apart to coöperate earlier than they actually did;

Tormasov.

nor were they strong enough until reinforced. In the czar's plan, the Riga forces were to move up river beyond St. Cyr and cut him off from the Grand Army, and Wittgenstein was to move towards the Beresina to join Chichagov; but delays intervened. Instructions in detail issued from St. Petersburg reached the Russian armies too late to be of value. As Chichagov and Tormasov might not agree, the latter was sent to report to Kutusov, and Chichagov with sixty thousand

men remained to face Schwartzenberg's thirty-five thousand. The latter had pushed Tormasov to the Styr, but when Chichagov arrived, he retired to Brest Litovsk, one division moving to Pruzhani. Chichagov followed, and on October 9 reached Brest Litovsk, eager for battle; but Schwartzenberg crossed the Bug to Vengrov, and his Pruzhani force retired to Bielostok; whereupon, instead of following up Schwartzenberg, Chichagov chose to move towards the communications of the Grand Army.

Admiral Chichagov possessed a strong character and fair ability. Kutusov had asked for his forces, but he could not have arrived until the time when Kutusov was able alone to face the wreck of the Grand Army; and his joining Tormasov proved wise. Although from Bucharest up he marched along her frontier, Austria made no protest.

In the 26th Bulletin, intended for the French people, the emperor gives his own explanation of the evacuation of Moscow. It must be read in the light of the actual facts, which have been stated impartially. Comment will not change it.

" The emperor, desiring to oblige the enemy to evacuate his intrenched camp and to throw him several marches to the rear, so as to be able quietly to move to the countries chosen for winter quarters and necessary to be occupied now so as to execute his ulterior plans, had, the 17th, ordered his vanguard to place itself behind the Viankovo defile, so that this movement could not be perceived. Since Moscow had ceased to exist, the emperor had projected either to abandon this pile of rubbish, or to occupy only the Kremlin ; but the Kremlin," not being strong enough, " would have weakened and been in the way of the army in its movements without giving a great advantage. . . . Moscow is to-day a real sewer, unhealthy and impure. A population of two hundred thousand souls wandering in the neighboring woods, dying of hunger, seeks in its rubbish heaps to find some débris, and a few vegetables in the gardens, to live on. It seemed useless to compromise anything for an object which was of no military importance, and which to-day has become without political importance."

" All the magazines having been evacuated, the emperor had the Kremlin mined. Mortier blew it up the 23d, at 2 A. M. The arsenals, the barracks, the magazines, all were destroyed. This ancient citadel, which dates from the foundation of the monarchy, this first palace of the czars, has ceased to exist. Of the four thousand stone houses which existed in Moscow, there were only two hundred left. They said that a quarter were left, because they included in them eight hundred churches. Of these a part are damaged. Of the eight thousand wooden houses, five hundred were standing. It was proposed to the emperor to burn the rest of the town, to serve the Russians in the manner they would act, and to extend this measure around Moscow. There are two thousand villages and as many country houses or castles. It was proposed to form four columns of two thousand men each, and to charge them to set afire everything twenty leagues around. That will teach the Russians, they said, to make war according to rule, and not like Tartars. If they burn a village, a house, we should answer by burning one hundred. The emperor refused these measures, which would so much have aggravated the misfortunes of this people. Out of nine thousand owners whose castles would have been burned, a hundred, perhaps, are the supporters of the Marat of Russia ; but eight thousand nine hundred are honest people, already too much victims of the intrigues of a few wretches. To punish a hundred culpable, we should have ruined the eight thousand nine hundred. We must add that this would have placed absolutely without resources two hundred thousand poor serfs, ignorant of all this. The emperor, then, contented himself with ordering the destruction of the citadels and military establishments according to the usage of war, without causing loss of anything to individuals, already too unfortunate in consequence of this war."

According to Chambray, whose figures are perhaps too high, the French infantry starting from Moscow was about ninety thousand strong, among them many veterans. They were ill-provided. No issues of shoes or clothing had been made in Moscow, though many had looted various articles of clothing. Except for this, the men were still wearing the uniforms in which they had marched in the summer. Much has been written about what might have been done in collecting equipment and saving victual in a better way. In part just, the fault was originally the emperor's for not creating a better staff — for provision and equipment are staff business.

Still, this is criticism after the event, and a staff corps like that perfected by Prussia fifty years ago is a thing that grows. It cannot be created by a word.

The cavalry was fifteen thousand strong, but so ill-horsed as to be of little use. The artillery was the same. The non-combatants, engineers, headquarters men, hospital and train men, and men of the reserve artillery were some twelve thousand, added to which were the useless non-combatants, fugitives, women and invalided soldiers. The sick and wounded who could march (some fifteen hundred were left behind) joined the column, but few escaped the Cossacks. This pitiful, but worse than useless crew, whose number can never be known, accompanied the column that marched on Smolensk; but it dwindled into a handful before the end.

The emperor forbade the abandonment of any guns, of which there were five hundred and seventy, and two thousand wagons. The sharp decisiveness of a Bonaparte, who abandoned the entire siege material before Mantua to march on and beat the enemy, was no longer present. Not one gun in ten was put to use, and all were left behind, a few at a time, along the fatal route. Wagons with the army chest and ingots of precious metal melted down from pillage of the Moscow churches had their place; but the private wagons half filled with loot were of as much use as the pearl to the cock in Æsop's fable.

The army marched slowly to begin with, on account of the enormous column and the difficulties in evacuating Moscow. No sooner had Mortier left the city than the Russians swarmed in, and the sight of the devastated sacred precincts must have lent a ferocity to their oath to pursue and punish the invader.

To mislead Kutusov as to its purpose, the main column began its retreat on October 19, along the old Kaluga road, in order Eugene, Ney, the Guard, Davout; and its head reached Vatutinki. The old road to Kaluga was the one where Kutusov had stood, and where Murat some miles further back still faced Miloradovich. Along the new road that runs through Borovsk more to the west, a small column under Broussier advanced to Fominskia to threaten Dorkov, who lay at Vereia; while, though Borovsk was his objective, Napoleon started by the old road to threaten Kutusov from such a direction as to keep him from moving on the line of retreat he intended to pursue, and most easily to draw in Murat.

On the 20th the Pachra was crossed, and Eugene, with
Poniatowski in his rear, filed to the right so as to reach
the new road and move towards Borovsk. Ney advanced
beyond the Mocha to get in touch with Murat at Voronovo.
"Have Ney understand," the emperor wrote, October 21, to
Berthier, "that he is to form the rearguard of the army; that
to this effect he is to have his corps increased by the division
of Claparède, his two brigades of light cavalry, and that of
Gérardin." But owing to subsequent manœuvres, Ney did
not become the rearguard until the army reached Smolensk.

Napoleon's instructions to Mortier to evacuate the capital
October 22 or 23 and march on Mozhaisk, were changed to a
march on Vereia. The Guard and Davout on the 21st followed
Eugene, who reached Fominskia, with orders to get on speedily to Borovsk; Murat, Ney and Morand remained along the
Mocha. The emperor followed in the track of the army; and
during the retreat headquarters was wont to be in nearby
castles, or monasteries, or churches in the villages. He was
convinced that he had deceived Kutusov, and that he would
reach the direct road to Smolensk before the Russians; but
Eugene disagreed with this opinion, as the hordes of Cossacks
would, he thought, report the actual facts. Murat, with Morand behind him, was to follow on the 22d, and Ney to cover
the march behind the Mocha, and catch up in the night of
October 22–23. The heavy pontoons were abandoned to complete the artillery teams, the light ones were taken; but as the
streams had already been bridged, even these did not go far.
The commissariat started fairly well supplied; but the soldiers
had had enough of poor victualing, and each one catered for
himself. Every company had two or three carts to carry provisions; others were filled with loot under the guise of extra
clothing. Non-combatants had a double supply. Every horse
near and far had been pressed into some one's service, and the

britska of the noble filed along behind the peasant's cart. The emperor knew that in a few days all this would be left behind; and in case of attack by Cossacks, the vehicles would make passable breastworks.

A few apologists for the Russian campaign have ascribed its failure to the weather. This is an error. So far no snow had fallen, and while on November 1 the temperature fell below freezing, yet the sky was clear. The testimony is overwhelming that the winter season was delayed, and that less cold and snow were present than usual. The temperature from Moscow to Krasnaia averaged from 25° to 15° Fahrenheit; few of the streams were frozen so as to bear troops or train. In the 26th Bulletin we find that "The inhabitants of Russia cannot account for the weather we have had for twenty days. It is the sun and the beautiful days of the trip to Fontainebleau. The army is in a country extremely rich, and which can be compared to the best of France and Germany." Sad exaggeration; and to what end? And on November 3 Napoleon wrote Maret: "The weather continues here to be very beautiful, which is extremely favorable." Gourgaud writes that in Prussia, Poland and even in Spain, the cold had been more extreme. According to Fézensac, it was November 7 before real cold set in; and the 29th Bulletin says: "Up to November 6 the weather was perfect."

Early on October 22 Napoleon ordered Eugene to dispatch Poniatowski to Vereia at once: "It is necessary to reconnoitre well and get news. The occupation of Vereia is the great affair for to-day." This was done. With Borovsk as objective, the viceroy himself crossed the Nara at Fominskia, Davout and the Guard came up there, with Murat and Morand in the rear, and Delzons' division got to Borovsk. Next day, out of Vereia, Poniatowski drove Dorkov, who retired by the south of Maloyaroslavez; Poniatowski was notified "not to send his wounded and sick to Mozhaisk, as it would encumber the road, which is already too much so; that it is better that he should carry them with him." Ney withdrew from the front of Miloradovich, who reported the fact to Kutusov. At midnight of October 22–23 Mortier left the Kremlin, having been able to blow up only the arsenal and part of the walls. The harm done was not irreparable.

When Kutusov at Tarutino heard of a French column near Fominskia, he dispatched Doctorov thither with twenty-five thousand men, believing it to be only a detachment which he might cut off. Doctorov soon ran across a heavy body, and a captured French officer revealed the truth. The Russian corps stopped at Aristovo and sent back a report that Moscow was evacuated; upon which Kutusov, hoping to head off the French, hurried a corps of Cossacks to Maloyaroslavez, and slowly followed with the entire Russian army, October 23. Doctorov clearly divined the facts and also pushed his column on Maloyaroslavez, the cross-roads of that section, and begged for reinforcements; but Kutusov was slow in movement, alleging that he must draw in his foraging parties. On the 23d Eugene, with his own and a cavalry corps, reached Borovsk, and Delzons hurried forward to Maloyaroslavez, drove out a few Cossacks, and began repairs on the Lusha bridge. Murat, Davout and the Guard followed on to Borovsk, Poniatowski was in Vereia, Ney was still in the rear. Napoleon in person reached Borovsk, believing Kutusov yet on the Nara, and that, instead of divining the retreat, he would look on the French march as a threat to turn his left; and that the Russian corps at Aristovo was sent out to fend off such an attack. Intending, as he notified Victor, October 23, to march to Kaluga and thence by way of Jelnia to Smolensk, he expected to reach this road first; should Kutusov attack, the army was to base on Vereia; but should Kutusov defend

Kaluga, Napoleon would deliver battle. Hence Junot, who had reached Mozhaisk, was ordered to send all troops ready for the march to Vereia. By holding Maloyaroslavez, which Delzons was to take and there face the enemy, Napoleon deemed the road to Kaluga safe, and thought that on the 24th he would be able to fathom Kutusov's designs.

"It is necessary that Delzons, as soon as he is master of this little town, shall reconnoitre well on his left," the emperor wrote Eugene, October 23, in the evening: "You should reconnoitre on your left, and should render an account to-morrow early of all that you shall have seen. You are to this effect to send along your left strong reconnoissances, an hour before daylight. We here are making front to the enemy from Delzons to Fominskia."

From Maloyaroslavez there was a new road to Smolensk, via Juknov and Jelnia, of which Napoleon desired to take advantage; Victor had some time before been ordered to send to Jelnia the division of Baraguey d'Hilliers, ten thousand strong, as a reinforcement, and the government of Viasma was to clear up this route. Maloyaroslavez for the moment was markedly a key-point; and Doctorov, marching ahead of his orders, early on the 24th came up.

The Lusha River has here a deep channel and but one bridge, and the fords were not used. South of the town the ground, accentuated everywhere and partly wooded, rises sharply up to a plateau, to fall away again gently. Learning that the town was weakly held, Doctorov attacked and drove out the two French battalions, but the bridge was firmly held. Delzons on the other side essayed to regain the town; and when Broussier came up, a serious contest ensued, in which the French showed such tenacity against the constantly reinforced fighting line of the enemy that Doctorov made no progress. The town was set afire, and in desperate hand to hand struggles it was taken and retaken as many as seven times. Mean-

while the main armies were approaching; Raevski, Kutusov's
van, came up to aid Doctorov, and Napoleon arrived about
noon, having near Borovsk heard the firing. Davout and
the Guard were placed in reserve on the right and left of the
road; and the leading Russian corps was put in to sustain the
hard-pressed troops which still held Maloyaroslavez; while
Eugene, sending in his last divisions, Pino and Lecchi, finally

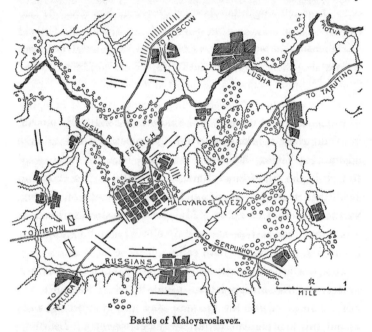

Battle of Maloyaroslavez.

secured the prize, but was unable to debouch into the open.
Gérard and Compans also crossed, and came up on the right
and left; and though at nightfall Kutusov made a last attempt
to force an entrance, he was thrown back and retired to the
heights, merely covering the town with artillery. Napoleon
had maintained his ability to cross the river and file to the
west through Medyni. Each side had put in twenty-five thousand men. The losses have been estimated at ten thousand

men on each side; they may have been six or seven thousand. Dorkov and Delzons were killed. The French won a tactical victory; but failing to utilize it, the real victory, so far as results go, remained with the Russians.

Maloyaroslavez has been called a decisive battle, as putting beyond Napoleon's power to operate his retreat after a victory. It has been called the turning-point of his career; but his decision at Smolensk to advance to Moscow appears to be more nearly that.

The entire Russian army gradually came up and bivouacked around Maloyaroslavez. At headquarters in Gorodnia, at daylight on October 25, it was reported from the outposts that there were signs of cavalry marching in the direction of Medyni. Napoleon called to his tent Murat, Bessières and Lobau, and on asking their opinions as to delivering battle, these officers agreed that retreat alone was advisable, the last suggesting Mozhaisk, the two former Smolensk; that the Grand Army should retire to the Niemen by the least opposed route. Napoleon rode out and spent some hours reconnoitring the enemy, but even then he seemed unable to make up his mind; he still hoped Kutusov would retire. This attitude of waiting on what the enemy would do is unlike anything we have so far seen in his career. Kutusov indeed had determined to retire to Kaluga, and the emperor may have noticed signs of it; but this fact emphasizes rather than lessens his indecision. He rode back to headquarters, and next morning renewed the reconnoissance under cover of his Guard. On this occasion he came near capture. Some Cossacks had been in hiding in a wood on the right; and had not the Guard galloped to the rescue, the Napoleonic scheme might have ended then and there. About nine o'clock the report came in that Kutusov was retiring, and that only a Russian rearguard was occupying the bivouac in the front.

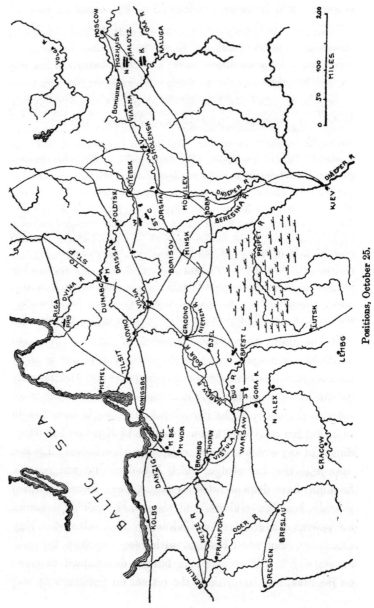

Positions, October 25.

As a description of the battle from his point of view, Napoleon told Berthier, October 26, to write to Junot: —

"That the Russian army moved on Maloyaroslavez ; that its vanguard arrived on one bank at the same time that our vanguard arrived on the other.; that the town is situated on the bank of the enemy, and in a very high position, which gave rise to a combat which lost the whole day of the 24th ; that while our vanguard sustained this combat, the whole Russian army arrived ; that on our side Davout's troops arrived to the relief of Eugene ; that we remained masters of the battlefield ; that the enemy lost seven or eight thousand men. Our loss is two thousand killed and wounded. Delzons was killed. We found the corpses of two Russian generals ; two hundred and fifty or three hundred prisoners remained in our hands. Write also that the 25th the army took position. The Russian army was opposite, a league behind Maloyaroslavez. That we marched the 26th to attack it, but that it was in retreat. That Davout followed it up, but that the cold, and the necessity of getting rid of the wounded that are with the army, decided the emperor to move on Mozhaisk, and from there to Viasma. . . . That the enemy's infantry, since the battle of the Moskwa, is much diminished ; that it is not composed of more than fifteen thousand old soldiers, but that they have recruited their Cossacks ; and that this cavalry, little dangerous in reality, is getting very tired."

It has been urged that Napoleon might have delivered battle to advantage ; but he could scarcely have put in more than seventy thousand men, as Poniatowski and Mortier were not at hand, while Kutusov had one hundred thousand men, with much cavalry. The French infantry would have fought well, but the odds were against them, and Kutusov had determined in any event to retire to Kaluga, if attacked. Looked upon with that knowledge, which Napoleon did not possess, he might have demonstrated for battle, have forced Kutusov sharply back on Kaluga, and then have quickly resumed his retreat via Juknov and Jelnia, well ahead of the Russian army. But when Kutusov withdrew, Napoleon, for some reason which will ever remain buried, determined to retire on Borovsk, and to continue the retreat on Smolensk by way

of Mozhaisk, Gshask and Viasma. For the purpose of retiring on Smolensk by this route, four good marching days had
been lost; and Kutusov, with his ninety thousand regulars
and thirty thousand Cossacks, was nearer than the French to
Viasma, Krasnoi, Kopys, on the French communications.

That Napoleon had called a council of war may not have
exhibited his growing loss of self-reliance, but his decision
certainly showed an unsoundness we little expect of him. The
manœuvre towards Kaluga was strategically sound, for, from
there, the retreat via Juknov and Jelnia led through an
undevastated region on Smolensk, and the holding of Kaluga
by a stout rearguard would prevent too sharp a pursuit. If
Kaluga could not be reached, then the next most favorable
route was from Maloyaroslavez via Medyni, Juknov and Jelnia on Smolensk. As a last resort only, as after a defeat,
was a withdrawal by way of Borovsk and Viasma excusable.
The very object of moving on Kaluga was to elbow Kutusov
off to the east or southeast, and gain the best route, through
Jelnia, on which line, moreover, were coming his reinforcements; failing in which, the battle of Maloyaroslavez was to
make sure of the next best route through Medyni. Either of
these routes would forestall attack except in the rear, whereas
the route chosen afforded the Russians time enough, and an
open road, to fall on the French flank, or head of column, or
rear, as they chose; and yet, after Napoleon had lost the first
route, and by hard fighting held the second, he deliberately
elected the third and worst route, back on Borovsk and Mozhaisk. That the great captain, on whose intelligence and spirit
the French had so long relied for victory, should call in
others to prop up his own powers may be pardoned, but that
he should delay his decision for two days exhibits a weaken-
ing will; and in his selection of the worst route possible for the
Grand Army to pursue, when he had just fought a hideous

battle to secure, and had secured, a better one, we fail to recognize the leader of 1805 and 1806. And when we compare this attitude with that of Frederick after Kolin or Hochkirch, of Hannibal after Zama, we are forced to the conclusion that

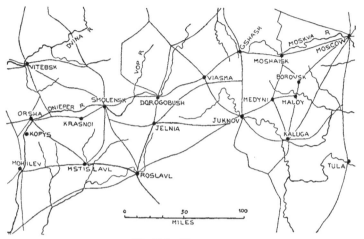

The False Manœuvre.

the emperor had already outlived his best powers, or was under a spell from this his first overwhelming disaster. If speed was ever needed, it had been since the Grand Army left Moscow; and instead of speed, there had been irresolution, and the consequent loss of four or more marches.

Napoleon now ordered what he might as well have done from Fominskia on the 21st. Davout was for some miles to pursue Kutusov with two divisions, leaving two in Maloyaroslavez, and one in Gorodnia; and then, with cavalry as rearguard, he was to follow the Grand Army at night towards Borovsk, to which place, during the day, Eugene was to proceed. Poniatowski, as flanker, was ordered towards Gshask by the southerly route of Jegorevskoi, Ney from Borovsk to Vereia, Mortier with Claparède and Roquet from Vereia to

Mozhaisk, whereupon Junot was to take the lead and march on Viasma. The forces ordered from Smolensk towards Jelnia were to file off on Dorogobush. Thus, left behind at Maloyaroslavez, Davout became rearguard instead of Ney; and on October 26 the Grand Army began the regular retreat, not again to be interrupted.

On October 28 Napoleon learned from Davout that there was no enemy in his front, which meant that Kutusov had either retired to Kaluga, or was moving westerly to cut off the French; and lest Viasma should be his objective, the emperor hurried the Guard ahead to sustain Junot.

Kutusov had retired on the 26th to Goncharovo, under cover of Miloradovich as rearguard. There was a defile in his rear on the road to Kaluga, and he had deemed it better not to fight the French thus placed. Next day he learned of their retreat, and assuming that they would move on Medyni, as they ought to have done, he at once headed his army towards this place, and reached Polotniani-Savodi; while the rearguard, now become a vanguard, returned towards Maloyaroslavez, thence to Adamovskoi, and was later ordered towards Mozhaisk. The main Russian body got to Adamovskoi on the 29th.

On reaching Vereia October 27, Napoleon found Mortier there, and the Grand Army retired in the prescribed order. On the 28th Junot and the Guard marched from Mozhaisk to Kolotskoi, preceded by Mortier, and with Ney and Eugene behind, at or near Borisovo; Davout was still at Borovsk, and Poniatowski was marching from Jegorevskoi to Gshask. Late this day a captured Russian officer reported that Kutusov was marching on Smolensk. As Davout sent in word from Borovsk that only Cossacks were following his column, the credibility of this news spurred Napoleon on; and with the Guard he hurried to Gshask on the 29th, so as to meet

Kutusov, should he first reach the French line of retreat; for soon after his decision, at Maloyaroslavez, he had recognized that his direction was dangerously eccentric thereto. As he passed the Kolotskoi hospitals, he ordered all the Borodino wounded to be carried along; but there being no provision for them on the road, they one by one died from the exposure. Left in the hospitals, the Russians would have given the sick some care, though stragglers in the open field were mercilessly cut down by the Cossacks or murdered by the peasants.

Gshask was reached by Junot, Ney got to Kolotskoi, with Eugene not far behind, and Davout Mozhaisk. This placed the whole army on the Smolensk road in one column, and to speed the march through the eaten-out country, Napoleon divided it into four sections, at half-day intervals. These were the Guard and Junot, Ney, Eugene, Davout; and thus the Grand Army retired, the hardships increasing from day to day, and lengthening the intervals. To the suggestion that for safety the army should have marched in three columns, one on, and one on either side of, the main road, it may be said that the emperor early made up his mind that Kutusov would not seriously attack.

By the end of October the soldiers had neither bread nor beef, the brandy was gone, and except a little plundered food in the private wagons, nothing was left. The men practically lived on horse-flesh, and as the cold nights afforded little sleep, every bivouac looked like a field of battle. To ease their load, the weak or cowardly threw away their muskets and ammunition and swelled the host of non-combatants, and the intermingled masses lost the appearance of an army.

The column kept on its ghastly route, and late on the 31st Napoleon, with the Guard and Junot, reached Viasma, fortunately ahead of the Russian van, and took position west of the town; Ney came on to Velichevo, with Poniatowski and

Eugene at Gshask, and Davout at Gridnieva. Davout had
been slow. Told not to abandon his artillery, he may, with
the sting of late faultfinding, have set his teeth to obey, if
he lost his last man. Left to himself, the marshal had a wonderful sense of what it was wise to do ; yet his delays may
have compelled the leading corps to wait, and given Kutusov
more time to come up. He and Ney were not working cheerfully together.

In Viasma dispatches were received up to October 14 from
Paris, from St. Cyr to the 20th, from Victor to the 24th,
and from Vilna to the 26th; and Napoleon spent the 1st of
November answering these. He learned that Schwartzenberg had on October 15 retired before Chichagov to the left
bank of the Bug at Drogichin, thus enabling the Russians at
Brest Litovsk to leave a containing force, and move towards
the Beresina to help net the Grand Army. Victor at Smolensk had received instructions to keep an eye on both right
and left, as the Army of Moldavia might join either Kutusov
or Tormasov; and as Wittgenstein was apt to be reinforced,
he was to be ready as a central reserve, to march on Minsk
or on Vilna. In accordance therewith, Victor had left fifteen
thousand men in Smolensk, and judiciously placed the rest
in Orsha, Sieno and Babinovichi. On November 2 Berthier
was ordered to write him in cipher " that the army is in
march, as I have already told him. Finding that the winter
was too long to pass it far from my flanks, that it is probable
that I shall place my right" (left) " on the Dvina and my
left" (right) " on the Borysthenes, and that by this means
we shall find ourselves in contact."

The news received accentuated the danger. From Brest
Litovsk and Polotsk alike the Russians were threatening the
line of retreat, with no sufficient French force to fend them
off; but beyond ordering the commanders in the rear to hold

their own and to keep him posted, Napoleon could do naught : for the first time he was at the end of his resources.

Leaving Viasma November 2, Junot reached Semlevo, the Guard behind him, Eugene and Poniatowski at, and Davout near, Fedorovskoi. In order that Ney, who had reached Viasma, might undertake the rearguard duty originally cut out for him, he was to remain there until the other corps had passed through.

There was grave danger of Eugene and Davout being cut off; and the Cossacks compelled the troops to march in closed squares, to fend off sudden dashes. " It is very important," Berthier was told to write Eugene, November 2, "to change the manner of marching in the face of the enemy, who has so large a crowd of Cossacks. He must march as we marched in Egypt, baggage in the centre, closed up in as many files as the road allows, a half battalion in front, a half battalion in rear, battalions by files on the flanks, so as when we come to a front, we can give fire towards every side." This could be carried out only in part — as were all other orders.

Meanwhile Kutusov, uncertain how to head off the French army, had from Maloyaroslavez been marching in a general parallel direction. His van aimed for Kolotskoi, but learning from Cossack scouting-parties that the French had already taken it, bore off to the left on Gubino, hoping to anticipate them at Gshask. With the main army Kutusov moved on Viasma, and by October 31 he was at Spas-Kusovi, the vanguard advancing between the two armies to Krasnaia, and Platov's Cossacks feeling Davout at Kolotskoi, and pushing him hard to Gridnieva and Gshask. Next day Kutusov got to Silenki, and the van came in touch with Eugene at Tatarikino. On November 2 the army was at Dubrovna with van at Spaskoi, and Platov still pressing Davout towards Fedorovskoi. The main army had moved through a country affording some supplies, but so slow was Kutusov that, although marching on the chord of an arc, the French got past Viasma before he reached them. A body of cavalry was sent forward on Jelnia.

The French delay on the Lusha was bearing bitter fruit: the Guard and Junot alone had got beyond danger of being cut off. Look again at the situation. Parallel to Ney at Viasma, twenty miles south, was marching the Russian main army; Eugene, Poniatowski and Davout were ten miles behind Ney, harassed by the Cossacks in rear, and with the Russian van on their flank. Should Kutusov on November 3 push sharply on Viasma, these three corps would be headed off and separated from the sections under Napoleon. Happily for the French, the Russian general kept up his policy of caution; but no wonder his lieutenants found grievous fault with his slackness.

Napoleon and the Guard, on November 3, made a short march from Semlevo to Slavkovo, Junot marching ahead to Dorogobush, Eugene and Poniatowski moving on Viasma. The cavalry of the Russian van, advancing beyond Maximovo, struck the head of Davout's column, while Platov harassed his rear.

Davout was filing through Fedorovskoi, ten miles to the east. Miloradovich posted some cavalry across the road in Davout's front, sustained by Eugene of Wurtemberg, and drew up his foot and guns parallel with it. Davout made a good fight against the cavalry, part of which he drove to the north of the road, where it joined Platov, who continued to harass his right flank, part to the south. But then he found a line of infantry in his front.

From this dangerous position Davout was rescued by Poniatowski and the viceroy, the latter sending back to his assistance the Delzons and Broussier divisions, which drew up so

as to enable Davout to file by in their rear, but later fell back
to Miesoyedova. Eugene of Wurtemberg claims in his Memoirs that he could have held his own against both Davout
and the viceroy, because the Russian artillery was in good
condition and the French ill-served and half horsed; Miloradovich may have been able to gauge the situation better. At
all events, Davout filed past, with Russian fire on his left and
Platov on his right and rear, and lost heavily, until he got

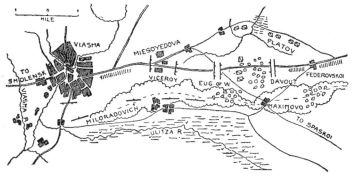

Battle of Viasma.

behind the viceroy; whereupon the French divisions formed
line and challenged the Russians to battle, but Miloradovich
did not attack. It was said at the time that Davout's men
had not behaved with their accustomed gallantry, but this
might be said of other divisions, and it was an awkward situation. The loss has been stated at five thousand men each
side.

Here had been a rare chance for a general Russian attack;
but knowing the French must keep up their retreat, Kutusov
was unwilling to force matters. He was loth to stake his
reputation on another pitched battle, when every day's retreat
made the chances of success greater. Yet had he cut the
French off, attacked them and been beaten, he could have
retired on either Chichagov or Wittgenstein; had he beaten

them decisively, he probably would have captured the emperor and put an end to the Napoleonic wars; and the campaigns of 1813, 1814 and 1815 would never have taken place. It will always be debated whether Kutusov was wise in adopting a Fabian policy. Once adopted, he consistently stuck to it; and it has been said that if his generals had not so constantly harassed him with demands for action, he might have been more willing to attack.

The isolated French corps commanders held a council and determined on retreat, which Eugene and Poniatowski conducted during the afternoon of the 3d, as a running fight, to beyond Viasma, Davout being in some disorder; Ney held Viasma until the other corps had got through the town; Napoleon remained in Slavkovo, busy with organization and supply — essential duties, but less so than what he owed to his endangered corps. Indeed, he spoke rather scornfully of their danger, and underestimated the forces of the foe, while overrating the ability of his lieutenants to surmount grave difficulties. On the day of battle Kutusov, with the main Russian column, advanced to Bykova. Had he been energetic, he might still have done the French column a fatal damage by sustaining his cavalry and cutting off Ney in Viasma.

From now on, Ney kept command of the rearguard. On November 3 Berthier was ordered to write him, " that as soon as he shall have taken the command of the rearguard, he is to make the army file along as fast as possible, for we are wearing out the remains of good weather without marching. Davout holds back the viceroy and Poniatowski for each Cossack charge that he notices." No one disputes the glory won for himself by Ney in this memorable retreat; neither does the military student forget the remarkable qualities of Davout. It was a pity these two great marshals, so excellent a complement each to the other, could not agree. With constant rearguard fighting, Ney organized his work in a marvelous manner. Beloved by the men, he treated his whole force as if none could ask better than " the glorious opportunity of getting himself killed " — as most of them did, and gamely.

Early November 4 Napoleon heard of the fight near Viasma, and complained to Davout that he had "received no account of what took place since he had been conducting the rearguard, and especially of yesterday." He planned to lie in wait between Slavkovo and Dorogobush, and to fall on Kutusov as he advanced, and he held the Guard and Junot there during the day, while Eugene, Poniatowski and Davout came up to Semlevo, for the most part in very bad order. Fézensac tells us that "the Royal Italian Guard almost alone marched in good order; the rest seemed demoralized

Ney.

and overcome with fatigue. An enormous mass of individual soldiers marched in disorder, and most of them without arms." And Ney wrote Berthier that " the roads were without exaggeration covered by . . . men of all regiments of the Grand Army, who could not be brought to march together." Fending off the onsets of the Cossack corps, Ney left Viasma and reached Semlevo late in the day; and on his report Napoleon decided to forego the ambush. Early November 5 he left Slavkovo for Dorogobush, and hither all the corps successively came, Ney still behind as rearguard. Kutusov spent

November 4 at Bykova, the van following the Cossacks on
the main road; on the 5th he marched to Krasnaia.

The embarrassment had become extreme. The provisions
from Moscow had long been consumed, the unfed horses fell
in their tracks and blocked the road; nearly two hundred
guns were abandoned between Moscow and Smolensk; the
French eagles, former emblems of victory, now seemed to lead
the soldier to certain defeat and death. Up to this date the
Grand Army had had to contend only with the Russians and
with hunger. Snow was now added. On November 5 there
was a slight fall, and next day a heavy fall of snow, with bit-
ing wind. Smolensk was yet distant, and winter was upon
them. Foraging was at an end. The beaten down snow got
slippery, and the horses had no footing. Only a part of the
Polish cavalry had means of sharp-shoeing, and the soldiers
had to push the guns up every slope. Few horses that fell
were strong enough to rise again, and fourfold the number of
vehicles were now abandoned each day. The army, which had
left Moscow ninety thousand strong, arrived at Dorogobush
with scarcely half the number.

On November 6, at Michailovska, Napoleon received news
from Paris of the Malet conspiracy of October 23, to spread
a rumor of the emperor's death and overturn the government.
Of small importance, it yet showed him how entirely the
empire rested on his single life, and how essential was his
presence in the capital.

Victor also wrote. St. Cyr had fortified Polotsk; Wittgenstein, reinforced by St. Petersburg militia, had intrenched
his camp, and prevented the French from foraging north of
the river. Macdonald had done nothing. He could have
accomplished as much with less forces, and the rest have ad-
vantageously strengthened Victor; but Napoleon feared an
advance down the coast around his left. By October 15 Witt-

genstein had forty thousand men, and Steinheil was bringing
him ten thousand more: St. Cyr had but twenty-seven thousand. Steinheil crossed at Druia to take Polotsk in reverse,
while Wittgenstein was to move on its front, and St. Cyr had
the chance of leaving part of his force to contain Wittgenstein, and destroying Steinheil; but he was cautious. Wittgenstein assaulted Polotsk the 18th without success. There
was no bridge by which the Russians could join; but fearing
the superior numbers, St. Cyr retired, October 21, behind the
Ulla to Chasniki, while Wrede moved to Glubokoi to cover
Vilna, and a division took post at Bechenkovichi to keep
touch with Victor. These operations cost each side about six
thousand men, and Victor, whose duty was to support either
wing, had to detach troops from Smolensk to aid St. Cyr,
some days previous to the evacuation of Moscow, and himself
followed. Even this reinforcement proved too small. Wittgenstein followed St. Cyr with caution, and on October 29
Victor took command at Chasniki, while Wittgenstein drew
in Steinheil to Lepel, and left thirty-five hundred men at
Polotsk. A force of five thousand men, sent down river to
watch Macdonald, reconnoitred as far as Dünaburg, and then
returned and faced Wrede, who was covering Vilna. Wittgenstein still had in line thirty thousand men; Victor had
three thousand more, and Dombrovski at Mohilev with ten
thousand men was also under his orders. With no idea of the
disaster to the emperor, Victor called in the force at Bechenkovichi, part of which joined; his cavalry had stayed behind.
He was now in force to attack, with a strong chance of success,
but he permitted Wittgenstein to do so; and although in the
ensuing action he was not defeated, he retired, apparently
thinking that his duty as general reserve did not comprise
attack. Happily Wittgenstein did not improve his opportunity. But, instead of retiring on Sieno so as to protect both

Orsha and Vitebsk, Victor retired to Chereia, November 6 —
a strategic error; whereupon the Russian left moved sharply
on Vitebsk, and captured it, November 7, with its full garrison.
The situation was becoming desperate.

Unaware of what had happened, especially of the disaster
to Victor, the emperor, on November 7, instructed Berthier
to "Write Victor the following letter: —

"In plain words: 'I have submitted your letter of the
2d to the emperor. His Majesty orders you to reunite your
six divisions, and to fall upon the enemy without delay and
push him beyond the Dvina, and that you are to retake
Polotsk.'

"In cipher (you must have received this cipher from
General Nansouty): 'This movement is most important.
In a few days your rear may be inundated by Cossacks. The
army of the emperor will be to-morrow at Smolensk, but
much tired by a march of one hundred and twenty leagues
without stopping. Take the offensive. The salvation of the
armies depends on it. Every day lost is a calamity. The
cavalry of the army is on foot. Cold has made all the horses
die. March! It is the order of the emperor and that of
necessity!'

"Send this letter to General Charpentier by the courier
who is to leave in an hour. He will send it by an officer to
Victor.   NAPOLEON."

But just as earlier orders to Victor had been impossible of
execution, so now was this. The conditions, unknown to the
emperor, had entirely changed.

Personally, on this retreat, the emperor rode in his coach,
or walked with the Guard, occasionally being in the saddle;
his thoughts were locked in his own breast. "He was pale,"
says Constant, "but his countenance was quiet; there was
nothing in his features which permitted his moral suffering

to be penetrated." Only such orders as that of November 7 to Victor show us how fully he gauged his danger : in no sense did he confide in his ancient fellows in arms ; neither indeed was he frank in writing to Victor, or Macdonald, or Schwartzenberg. How far he had lost the art of dealing with facts; how far, in misrepresenting them to others, he deceived himself, is a question hard to solve ; but that he was no longer the same man is plain. He looked towards Vilna, which he determined personally to reach at any loss, and believed that, once out of the horrible situation into which his own faulty judgment had plunged him, he

Victor.

yet had means and characteristic force enough to meet whatever might happen.

Every virtue carried to excess becomes a vice. The emperor's habit of exaggeration had grown beyond reason. It had been deliberately assumed, and within bounds had accomplished its purpose, but it was now abused. Yet although much fault may be found with this misleading method, it remains a question whether war can be carried on by always stating the exact facts to subordinates. There is in history no more heroic moment than that of the evening before Leuthen, in which Frederick the Great collected about him his officers, and told them that the enemy intrenched on the heights beyond was three to one of them, and that they must beat him or fall one and all at the foot of his batteries ; but

Napoleon never exhibited just that quality, nor did he ever
have officers or men of the temper of those the king's father
had passed through his training furnace, and the king had
welded into steel. It is unwarranted to tax the emperor
with mendacity on account of these lapses: the diplomacy of
the day was full of lies on both sides, and military reports
were then, as they commonly are now, utterly misleading.
Napoleon kept up a habit which had worked well, but which
under existing abnormal conditions would not work. It did
mislead Victor as to Wittgenstein's strength, but what soldier
would have had the emperor say to Victor: "You are outnumbered, the enemy has resources which you lack, and yet
you must move against him and beat him"? The emperor
was wiser, within bounds, to keep up his ancient habit; his
fault was in exceeding reasonable bounds. Only Davout and
Ney were fighters against fate. With twice his force Victor
would not have been too well equipped for his work; but to
tell him he had not resources enough and yet must accomplish
results, would have been very much like hanging an unsuccessful admiral to the yard-arm *pour encourager les autres.*

For ordering certain things to be done at a distance, which
he ought to have known could not be executed, Napoleon
is in a way justly criticised, in a way not. Should he at Moscow, even if conscious of the dangers in his rear, have ceased
from giving such instructions? Should he have assumed that
his foundations were crumbling, and issued orders accordingly? Which system of care for his base and his reinforcements would work the best: the assumption that little can
be done with weak orders, or the assumption that much can
be done with vigorous instructions? Had the emperor sent
dispatches, for instance to Maret, that he was in a desperate
strait and it was a question if he would ever reach Vilna,
would he have held the allies to their work until he fairly

got out of the clutches of the Russians? It seems that, taking the man as he was, with all his strong and weak points, it bred more accomplishment for him to order too much than too little. He probably foresaw disaster before he left Moscow, and he would scarcely have acted a Napoleonic rôle by accepting this, and requiring less of his subordinates. We know what happened while he acted the stronger rôle; had he acted the weaker one, would he have been able to reach France, and within a few months raise so mighty an army again as to march back to the Elbe and defeat his enemies in the first two battles? Much fault must be found with Napoleon in this campaign, but this may be carried too far by characterizing his orders as absurd because he knew, or might have guessed, that they could be carried out only in part. There was no man in the Grand Army who could have got any part of it from Moscow back to the borders of Prussia; Napoleon himself saved only a skeleton of it — and its head; and sharp and constant and even unreasonable requirements seem to have accomplished the end. Napoleon had been spoiled by the hitherto universal obedience to his commands; but to assume that he had lost all perception of the limits of his power, or that he did not realize his difficulties, is as far from the truth as to assume that he was, before starting from Smolensk, as accurate and far-seeing in his calculations as he had previously been. During the first week at Moscow he probably foresaw nothing worse than another year's campaign in Russia, but after Maloyaroslavez he did foresee disaster. Even then, to weaken in his self-assertion was to invite a greater calamity than actually followed. Much must be said against Napoleon's inaccurate gauging of possibilities in the Russian campaign; but during the retreat, it was only his strong will, his almost abnormal control over his lieutenants, which enabled him to guide even the ghost of an army beyond the Russian frontier. To exhibit weakness was but to invite a *Sauve qui peut !*

As an instance of this hypercriticism, Chambray quotes a dispatch from Berthier to Victor ordering immediate attack, and telling him that if Wittgenstein has too difficult a position, he must turn him out of it; adding that if Victor can win a handsome victory, the emperor will be able to take up winter quarters on a line from Polotsk to Vitebsk, Orsha and Mohilev, which would bring about peace during the winter, or a chance to menace St. Petersburg in the spring; that Wittgenstein must not be allowed to join Kutusov at Vitebsk, which would cause the loss of Lithuania ; that the campaign could not close without a battle between Victor and Wittgenstein, and the sooner this took place the better. Because this order was not capable of execution, the emperor is blamed for misleading Victor. Over this point never-ceasing arguments could be had, but it is answered above. If it be held that in disaster the commanding general should weaken in his purpose and in his orders, then Napoleon was in the wrong; but the strong commander is slow to acknowledge defeat. By conduct leaning towards weakness, it would have been easy on any day during the retreat to change the Grand Army into a mob of fugitives, of which not one could have crossed the Beresina.

As another instance, the emperor, on October 5, ordered the removal of the wounded to begin, and made Junot and Baraguey d'Hilliers responsible for the collection of vehicles and horses, although the country had already been stripped of everything of the kind. Despite all this, many wounded were actually got to the rear, as with less crisp orders they would not have been. This is quite apart from whether it was wise to move the wounded; as a matter of fact, most of them perished from exposure. They could not have been worse off had the Cossacks cut them down; but the situation was such that, even if he knew that all the wounded would die, Napoleon also believed that if he abandoned them, they would all meet a like fate, and he would be bitterly held to task for so doing.

When, however, it comes to judging the emperor's lapse from the clear, vigorous thought and action to which he has accustomed us, then criticism becomes fair. The old Napoleon would not have gone beyond Smolensk; or, having done so, would not have dwelt so long in Moscow; he would have better harbored his resources; he would have attacked Kutusov a second time; he would have more constantly looked after his lieutenants and disciplined his divisions, and have personally directed their movements. There is no desire

Napoleon.
From a sepia by Horace Vernet.

to cover up the manifest decrease in characteristic power of the great soldier. He was no longer the man he had been in the Ulm and Austerlitz and Jena campaigns, when his intellectual force and vigor of character and clearness of vision may be said to have been at their highest. There are so many open questions in this campaign that it is easy to insist that Napoleon erred every day in what he did: he certainly com-

mitted errors enough. So did Kutusov, unless we assume
that he intended to play only the Fabian game. But it is not
necessary to seek for mistakes in order to combat them.

The further march on Smolensk continued. The weather
grew colder and the men suffered more; the Grand Army
was fast dissolving. There was no more cavalry; the guns
grew fewer each day; the water-courses all ran in deep chan-
nels in the plain, and it was impossible to cross them with
unsharpened, ill-fed horses and heavy loads. At each of the
crossings, the guns, caissons and munition wagons had to be
dragged up the steep bank on the further side by hand.

The men ate horse-meat, or dogs found in the burned villages they passed. Stragglers fell into the hands of the
enemy, and were mostly cut down or saved for a worse fate.
The roads were covered with men without weapons, each
looking out for himself. Every nightly bivouac saw hundreds perish with cold and hunger. Dead men and horses
lined the road; the men were passed without heed — 't was
but one more; the horses were seized on to keep alive the
famished wretches for another day's trials. Men went mad
from the terrors of the route: hosts committed suicide.

No description can equal the horrors of this retreat. Old
comrades plundered each other to keep from starvation. The
man who fell by the way was stripped of his clothing to keep
others from perishing by cold. The scenes among the actual
or self-made non-combatants were too sickening to describe;
but there was, as there always is, a nucleus of true heroes,
who did not forget their manhood or the ancient ties of blood
and service. The proportion of officers who got through was
greater than of men, not only because they could in a sense
better care for themselves, but because they were of a higher
type, with moral courage to outlast the others.

So many volumes have been written on this subject that the

mere recital of the losses must suffice. The hideousness of these weeks has nothing to do with the History of the Art of War.

On November 9 Napoleon with the Guard and Junot reached Smolensk; he and all his military family afoot, for the saddle-horses could not stand. All the corps shortly

Russian Landwehr.

arrived: Poniatowski on the 10th, taking position on the Mstislavl road, Davout on the 12th, Eugene and Ney on the 13th. From Dorogobush Eugene was sent by way of Duchovchina, so as to move on Vitebsk.

At Smolensk Napoleon heard of the loss by Baraguey d'Hilliers of a brigade surrounded at Lakovo on the road to Jelnia, showing that Kutusov was active, and that the Grand Army could not rest in Smolensk. He also heard of the fall of Vitebsk. The weather continued cold, but the snow had the one good effect of forcing Kutusov farther to the south to forage his horses.

In his circuit via Duchovchina, Eugene was followed by five thousand Cossacks under Platov; and at the Vop, on the 9th, being unable to throw a bridge, he was in grave danger. In summer the Vop is easily fordable; but now its channel was full, the bridges broken, and the steep banks covered with ice. The men waded the river in water up to their shoulders; and with loss of half his men, all but a dozen of his sixty guns and his entire train, Eugene reached Duchovchina, where he found a little food. Had Vitebsk been open to him, he could not now march thither on account of his depletion.

At Smolensk the Grand Army numbered barely fifty thousand men, a large part unarmed — less than a third of its strength here seven weeks before. Meanwhile Kutusov marched via Gavrukovo, Jelnia and Lakovo, and on November 13 reached Chelkanovo, two marches south of Smolensk; and his van, which had kept between the main column and the French army, stood at Chervonoi, leaving a cavalry force to follow the French rearguard. Though nearer his base, Napoleon's position had not improved, for the Russians, advancing through a country as yet undevastated, were in the better condition; and with ordinary exertion Kutusov could reach Krasnoi, or Orsha, in time to fall on the flank of the French, or head them off.

Napoleon had expected to pause at Smolensk for rest and for reorganization, with the fresh men under Baraguey as leaven to call back the soldiers to their duty. The army was raveled out of all recognition in spirit, leg-weary and starving, and heart and body alike needed to be knit up; it had looked forward to Smolensk as furnishing repose and food. In summer, though burned, this town had shown them pleasant environments and rich grain-fields; now, towards winter, they found but half-roofed houses, filled with sick and dying, empty shops and misery. The garrison, the sick and wounded, the passing troops and trains, had eaten everything: Smolensk was as naked of food as the road from Moscow. Had the army come through the less poor Jelnia country, it would have kept its ranks better. It was no longer an army.

Victor was still at Chereia, Wittgenstein on the Ulla, a detachment in Vitebsk. To Victor's report, received on the 11th, Napoleon replied, " His Majesty will turn with a part of the army on Orsha; but this movement can be made only slowly; it is all the more essential for you to attack Wittgenstein." He appears to place the danger of Wittgenstein before that of Kutusov.

French Cuirassier on Cossack Pony.

From the French right came like ill news: Schwartzenberg and Reynier, after crossing the Bug, had retired to Vengrov about mid-October, while Chichagov held Brest Litovsk and Pruzhani. Essaying a partial blow against Schwartzenberg by passing the Bug, he was driven back; but by the end of the month he left Sacken in Brest Litovsk with twenty-five thousand men to contain Schwartzenberg, while he, with thirty-eight thousand, marched towards Minsk, and reached Slonim November 6. Reinforced by Durutte's division, Schwartzenberg recrossed the Bug October 30 at Drogichin, and marched on Volkovisk, being near Svichloch when Chichagov was at Slonim, and Sacken, following him up, was at Orlia. It would have been better strategy for Schwartzenberg originally to leave a containing force behind the Bug and march on

Minsk, so as to rally on his chief. His half-hearted aid was now useless.

The attempt to reorganize at Smolensk largely failed. What cavalry was left was consolidated under Latour-Maubourg, but with the half-starved horses, it was a sorry body. It sounds pathetic to read : " The first and second divisions of cavalry, each composed of three regiments, will be formed into one company, or one squadron, according to their forces." This reorganization was temporary, but the dismounted men were to be held, " up to the moment when, on the arrival of remount horses, each regiment can have three hundred or four hundred men to put in the field, at which period everything will go back to the original status." In victualing, too, the hungry troops would not wait for regular distribution ; much was pillaged and more wasted. Many impossible orders were issued in these days. They speak of stores at Lepel, but the Russians had possession of Lepel. Dombrovski's five thousand men extended over hundreds of miles from Slutsk to Mohilev, but he was ordered to defend Minsk, when this was already held by Chichagov. It seems as if the emperor paid insufficient heed to Chichagov, but he had rightly gauged Kutusov, and believed he would not press for a decisive battle.

As another sample of the impossible orders of these days, on November 11 Berthier was ordered to write Poniatowski :—

" That it is necessary for him to march with his army corps to Mohilev. . . . That arrived there he will strive to reorganize his corps, in joining to it the march-regiments which belong to him, and which the governor of Minsk has kept back. After this first operation he will occupy himself in gathering all his cadres into one division, and that afterwards, the cadres which are found disposable he is to lead back to Warsaw to take the men there present and complete his division. He can leave the 12th."

But the road to Warsaw had long been closed — as perhaps Napoleon might have guessed, if he did not know it.

Whether to halt at Smolensk or not was a question. Ney and Davout were far in the rear, and Eugene's eccentric march kept him at a distance. To disperse meant destruction in detail; to wait to assemble would enable the several Russian armies to close the trap. The army was now so small that the little food went farther: and the snow made separation for subsistence unnecessary. On November 13 Davout was nearing Smolensk and Eugene coming down from Duchovchina. The army could have been concentrated; but Napoleon pushed forward Junot's van, and it was again strung out to a length of fifty miles.

The march of the army along a single road had made victualing more precarious, and afforded the enemy a better chance of attack ; three columns, upon the main road and along parallel by-roads, would have proved safer. It was thus Napoleon advanced ; he would have done well so to retreat; for it was Kutusov's avoidance of battle alone that saved the army.

Though the Grand Army was perishing of exhaustion, yet Wittgenstein and Chichagov, not ready, as Kutusov seemed to be, to let it so die, were striving to encircle it. Napoleon was fully aware of the gravity of the case, yet neither in orders, dispatches, conversation, nor bearing did he give his marshals, correspondents, or staff the remotest conception of what was passing in his mind. On November 14 he left Smolensk with Junot, Poniatowski and part of the Guard, the headquarters baggage and treasure, under escort of another part, having preceded him two days, and Claparède one day. Davout remained in Smolensk, with Eugene and Ney to arrive. Eugene was to follow on the 15th, Davout on the 16th, and Ney on the 16th or 17th, after having blown up the walls and towers. Should the rearguard be attacked, Davout was to aid Ney.

On November 14 Berthier was ordered to write to Ney that the emperor was going to Krasnoi : —

"That it is necessary that he should continue to lead the rearguard, that Davout will sustain him. . . . That on the 16th he will blow up the town" (Smolensk) "on leaving, or simply take up a position at the bridge-head, so as not to blow up the town until the 17th, if all should not be ready. That it is necessary to make his arrangements with Davout ; that I recommend him especially so to act that the guns and munitions are destroyed, and that the least French possible should be left in the place."

Meanwhile Kutusov slowly advanced towards Krasnoi, and the light horse of his van ran against the French head of column and was driven back. Napoleon passed the night of November 14–15 at Korytnia. The situation had become worse than at Viasma, for the Russians had relatively gained in strength and morale ; and the French army was strung out over four days' march — unquestionably an error in logistics.

In other campaigns frequent extracts have been given from the Bulletins of the Grand Army. Those issued during the Russian campaign are almost entirely omitted in the Correspondence. The following explanation of this fact is given after Bulletin 1 : —

"There will not be found hereinafter all the Bulletins of the Grand Army during the campaign of 1812. The commission has thought that it should reproduce only the Bulletins of which the manuscript text bears some corrections of the emperor, and those which by reason of their exceptional importance cannot be considered as the work of the staff, and can be attributed only to the emperor."

Sword of the Period.

CHAPTER 7

THE BERESINA. NOVEMBER 15, 1812, TO JANUARY 31, 1813.

KUTUSOV played a Fabian game, when by an attack he could have destroyed the wreck of the Grand Army. On November 17, at Krasnoi, Napoleon stood with the Guard to let his rear close up. Kutusov weakly attacked, and all came up except Ney, who, left to his fate, by a circuit fought his way through to the army, reaching it with less than a thousand men. At Orsha a slight reorganization was made, and much material was burned. Napoleon intended to move through Minsk, but when this place went lost, Studianka was chosen for crossing the Beresina. Meanwhile Wittgenstein had pushed back Victor, who had gone to St. Cyr's aid, and Chichagov had come up to the Beresina. At frightful loss the Beresina was crossed November 27–28, and the army kept on towards Vilna. On December 5 the emperor left Murat to command the army, and made his way to Paris by December 18. At Vilna and at Kovno the army — now only a mob — expected to pause, but could not. Pursuit stopped at the Niemen. The Prussians and Austrians made a Convention with the Russians. The French losses in the campaign were probably four hundred thousand men, the Russian a hundred and fifty thousand. Murat turned over the command to Eugene, who conducted the army back to the Oder, and later to the Elbe. Napoleon at once began creating a new army, with which he proposed to march back to the Niemen.

THE emperor's judgment of Kutusov's enterprise proved accurate ; and although every day added to the danger as well as the difficulties of the French, yet the Russian general clung to his policy of letting distress do the work of battle. On almost any day he might to advantage have attacked in force, but he refrained. On his side, the emperor might have foreseen that the Russians could anticipate him at Krasnoi, and have evaded them by marching on Orsha north of the Dnieper; but poor maps and uncertain news induced him to keep to the route he knew, bad as it was.

On November 15, at 8.30 A. M., Napoleon and the Guard

started from Korytnia for Krasnoi, while the Russian van
under Miloradovich, advancing towards the main road, reached
it at Rshavka just as the Guard appeared. Instead of attacking smartly and pushing on to Krasnoi, Miloradovich, held
back by Kutusov, only opened artillery fire, and Napoleon
filed by with small loss. Junot and Poniatowski were already
beyond Krasnoi, Eugene had left Smolensk and reached Lub-

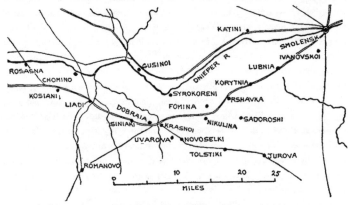

Smolensk-Krasnoi Country.

nia, Davout and Ney were still in Smolensk. Kutusov's main
force was at Jurova. Sending Roguet's division of Guards to
drive off the Cossacks, Napoleon remained at Krasnoi during
the 16th to allow the corps in the rear to close up. During
the day Kutusov came along to Novoselki and his van to
Nikulina, both close to Krasnoi; but he seemed still to avoid
attack, though this was the auspicious moment. There was
good reason for the loud complaints among Kutusov's lieutenants; to end the matter would be to save thousands of
Russian as well as French lives; for although they were not
perishing in droves, the Russian force was also dwindling in
the extreme cold. All his officers urged action, but Kutusov
stuck to his own course. He was hyper-conservative.

When Eugene reached the Russian van astride the road east of Nikulina, his smart attack was repulsed, and Miloradovich sent in a demand for surrender. But, made of rugged stuff, Eugene started on a circuit around Miloradovich by way of Fomina, and reached Krasnoi at night of the 16th with thirty-five hundred men left of the six thousand with which he had left Smolensk. Davout was at Korytnia, and Ney still at Smolensk. Junot and the Poles had kept on to Liadi. During this threat against Eugene, Napoleon might to advantage have attacked Miloradovich's rear, but he had only the Guard to put in, which, although still consisting of thirteen thousand foot, two thousand horse and a few guns, he must keep intact, as a nucleus for the army, and, as he never forgot, for his own personal safety.

A worse situation could scarcely exist. Strung out over a distance of forty miles, Kutusov by one strong push could cut the French army in two, and successively demolish the several corps; or, should Napoleon await their arrival at Krasnoi, Kutusov, by extending his left, could seize the road to Orsha and cut the army off from its one line of retreat. This was, in an uncertain way, the Russian leader's idea. He thought to throw Tormasov to the left, hold Galitzin in front of Krasnoi, and let Miloradovich, from a position south of the road, handle Davout and Ney; but the whole scheme was lamely carried out. Napoleon, however, had to choose between abandoning Davout and Ney, and running this risk; and at the point of fatal danger the old Napoleon flamed up. Relying on the dread inspired by his own personality and the Guard, he stood his ground, and enabled both Eugene and Davout to join the army. At first blush, this act appears foolhardy, but it was the only thing to do; the least risk lay in the boldest course; he could not remain passive and encourage the enemy to offensive measures; it was safer, even with his

handful, to attack, himself; and as after Eugene's escape
Miloradovich still held the road at Nikulina by which Davout and Ney must reach him, he advanced on the enemy,
hoping Kutusov might call in Miloradovich to strengthen his
own line.   Both from an individual and a military point of
view, his act commands our admiration.

Early in the morning of the 17th Napoleon sent out Mortier, who took Uvarova after a slight combat; and so soon as

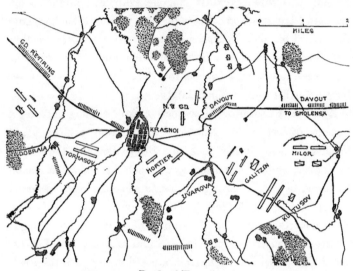

Battle of Krasnoi.

the emperor with the Guard demonstrated along the Smolensk
road at Nikulina, Miloradovich was called in from the right
to the main army, drawn up in order for battle.   Recognizing his danger, Davout pushed through and reached Krasnoi
before noon.   But as Tormasov had extended far beyond the
French right, this fragile offensive could not last.   Napoleon
must withdraw before Ney could come up, and leave the rearguard to its fate.   This was done.   It was a sad necessity,
but unless we go back to Hannibal at Crotona in 203 B. C.,

perhaps no finer figure can be found in the annals of war than Napoleon standing here with fifteen thousand famished men facing an army of eighty thousand effective, for many hours, to enable ten thousand comrades to escape annihilation. There was no particular fighting. Kutusov's purpose to throw his left around the French, to cut the road to Orsha, weakened when he ascertained that Napoleon and the Guard were in his front, and he let them pass on towards Dubrovna, intending to harass their rear and then turn on Davout. Thus when the emperor retired through Krasnoi, he met only the light horse which had been sent beyond the town; this fell back, and the handful reached Liadi. In covering the retreat Davout suffered considerably; especially Friedrich's division at the rear was harassed. The army generally lost heavily in prisoners, mostly, however, non-combatants, without whom it was better off. Eugene was at Liadi, and Junot and Poniatowski beyond the town. Kutusov assembled his army at Dobraia.

Ney was thus cut off. With six thousand men, and an equal number of unarmed stragglers, he had left Smolensk before daylight, November 17, and had marched to Korytnia, unaware that the Russian army stood across the road. There had been another quarrel with Davout, because Ney, reaching Smolensk last, found no food; and he afterwards accused Davout of deserting him on the march to Krasnoi; but Davout was drawn in to Krasnoi by the emperor's order, although Ney claimed that he received no intimation of this fact. It was not like Davout to fail to communicate important instructions, and it is not fair to assume that he did so fail: the numberless Cossacks on the road would have made the loss of a dispatch probable. Ney was, however, not fully informed; and Fézensac, who was with him, says that he had no news for three days before he left Smolensk. Of the two

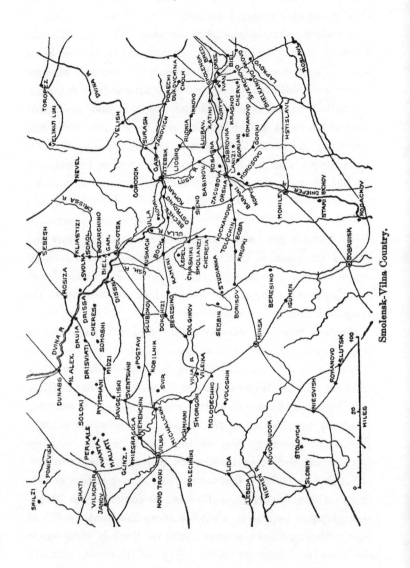

Smolensk-Vilna Country.

men, Ney was the more given to prejudice ; but in such awful days much must be forgiven.

Next day, about three, Ney ran across Miloradovich, standing athwart the main road east of Krasnoi. As the fog prevented his seeing what was in his front, he attacked sharply and was repulsed. In a worse position than Eugene, he adopted the same course : Miloradovich demanded surrender, at which Ney laughed ; and at dark he left his bivouac-fires burning, and moved away to the north, knowing nothing about the roads or country. At one place he broke the ice on a stream to ascertain which way the water flowed. His direction proved to be towards Syrokoreni on the Dnieper. Crossing during the night with the loss of a number of men drowned, frozen, shot or sabred, by morning of the 19th he was at Gusinoi, with but half of his men. Those who could not follow were captured. At Gusinoi he met the Cossack corps from Smolensk, and had to fight for every mile of his route. Luckily, the extreme cold had ceased. During the 19th and 20th he reached Rosasna, and next night the main road to Orsha, sending couriers ahead to establish touch with Napoleon, who at once ordered a body under Eugene back to his aid. Ney reached the wreck of the Grand Army with eight hundred braves left out of the thirty-nine thousand men his corps had counted under the colors on the 1st of March. Nor was his case an exception.

Napoleon blamed Davout for abandoning Ney : he had to blame somebody. The charge was unfounded, as Davout had only obeyed his orders. If any one abandoned Ney, it was the emperor. There was probably no man he would not rather have left in the lurch ; but abandoning rearguards, as every old soldier knows, is too old and essential a matter in war to need defense. The author has twice been in such a case. To save the rest of the army, Ney had to be sacrificed ; but his

marvelous escape was a great relief to Napoleon. Early on
November 20 he had written Maret: "I have no news from
Ney. I have almost given up hope of him." But when, after
leaving Orsha on the same day, he learned of this gallant
marshal's arrival there, he wrote Maret: "My anxiety for Ney
is ended. He has just rejoined us. I have determined to set
the whole army, even Oudinot and Victor, on the march to
Borisov, and from there to Minsk." And he added: "My
chief anxiety relates to victual."

Why Kutusov did not send cavalry towards Orsha to capture the garrison and to cut the bridge can be explained no
better than his other inactivities. The river here is wide,
and a broken bridge would have caused the Grand Army as
much trouble as they had at the Beresina; but after Krasnoi,
the Russian leader pushed even less than before.

The army was to halt for a short respite behind the
Dnieper at Orsha; but on reaching Dubrovna on the 18th,
the emperor was met by serious news. Minsk had been lost,
and though Oudinot was ordered to Borisov, to join Dombrovski and retake the place, it was too late. Victor with
his own and Oudinot's corps, some twenty-five thousand men,
had advanced, November 13, from Chereia on Smolianzi to
turn the Russian left; but Wittgenstein did not move from
his strong position on the Ulla, and Victor fell back to Chereia. Had Wittgenstein pressed Victor seriously, he might
have seized the main road of retreat, but he neither knew the
condition of the Grand Army, nor where stood Chichagov, on
whose advent he was counting to assume a bold front. On
November 19 Napoleon wrote Berthier to order Victor to
operate as if the emperor were moving against Wittgenstein
— "a very natural manœuvre. That my intention is to move
on Minsk, and when I shall be master of this town, to take
up the line of the Beresina; that it would therefore be possi-

ble that he might receive the order to move on Beresino to cover there together the route to Vilna, in communication with the 6th Corps. Let him study this movement and let you know his observations."

News also ran in that the Minsk garrison had, on the approach of Chichagov, retired towards Borisov, and had been joined by Dombrovski from Mohilev. It was evident that unless a Beresina crossing could be held, the Grand Army must perish to the last man; and Oudinot and Dombrovski were ordered to hold Borisov at all hazards, as a means of arresting the junction of Chichagov and Wittgenstein.

This idea of marching on Minsk appears in several documents at this time — the emperor had harbored it some days. To Maret, November 20, he wrote: "Notify Schwartzenberg that I am marching on Minsk, and that I count on him;" and next day he mentions the same thing to Berthier; but he soon found that his route might not lie that way: after crossing the Beresina, it would depend on the operations of the Russian armies.

Headquarters now came on to Orsha, and from here Victor was ordered to maintain Chereia, and was notified that Oudinot would get to Borisov by the 24th and the army by the 25th and 26th, and that Victor was then to undertake the rearguard duty.

At Orsha were food, arms and ammunition, and some artillery. Six new batteries were formed, and an effort made to rearm the stragglers, and get them back to their corps; but the obedience of a mob cannot be compelled without rougher methods than could then be used. The infantry was not reorganized as the cavalry had been, the corps being left as they were: a change would have made public the grievous losses, and have unnecessarily puzzled the soldiers. The Russians always exaggerated the French numbers, and as the Romans with Hannibal, so the Russians cared not to bring Napoleon to bay.

The emperor did succeed in reducing the train.

On November 22, in an order of the day, he said : "The baggage is to be reduced. Every general or administration officer who has several carriages will have half of them burned, and will turn in the horses to the artillery park. The Major-General is charged with the execution of this order." Two days later an order was given to Berthier, "To have burned half of the carriages, cabriolets, carts, coaches, etc., in the several corps . . . it being indispensable that all the provisions should be carried along, and that no guns or munition-caissons should be left along the route."

In addition to private seizures, a number of small country horses had been got for the artillery, and while general officers kept one wagon, no horse was left in the possession of a regimental officer. That these orders were but partially carried out was shown by the crowds at the passage of the Beresina, but something was accomplished.

Lest they might be captured, the emperor burned his own papers. Davout's, and doubtless other corps headquarters records, fell into the Russian possession.

The pontoon train was burned, although Eblé was able to keep a few tools. This was a curious mistake, as the pontoons might have been of critical value at the Beresina; but Napoleon at the moment proposed to cross on the Borisov bridge, and though he did not know it had been burned, this was an accident which might at any moment occur.

It was a time, however, when mistakes were natural. It is easy to place dates in juxtaposition to orders, to prove that Napoleon should have done this or that; but no man could have kept breath in the body of the Grand Army until it reached the Niemen, so well as he. All the mistakes he committed, any leader would have committed, and more.

It is often assumed that Napoleon did not hurry the retreat as was required, but he probably moved as fast as was possible for the exhausted men. He is charged with undervaluing the danger threatened by Chichagov and Wittgenstein. He had already discounted Kutusov, and his old habit of not estimating obstacles until he reached them may here have made him underrate the two others; but had he gauged them at their true value, he could not have moved much faster.

It must not be forgotten that none of the Russian generals knew much about his colleagues' movements; Wittgenstein and Kutusov exchanged some dispatches, but the other armies were much in the dark; and despite orders from St. Petersburg, each of the army commanders had been acting on his own ideas, with only a very general view of coöperation.

The retreat continued along the main road, and on November 21 Junot and Poniatowski were at Tolochin, with seven hundred men between them fit to put in line. The Guard and headquarters were at Kochanovo, with Eugene and Davout closing up. Kutusov lay at Lanizi, with van at Goriani. Except the Guard, which the emperor now accompanied afoot, no semblance of an army was left. From Kochanovo Borisov was the objective, and thither, as the key-point of the movement, had been ordered all the nearby corps. But Napoleon's calculation failed: he could not get there before the Russians. Chichagov had reached Minsk the 17th; his van advanced on and carried the bridge-head at Borisov on the 21st, and next day he crossed the Beresina.

It is interesting to compare with the forces at the opening of the campaign the numbers left at this time. On the 21st of November Junot and Poniatowski, seven hundred armed men in all, were at Tolochin; Napoleon and the Guard, forty-eight hundred strong, and the cavalry, reduced to sixteen hundred men, were near Kochanovo. On the 20th Dom-

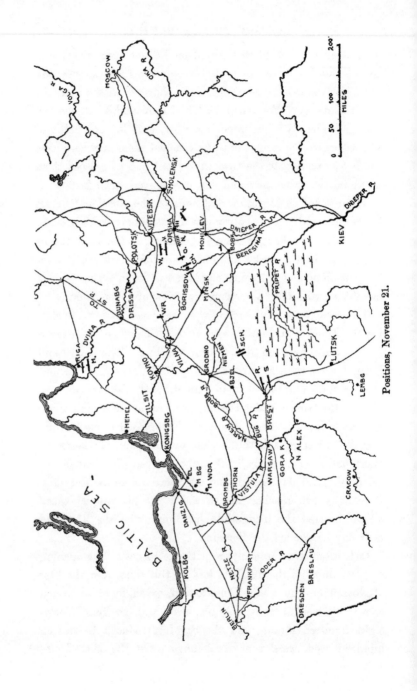

Positions, November 21.

brovski with four thousand men had joined the garrisons of Minsk and Borisov, some fifteen hundred men, at the latter place ; but Chichagov's van drove him out on the 21st after a noble defense, and he retired with but fifteen hundred effective on Bobr, where he met Oudinot with eight thousand men and the Mohilev garrison of twelve hundred. There had been a little French garrison in Minsk under Bronikovski, and a small Russian force at Bobruisk, together with a larger one at Mozyr under Ertel, but the latter took no part in the Beresina manœuvre. Victor with eleven thousand men stood at Chereia. The Grand Army had thus dwindled to less than thirty thousand men all told. Opposite this handful of desperate soldiers stood Kutusov at Lanizi with sixty-five thousand men; Wittgenstein with thirty thousand men at Chasniki; Chichagov at Borisov with thirty-four thousand, — a total of one hundred and thirty thousand men fit for duty. Thus Napoleon had so managed as, out of half a million, to have left for his desperate struggle only thirty thousand armed men — one in seventeen ; while out of a quarter of a million men the Russians could put in line over one half.

Let us see how Chichagov had come into the present problem. When Schwartzenberg crossed the Bug and marched on Volkovisk, October 30, he left Reynier opposite Sacken. Sacken attacked November 14, but was beaten; and Reynier followed on to Volkovisk, while Schwartzenberg was at Slonim. A second attack had no better result, and Reynier then followed Sacken back to Brest Litovsk, which he captured November 26. Still, though defeated, Sacken had actually contained both Reynier and Schwartzenberg. The latter has been charged with acting treacherously. He was half-hearted, but his task was to protect the Warsaw country; and that he did not know the grievous case of the Grand Army was Napoleon's fault, for Schwartzenberg got his warped facts from Maret. Being in the campaign only as auxiliary, he did not care to march to the emperor's relief without definite orders. When Chichagov left Slonim, November 8, he sent the czar's aide, Chernishev, with a body of Cossacks to Wittgenstein, asking for coöperation to stop the French on the Beresina. Chernishev managed to push through, after

a combat with some cavalry under Corbineau, which was marching from Vilna to the Beresina. Chichagov reached Niesvish November 12, his van under Lambert drove back at the Niemen a party from the Minsk garrison, and on Lambert's further advance, Bronikovski abandoned Minsk with its stores, retiring to Borisov to join Dombrovski. Chichagov again moved

Chernishev.

forward, and Lambert, sending a detachment up to Sembin, reached Borisov November 20. On being attacked, Dombrovski, after a stubborn defense, was driven out without destroying the bridge, and Lambert, wounded, was replaced by Phalen. In Borisov, Chichagov found dispatches which gave him a slight knowledge of the French disaster, but having no idea how weak the Grand Army was, he dreaded meeting it. The importance of Borisov and the danger of Chichagov's presence were not lost on Napoleon. Berthier wrote Oudinot, November 22: "Should the enemy have seized the bridge-head and burned the bridge so that we might not cross, it would be a great misfortune;" and should other crossings be hard to find, "we should have to be prepared to march on Lepel."

The weather had changed after November 14, and by the 19th it was thawing; rain fell, the roads were deep and the Beresina full of floating ice. The news of the fall of Borisov reached Napoleon at Tolochin the 22d, and here, says Ségur, "he felt that his only chance was to offer up the army piece by piece, one after another, beginning with the limbs, to save the head." He wrote Oudinot that he was to capture the Borisov bridge; or if it was broken, to seek a fresh crossing, either at Beresino or at Sembin, build bridges and bridge-heads, and hold them. This was really a week's work, which Napoleon in his hurry ordered done at once. Later, he selected the ford at Viesolovo, and on November 22 wrote Oudinot to prepare the bridges there. Next day he established head-quarters at Bobr, having of late constantly been with the van. Oudinot with Dombrovski, who had reached Loshniza the 22d, at once continued his march towards the Beresina; and meeting the Russian van, which itself was marching on Bobr, he so furiously attacked it on the 23d, that he drove it back in panic sufficient to infect Chichagov and his staff, and to bring the whole Russian army into disorder. This did not argue well for its condition. The success was a misfortune; for though it enabled Oudinot to seize Borisov, it induced Chichagov, who believed the whole French army upon him, to recross and destroy the bridge. From Bobr, November 24, Napoleon wrote Maret that Dombrovski had lost Borisov, but that Oudinot had recaptured it. " But the bridge is burned. They hope to make another one during the day. It is cold. My health is very good. I am very anxious to have letters from Vilna and Paris. I have received no messenger from

you. This, however, was easy. I have no news from Schwartzenberg. Where is he? See that you collect at Vilna a great
quantity of victual."

The Guard had been the one body cared for, and was in least
ill condition; and owing to its excellent material, as well as
to the constant presence of the emperor, it had kept its discipline. On November 19 Napoleon addressed the men: —

"Grenadiers of my Guard, you have been witnesses of the disorganiza-
tion of the army. The majority of the soldiers, from a deplorable fatality,
have cast away their arms. If you should imitate this fatal example, all hope would be lost. The safety of the army is confided to you.
You will justify the good opinion that I have of you. Not only must
the officers maintain a severe discipline, but the soldiers must exercise
among themselves a rigorous surveillance, and themselves punish those
who fall out of their ranks."

Quite apart from his own safety, the emperor was aware
that the only hope of the army again seeing the Vistula was
to hold together the Guard as a nucleus on which to rally the
disorganized forces. Orders to the line to stop pillaging,
or to maintain discipline, were useless: starving men cannot be held together. Yet the spirit of the troops and their
admiration of the emperor never ceased; the blame for their
troubles was not cast upon him; and Napoleon could have
accomplished more towards holding the Grand Army together
by himself moving among the troops to encourage them, instead of rarely leaving the immediate environment of the
Guard. All agree in testifying that the soldiers of the Grand
Army, even those who were taken prisoners, maintained their
fealty to the Great Captain. Heine's poem of "The Two
Grenadiers" is not an idle thought.

At this time Napoleon considered several manœuvres for
freeing himself from his fast encroaching foes. One idea was
to add the arms-bearing men of the Grand Army to those of

Victor, and drive back Wittgenstein, so as to open the route
on Vilna via Lepel; but as that country was full of marshes,
which might not be frozen so as to bear troops, and as Wittgenstein might arrest him until Kutusov and Chichagov came

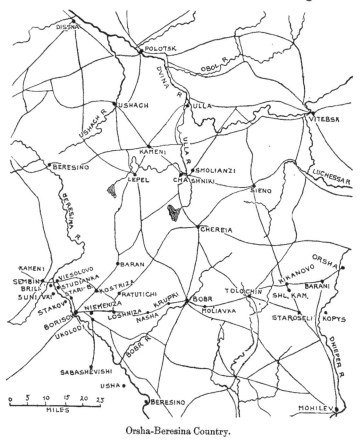

Orsha-Beresina Country.

up in his rear, after mature reflection, on consulting various
staff officers who had studied the country, — among them
Jomini, who recommended a crossing as near Borisov as possible to get on the straight road to Vilna, — Napoleon decided
rather to force the Beresina at a point between the three

Russian armies, and to head for Molodechno through what was a less barren country. It was hard for him to give up the idea that he could yet brush aside Chichagov, march through Minsk, join Schwartzenberg, and finish the retreat by a tactical if not strategic victory. Had the Borisov bridge stood, he might have attempted this. He dreaded to reënter France a defeated man. But the information brought in by Corbineau, who had just come from Wrede with some cavalry, — and met Chernishev on the way, — showed such facts that he finally chose the straight road to Vilna; and when he heard that the Borisov bridge was definitely lost, nothing could be done but bridge the river somewhere else; and this he set about with his usual skill.

Meanwhile Victor retired before Wittgenstein, who reached Chereia. Exaggerating the numbers of the Grand Army, and unaware that Chichagov had taken Borisov, the Russian leader was cautious. He might to advantage have marched to Viesolovo and Sembin, but he believed the Grand Army was moving to Borisov, and indeed heard that part of it was heading towards Bobruisk. With growing inertia, Kutusov had got only to Morosovo, while his van crossed the Dnieper at Kopys.

When Oudinot reported that he still held Borisov, but that the bridge could not be repaired in season, he added that Corbineau had found a good ford at Studianka, and that this was a safe place for a passage; and on November 24 Napoleon sent Eblé with Chasseloup and Jomini to him, with what was left of the pontoon tools and the sappers; and to protect the operation, formed under Ney, out of the Mohilev garrison, the Poles and the relics of his own corps, a body to follow the Guard, and hold Bobr until Davout and Eugene came up. Davout was notified not to march so fast as to prevent the wounded and the stragglers from keeping up. Headquarters was transferred to

Loshniza. Oudinot reconnoitred the Studianka ford and those at Stakov and Ukolodi, and reported next morning that he was striving to deceive the enemy, of whom some twenty thousand men stood on the other side. At noon he further reported: " I have decided for Studianka as the point where I intend to make my crossing the coming night, and to-morrow early I will make diversions at Ukolodi and Stakov." A later report was that the lay of the land was not favorable, and towards evening Oudinot sent this information to headquarters at Loshniza.

Chichagov.

The emperor was much disappointed; he had hoped Oudinot would force a passage that night, and wrote him that Mortier and two divisions of the Guard had been ordered to Borisov to his support, and that he must cross on the 25th, if he had not done so previously. Victor was ordered to fend off Wittgenstein at all hazards, and pushed to Kostriza to attack whatever he met. While Eugene and Davout were coming up to Loshniza and Nacha, Napoleon went on to Borisov, and near that town heard from Victor that he was falling back on Loshniza, thus opening the Studianka ford to Wittgenstein. With a sharp rebuke for this retreat, Napoleon ordered Victor forward again to Ratutichi, as the only means to prevent the Russians from cutting the army in two on the Borisov road.

The Grand Army was indeed in a critical state. Nothing better shows the bad condition of the line of communications than the fact that, at the Beresina, Napoleon received the first letter from Maret for a fortnight. Strategically, the

army was pressed by Kutusov in the rear, threatened by
Wittgenstein on the right and by Chichagov on the left
front, and had a difficult river to pass in the teeth of far superior forces. A problem for an army in perfect condition,
what a task it was for the wreck of an army, dying of
famine! Had the Beresina remained frozen, Napoleon might
have crossed and beaten off Chichagov, for there were still
of the Moscow troops some fifteen thousand armed men, and
Victor and Oudinot had fifteen thousand more; but the river
was open, and while once crossed it would be a protection,
it was now a difficulty of the first order.

When Eblé and Chasseloup reached Studianka in the
afternoon of November 25, they found that demonstrations
had been made up and down the Beresina, but that little
had been done towards bridging it, and they at once took
matters in hand. Chichagov had at hand twenty thousand
foot and eight thousand cavalry, the latter useless on this
marshy terrain. Wittgenstein and Kutusov had given him
the impression that the French army was going to cross at
Borisov and below it; and thus misled, he sent a division
under Chaplitz up river as far as Brili, which pushed a
reconnaissance out to Sembin, and leaving Langeron at Borisov, he marched, at Kutusov's suggestion, down river nearly
twenty miles. Reconnoitring on the 25th, he found no enemy,
returned to Borisov, and dispatched Langeron on Sembin,
but too late to dispute the crossing.

The French forces on November 25 stood as follows: the
Guard in Borisov, headquarters at Stari-Borisov, Oudinot at
Studianka, Ney on the road from Loshniza to Niemeniza,
Eugene at Nacha, Davout between Krupki and that place,
Victor at Ratutichi. Of the Russians, Kutusov was at
Kopys, out of harm's way, and his van at Tolochin; Witt-
genstein had advanced to Baran; Chichagov was at Saba-

shevishi and Usha, with Chaplitz watching Borisov, and a division opposite Studianka. Good luck had for a moment smiled on the Grand Army, and had left its passage of the Beresina open; frosts set in and hardened the roads so that

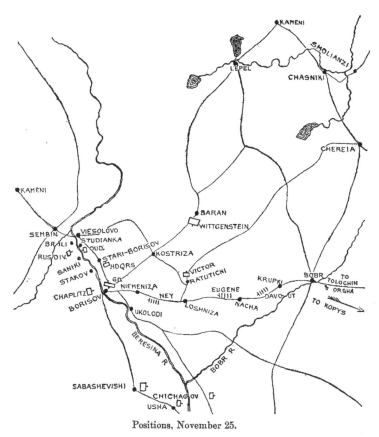

Positions, November 25.

wheels could travel; and at Studianka, where the bridge was thrown, there was plenty of timber in the houses for use for the bridges.

Early on November 26 the emperor left Stari-Borisov, the Guard ahead, and on reaching Studianka, found that the

material for two bridges had been assembled.   The throwing
was begun by 8 A. M., under cover of Oudinot, while his artillery, placed on the heights back of Studianka, commanded
the plateau, and staved off attack by the Russians.   Corbineau's cavalry crossed by wading and swimming to clear the
farther bank, and a battalion of five hundred sharpshooters
was put over on rafts.   Although the marshy ground would
now bear the troops, the river was still open except at the
edges, and was floating down huge blocks of ice.   Of the two
bridges, the upper was a fragile one, suitable for foot-troops
and, according to some authorities, cavalry, and the lower
was a stronger one on trestles, nearly five hundred feet long,
to serve for the artillery and train.   The brave sappers stood
chest-deep in the water to do their work, and more than half
of them died of the exposure — few soldiers are called on
to equal such heroic work.   Eblé, an old man, showed great
devotion.   At one o'clock, November 26, the upper bridge
was finished, and Oudinot and part of Ney began the crossing.   The lower bridge was finished at about 4 P. M., and
the artillery started across, followed during the night by the
rest of Ney and Claparède; and by morning of November 27,
over ten thousand men were on the right bank.   Had Davout
been ordered to hurry up his column, there were enough hours
for the whole body of the non-combatants to cross.

A long causeway ran over marshy ground from Borisov
to Sembin, and was provided with three bridges.   Had the
Russians seized this causeway, the French army would have
been lost; but Oudinot was quick enough in throwing forward some of his first troops over, and held it; and once
well across, he fell smartly upon Chaplitz, who had started
back towards Borisov, but had returned, sustained by Pahlen.
Holding the woods, which were plentiful, Oudinot fended off
several Russian attacks; and finally, though hotly withstood,

pushed the Russian division back on Stakov, and also occupied Sembin, which freed the road. Men of all nationalities and corps fought side by side, French, Poles, Swiss, Croats, and all did well. On the other side the Guard and Ney came up; Victor, leaving Partouneaux at Loshniza as corps rearguard, fell back to Borisov; Davout reached the same place, and Eugene Niemeniza. Puzzled by the situation, Chichagov had not moved; Wittgenstein advanced to Kostriza; Kutusov crossed the Dnieper to Staroseli, with van at Moliavka. The French were favored by the slowness of the enemy; for instead of marching on Oudinot, Chichagov, who feared to meet the Grand Army singly, strove to get in touch with Wittgenstein. The latter, from Baran, should have marched on Sembin, but on November 27 was still at Kostriza. From here there was no direct road to Studianka, but he slowly marched on Stari-Borisov with part of his force, and sent the rest to Borisov. Victor, with the main column, had already got above Stari-Borisov.

The crossing was not accomplished without accident. At eight in the evening and six next morning, the heavy bridge broke, and, requiring hours to repair, occasioned dangerous delay; but Victor, reaching Studianka at 4 A. M. of the 27th, took position to cover the operation. When, on the 27th, Wittgenstein reached Stari-Borisov, Partouneaux, who had acted as rearguard, found himself cut off. He strove to push his way through, but had to retire to Borisov, and there surrendered, with over two thousand men and more stragglers. One battalion found its way to Studianka by accidentally taking a little river road, unknown to Partouneaux.

About noon of November 27 the emperor and Guard filed across the bridges, and headquarters was set up in Sanivki; Eugene and Davout came up during the day, and got over that night. Napoleon took Victor to task for not better fending off Wittgenstein, but he had been outnumbered two to one.

On November 27 the emperor wrote to Maret : " I have just passed the Beresina, but this river, which is floating much ice, makes the stability of our bridges very uncertain. The army which was opposed to Schwartzenberg wished to dispute our passage. It is concentrated tonight on the right bank of the Beresina, opposite Borisov. The cold is very considerable. The army is excessively fatigued. Thus I am not losing a moment to get nearer to Vilna, so as to restore ourselves a little. . . . Have a great quantity of bread baked and biscuit made. I suppose you have constantly given news of us to Paris. I have received your letter of the 22d, of which Monsieur Abrahamoviz was bearer. This is the first I have received. What is Schwartzenberg doing ? "

Learning the facts early the 27th, Chichagov came down to Borisov, repaired the bridge, and, opening connection with Wittgenstein, it was determined to attack next day along both banks. Accordingly, on the 28th, by 8 A. M., Chichagov advanced upon the French line, standing astride the Sembin road, with Oudinot on the right, Ney on the left and the Guard in reserve. Ney first attacked and drove back the Russian van on Stakov. Unable to manœuvre in the heavily wooded country, and cavalry being useless, Chichagov made no headway. An all-day battle was gallantly contested, and bloody on both sides, but Ney so far won as to prevent the Russians from debouching from Stakov. On the other bank Victor, with six or seven thousand men and little artillery, defended the heights beyond Studianka, on a three-mile front ; but being almost surrounded by Wittgenstein during the forenoon, drew in nearer the bridges. He fought with determination which did him the highest credit.

It was supposed that when Eugene and Davout and the non-combatants arrived, the bridges would be in constant use to get the masses over ; but the mob could not be handled. With the management required to pass a defile, such as a

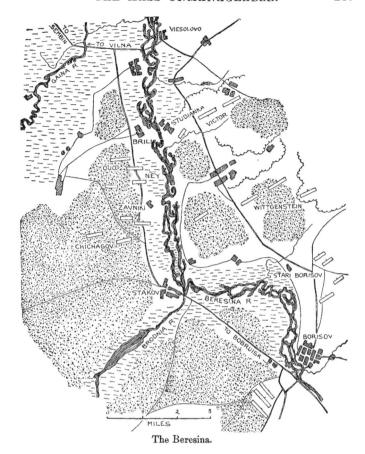

The Beresina.

bridge, and the undisturbed parking of all vehicles so as to cross in order, three or four thousand guns, caissons and carriages might well have been got over; but without discipline, and Napoleon and his staff being absent, with no particular person in charge, the mob acted as mobs generally do. There were many men still available in line, if they could be put over, but not only was the mass unmanageable, it was so crushed by its disasters, and so torpid and apathetic, that it could not be got to move until the Russian cavalry van appeared, and from the heights shelled the mass of human beings on the banks and produced a panic. All at once fled. Thousands were driven into the river; and the camp followers, men and women alike, fought for precedence like wild beasts. Carts, wagons, guns, caissons, were inextricably mixed in the effort to reach the entrance to the bridges, thus blocking the avenues of escape. Hundreds fell from the bridges into the river, to be carried down and perish. Other hundreds fell by the hands of comrades. Neither age nor sex protected any from the mad rush for safety. At nightfall Victor began his passage, and by midnight all the armed troops that were left, some three thousand men, were over; how many stragglers and non-combatants were abandoned, to be cut down by the Cossacks, will never be known. By morning the bridges were set on fire and soon consumed. The fight of both Victor, and Ney and Oudinot, to protect the crossing, had been praiseworthy to the last degree.

The Russians had not exhibited their wonted vigor: the mass of human beings along the river led the commanders to overestimate the French numbers. Had the three Russian armies better coöperated, neither the emperor nor any French soldier would have crossed the Beresina; the few who did escape owed their safety to the laxness of the enemy. During the 29th the Grand Army filed through Sembin towards Vilna in great distress; and, within three days, the armed men under the colors numbered less than ten thousand. Once across, Napoleon appears to have paid little heed to the rear: he could not or would not exert himself as in earlier years. He had hoped for a respite in Molodechno, but there was none. Wrede had some four thousand men there, protecting the army on the north, but as Wittgenstein was following on a parallel line still farther north, hoping to reach Vilna first, no delay was afforded. Yet from Molodechno the Poles were

sent towards Warsaw, which they reached in safety with all
their guns, their route lying outside the region of operations.

It was manifest to Napoleon that his place was no longer
with the relics of the army, but in France, where he might
create another.

On November 29 he wrote Maret : "The army is numerous, but disbanded in a fearful manner. A fortnight is necessary to get it under the
colors again, and a fortnight, where can you find it ? Cold, privations,
have disbanded this army. We shall reach Vilna; can we hold ourselves
there ? Yes, if we can stay there a week; but if we are attacked there
the first week, it is doubtful whether we can remain there. Food, food,
food ! Without that there are no horrors to which the undisciplined
mass may not be carried against this town. Perhaps this army cannot be
rallied till behind the Niemen. In this state of things, it is possible I may
deem my presence in Paris necessary for France, for the empire, for the
army itself. Tell me your opinion. . . . I desire there shall be in Vilna
no foreign agent : the army is not fine to show to-day. As to those who
are there, you must send them away. You must tell them, for instance,
that you are going, and that I am going to Warsaw, and send them
thither at once, indicating to them a day on which they are to leave."

As in Egypt, the emperor had already predetermined his
action, and for the first time he was quite frank in telling
Maret the condition of the Grand Army. He wrote him, but
in a less direct, coherent style than usual, on November 30.
In these letters much can be read between the lines.

"Send victual, bread, biscuit and meat to us. Establish a good garrison to do the policing and to arrest stragglers. I have more than forty
thousand men whom fatigue, want of food and cold are making travel
like vagabonds, or rather like brigands. If they cannot give us one hundred thousand rations of bread at Vilna, I pity the town.

Victual in abundance alone can restore order. . . . The army is horribly tired. It has been marching forty-five days. It has needs of all
kinds. . . . The stragglers must have food; but they must be stopped and
sent to their flags. Much firmness and food everywhere, and it will be

restored in a few days. . . . I sent you word that I beat Chichagov and his four divisions, and that I made six thousand prisoners. I have reduced him to seven thousand foot and six thousand cavalry. I have beaten Wittgenstein at the passage of the Beresina. . . . I desire to enter into winter quarters, and my army needs to be restored from its exertions. . . . Victual in Vilna, victual in all the districts, bread, meat and brandy ! Where in the neighborhood are there cantonments where it could best live ? Are there any horses there ? Where and how many ? We need them much. Bourcier must not count on any harness. We bring back nothing but men and a few sabres. The operation of the enemy on Minsk, which obliged us to prolong our retreat twenty-two days, and the shameful inaction of Victor, who did not attack, have done us a grievous harm. Without these accidents I should have remained at Smolensk, Vitebsk, Orsha, Mohilev. Schwartzenberg has cruelly compromised me. You do not speak to me of Paris, yet it is twenty days since I have heard from there. Where are the eighteen couriers ? How is the empress ? "
Again he wrote Maret, December 3 : " We are horribly tired and very hungry. Send to meet us bread, wine and brandy. I have one hundred thousand isolated men who are trying to keep alive and are no longer with the colors, which makes us run horrible danger. My Old Guard alone holds together, but hunger is reaching it too.

" Let the governor remain in Vilna, where he is necessary. Let him assemble all the stragglers by army corps and in the convents, and let him feed them well with a complete ration of bread, meat and brandy. Let him arrest all stragglers and prevent their passing Vilna. Let him condemn to death any soldier having left his flag and gone beyond Vilna.

" I need to know what food there is in Vilna and Kovno, as well as clothing and munitions of war. Has Kovno been fortified ? "

And again: " We must have one hundred and twenty thousand rations of bread a day, that is a *sine qua non*." Next day he wrote Maret : "I want you to come to meet me at Smorgoni. Send to Warsaw the ministers of America, of Prussia, and all the other ministers, and you will announce that you are going there yourself."

On December 2 Berthier's aide-de-camp, Montesquiou, had been ordered to Paris with a letter to the empress : —

" He will announce everywhere the arrival of ten thousand Russian prisoners, and the victory won on the Beresina, in which we made six thousand Russian prisoners and took eight flags and twelve guns. He will announce it also at Kovno, at Königsberg, at Berlin, . . . and will everywhere have put in the gazette: ' Monsieur de Montesquiou, aide-de-camp, has just passed, bearing news of the victory of the Beresina, won by the emperor over the reunited armies of Chichagov and Wittgenstein. He carries to Paris eight flags taken from the Russians in this battle, where we made six thousand prisoners and took twelve guns. When this officer left, the Emperor Napoleon was in Vilna in very good health.' . . . Montesquiou will go as fast as possible, so as to contradict everywhere the false reports which have been spread. He will tell that these two corps " (Chichagov and Wittgenstein) " desired to cut off the army, and that it marched over their prostrate bodies (*qu'elle leur a marché sur le ventre*); that it has arrived at Vilna, where it will find numerous magazines, which will soon restore it from the suffering it has undergone. In Paris he will be able to give the empress details of the good health of the emperor and of the state of the army."

On December 5 the emperor reached Smorgoni. Here he wrote in his own hand the 29th Bulletin, dating it Molodechno, December 3, called his marshals together at supper, apparently well at his ease, and had Eugene read it to them. He then placed Murat in command, with Berthier as Chief of Staff; but it was Berthier who was the real commander. There was necessity for no more than one marshal: Ney or Eugene could have done the work ample justice. Few agreed among themselves, and to leave them behind under Murat could not work well. Yet to leave them there kept up, as it were, the cadres of the Grand Army, so as to be filled by future levies, and, in a manner, imposed on the enemy.

Just before leaving, Napoleon wrote to Berthier, December 5 : " My Cousin, two or three days after my departure, the following decree will be put in the orders of the army. You will spread the rumor that I have gone to Warsaw with the Austrian corps and the 7th Corps. Five or six days afterwards, according to circumstances, Murat will issue an order of the day to let the army know that, having had to go to Paris, I have confided the command to him." The decree spoken of is that " Murat is named our lieutenant-general to command the Grand Army in our absence."

Having done this, the emperor left Smorgoni before mid-night, with Caulaincourt in the carriage beside him, and Rustan on the box, with Duroc and Mouton following, and drove towards Vilna: On the road to Oshmiana he barely escaped capture, as some Cossacks had raided and only just left the town. After consulting with Maret at Vilna, he drove to Warsaw and thence to Dresden and Paris, traveling day and night, as was his lifelong habit. He reached the Tuileries December 18.

Criticism upon Napoleon's abandoning the army may be overwrought. As a commanding general has no right to expose himself in battle, so is the duty imposed upon a ruler to protect his person for the safety of the state. Whether he be a good or bad monarch makes no difference in the princi-ple, and unless Napoleon was to abandon his empire, it was essential that he should go back to France and raise new levies. Nothing he could personally do would alter the fate of the Grand Army: that had long been sealed. Not only so, but unless his enemies were to be given opportunities to join against him, France first, and the rest of the world next, must understand the retreat from Moscow and the fate of the Grand Army from the Napoleonic standpoint. To give the matter proper color, Napoleon's presence in Paris was imperative; and while the limited information afforded during the campaign by the Bulletins and Napoleon's letters to the rear had deceived his subordinates and his own people, it also prevented the rest of the world from too soon gauging the immensity of the disaster.

The constant insistence on the emperor's good health has been pointed out as a selfish characteristic; and that Napo-leon was profoundly selfish, there is no one to deny. But has not the health of the sovereign always been the first thought of his people? So long as he was to keep alive the Napoleonic scheme, so long must he foster the French interest in his personal welfare. Are there not Court Circulars to-day in which, in times of profound peace, the simple ailments of the sovereigns are announced as matters of prime importance to the state? How much more, then, the health of the emperor in the midst of a great campaign.

The campaign had ended at the Beresina, but the mob of mostly unarmed men, once the Grand Army, was followed sharply to Smorgoni, where were some small supplies. The cold again came on; few escaped frozen members, and all were dulled in body and mind. Twenty thousand men fell from exhaustion from Smorgoni to Vilna, which was reached December 8. Gallant Ney, who had successively commanded every part of the army, and now led a rearguard of some two thousand men of Wrede's and Loison's divisions, was harried by the Russian light troops every step of the way, and had Chichagov and Wittgenstein in his rear, and Kutosov back two marches.

The demoralization spread to the reserve corps, which in its retreat the Grand Army had picked up. Loison had arrived at Vilna from the rear with ten thousand men, and was sent out to receive the Grand Army, but in three days two thirds of this number had fallen in their tracks. If we can credit Chambray, the number under arms had dwindled from thirty thousand at the Beresina to nine thousand men. Of these, ten thousand may have been lost in the crossing, and the cold which began on December 3 may have frozen the last resistance out of an equal number.

Vilna was full of stores, accumulated from Königsberg and by levy throughout Lithuania. The famished men — no longer soldiers — pillaged at will; and what was not consumed or destroyed fed the oncoming Russians. Devouring food with the voracity of animals and over-drinking brandy threw the bulk of them into every house, sick with dysentery; many died; every church and public building became a hospital. Nearly twenty thousand men who entered Vilna were unable to leave it.

Five miles west of Vilna is the steep Ponary hill, and this, covered by ice, arrested everything on wheels. Here were abandoned nearly all the guns that were left; and even the treasure chest, with six millions in coin and the Moscow spoils, stalled with four thousand other wagons, fell a prey partly to the French soldiers, partly to the Cossacks. Orders to hold Vilna for winter quarters could not be executed; those who could drag themselves away followed the army, to perish in the snow; and so Murat continued the retreat.

A fortnight later Alexander arrived at the Russian head-quarters in Vilna, and did everything to aid the French invalided, as well as to reorganize his own forces. There were almost as many Russian sick as French in Vilna, and no discrimination was made: the czar and Constantine were equally active in the good work. Want of care brought on gangrene, and this was followed by typhoid. The distress left room for naught but charity. Vastly to his credit, the czar issued an immediate amnesty to Poland.

Kovno, seventy miles from Vilna, was reached in three days, December 12, and was also looted. Ney defended this town until some Cossacks passed the Niemen on the ice and cut him off; he then moved down the left bank on Tilsit, and eventually got to Königsberg with five hundred men. The Russians did not move into Prussia for some days: the pursuit ended at the Niemen, although this was frozen over so that artillery could cross. At the Beresina, with still a semblance of organization, this might have been a benefit; at the Niemen, where barely six thousand men had muskets, it aided the Cossacks to harry them; and the Grand Army, which

had made so proud a show here in the early summer, took
refuge in every direction through the woods and along any
roads from the pursuing swords. The most part fled with
Murat and headquarters towards Königsberg. From Kovno,
December 12, Berthier wrote Napoleon : —

"I must say to Your Majesty that the whole army is dissolved; even
your Guard, which is barely four or five hundred strong. Generals, officers, have lost everything they had; nearly all have different parts of the
body frozen. The streets are covered with corpses, and the houses filled
with them. The army makes up a single column of several hours' length,
which breaks up mornings, and comes in evenings without order." There
was no possibility of stopping even at the Niemen, and the mass kept on
towards Gumbinen. "I will not relate to Your Majesty the sorry details
of plunder, disobedience, dissolution," wrote Berthier, December 16;
"everything has reached its worst."

On December 19 Murat got to Königsberg with four hundred men of the Old Guard and six hundred of the Guard
cavalry, followed by a few thousand stragglers.

The Russian generals had striven to conserve their own
force rather than inflict further defeat on the French. But
they themselves had not come off without losses. On December 4, says Buturlin, there were, out of eighty-eight thousand
aggregate, only forty thousand men in line.

Wittgenstein marched on Tilsit, hoping to cut off Macdonald, who had gone into winter quarters before Riga.
Napoleon might have made the latter more useful, but his
men would have dwindled fast like the rest. Macdonald and
Yorck, who commanded the Prussian contingent in his corps,
were on bad terms, yet Yorck had done his work well. On
December 18 Macdonald received orders to withdraw to Tilsit, which with the bulk of his corps he reached in about ten
days, before Wittgenstein got so far along. Yorck, who was
in the rear of his column, in the course of the manœuvre got

isolated. He might perhaps have fought his way through, but being first a Prussian patriot and next an officer serving Napoleon, he entered into the Convention of Tauroggen with the Russians.

Yorck's Convention, received January 1, 1813, proved to Murat that Prussia was not an ally to trust, and he retired to Elbing. Including Macdonald, who just managed to reach Königsberg, the garrison of that city and the Poles, Murat could number twenty thousand men on the Vistula. The

Yorck.

Poles were later thrown into Danzig, where Rapp was in command. At the Vistula a few men gradually came in. As an instance, the 3d Corps, says Fézensac, reached its headquarters at Marienwerder one hundred and twenty strong, and in a fortnight had one thousand men. But when the Russians took Marienwerder, and thus cut the French army in two, the left fled towards Danzig, the right towards Thorn. Thereupon Murat retired to Posen, turned over the command to Eugene on January 16, and left for his kingdom of Naples. Thus was even the line of the Vistula forfeited. On the side of the Russians in January, 1813, Chichagov came on to Marienwerder, Wittgenstein to Elbing, Kutusov slowly marched to Plotsk. Schwartzenberg, ordered back to Bielostok and Warsaw, also concluded an armistice, which released the Austrian corps from further activity, but permitted Reynier to retire, though he was attacked by the Russians at Kalish.

It is possible only to guess at the losses of the Russian campaign. Chambray gives the total number that crossed the Russian frontier as six hundred and thirty thousand. Some sixty thousand, mainly the right and left wings, returned. Buturlin says there were two hundred thousand prisoners, but how many of these died, no one can say. All told, over four hundred thousand lives must have been sacrificed. How many Russians perished has never been estimated, but it may have been one hundred and fifty thousand men. The loss was an enormous drain on France; that it included the veterans on whom Napoleon relied for victory made it still greater. Had not the proportion of officers who returned been superior to that of the men, Napoleon would have been unable to raise an efficient army in 1813. Especially was this true with the cavalry and artillery.

It is curious that not one of the French officers above the rank of division general lost his life. They one and all fearlessly exposed themselves and some were wounded, but all got back to the base. As the greatest losses in the campaign were not from battle, that these men could better protect themselves and had higher morale explains the fact.

In Posen Eugene received the first sketches of Napoleon's plan for recreating the army. Gradually the Oder was reached, and, with the aid of fifteen thousand men from Italy under Grenier, Eugene made his way back to the line of the Elbe.

It was months before the world understood the meaning of the failure in Russia. Prussia was ready for anything. Austria was still debating, and Alexander was willing to go on with the work he had so well begun. England cared only for the overthrow of the Continental System, and the return of peace. The English press was outspoken, but England continued to work slowly. Despite discontent, France was still Napoleon's tool. The French press was muzzled and unable to say much, although the commercial element kept on crying for its ancient trade, which the Continental System had sapped to its roots, and the peasantry protested against continuing to send their sons to the shambles. The real truth was long hidden, but invalided officers, who had managed to return, gradually told the story. France has always been patriotic, and though the people cried out against further wars, few words were spoken against the imperial régime. Napoleon was almost as strong in France after the Russian campaign as before : it was the country that was weaker.

Great and distant enterprises, says Montesquieu, perish by the greatness itself of the preparations which have been made to insure their success. The reasons for the failure of the 1812 campaign are marshaled by Jomini. Each of the many errors has already been commented on; but they may be crudely rehearsed. The principal error was in not recognizing that an army numerous enough to conquer peace in Russia could not be subsisted there, if the Russians conducted a re- tiring campaign and led it into the heart of the country. If a decisive battle could be early won, success was probable ; if not, Smolensk was the farthest point that, in 1812, could with safety be reached. Jerome did not act with sufficient vigor against Bagration : but so important a charge should never have been confided to him ; the best men, not relatives, should have been chosen for high command. The Poles were not as valuable allies as had been expected, but Napoleon did little to win their support. Russia furnished less grain than Napoleon calculated on, and no means of grinding the corn had been provided. The beeves bought in Poland and Galicia could not travel rapidly enough. Food could not be transported from the magazines on the Niemen and the Vilia — no campaign has ever better proved that an army travels on its belly. Napoleon remained two weeks at Vilna instead of pushing to Glubokoi and Polotsk against Barclay, or on Minsk against Bagration, and lost the precious moment. The grand-tactics of Borodino was faulty: the mass should have been thrown upon the Russian left along the old road, and with more *ensemble*, while the viceroy merely contained the right and centre; and the Guard could have been put in to advantage, though not to do this was a proper precaution in any one but a Napoleon. The Russian army should have been pushed more sharply after reaching Moscow, for it was not then in good order; and if Kutusov could have been beaten at Tarutino, the campaign might have been less disastrous by a retreat via Kaluga. The delay in Moscow, expecting Alexander to yield, showed Napoleon's power of gauging facts to have deteriorated. The eccentric retreat after Maloyaroslavez lost several days. The French army markedly lacked topographical knowledge about Russia, and there was no suitable staff to acquire it; Napoleon used only the main roads, whereas there were fair roads, unknown to him, in every direction. Napoleon did not work the Swedish problem wisely. Turkey might have been of great assistance to the invaders; the peace won by Chichagov was concluded when Napoleon's plans reckoned on Turkey to push operations; and when Bernadotte joined the Russians, the two armies from Moldavia and Finland took the field. The Russians showed more aptitude for modern war than Napoleon had credited them with. The manœuvre by which Barclay abandoned his proposed Drissa defensive and fell back on Smolensk to receive Bagration, was as masterly as Alexander's courage in refusing to make terms was noble. Macdonald, Oudinot, Victor and St. Cyr should have operated under one head on the Dvina; such a mass might have destroyed Wittgenstein. Though strategical and tactical errors were committed, the logistics was most at fault. While the military errors are more open to criticism, yet two broad reasons lay at the root of Napoleon's failure: he could not feed his army, nor did he measure the stanchness or ability of his oppponent.

Those of Napoleon's panegyrists who underrate the Russian resistance, either from its military or characteristic standpoint, do ill-service to the Great Captain's reputation. Cut in two at the opening of the campaign, they retired five hundred miles without leaving a trophy to the pursuer. Not one of the Russian commanders was a great soldier; but they all did excellent work. Barclay and Bagration, cut asunder, made their junction, and the men so held themselves that, after the serious defeat at Borodino, they could yet harry the Grand Army and face Napoleon at Krasnoi. Wittgenstein, inferior to the joint French armies opposed to him, yet managed to overcome them all. The Russians opened the campaign by a series of faults; they corrected these errors while operations continued, and succeeded in destroying the Grand Army as no other army of modern times has been destroyed, their own forces meanwhile being kept fairly intact and in good order. When Kutusov could hold head to the diminishing French forces, the Russians, instead of permitting their wings to fall back with the central army, brought them forward against the French rear with wonderful effect. And while the campaign lacked method, in a sense, yet the direction given the Russian armies in its second half by Alexander and his staff was accurate and resultful. It has been common to give many explanations of the failure of the Russian campaign. We have rehearsed those of Jomini, with a few added. Perhaps they can all be summed up in one: that the enterprise was too great an one for any human being to carry through, with the then methods of transportation and communication.

Prussia and Austria were still discussing; Hardenberg and Metternich exchanged letters. When, after the burning of Moscow, Cathcart was assured by the czar, whose words speedily reached the powers, that the disaster in no wise changed his mind, Prussia and Austria began to see their chance. Prussia refused reinforcements on the ground that she had no more men, and that the contributions exacted by force vastly exceeded the war indemnity due. Austria still continued distrustful of Russia. During November, Austria had essayed mediation, but it did not go far: she was afraid to break with France. But when Napoleon asked Francis for thirty thousand more men, and stated that Prussia would send reinforcements to stave off Russian invasion, he taxed Austria too far.

That Napoleon had scant praise to bestow on the brave men who fought his battles in the Russian campaign has often been made a serious reproach. This may be just, but it has a parallel in the dispatches of the Duke of Wellington. Neither is justifiable.

It may be interesting to note that the Grand Army, on the average, marched from the Vistula to Vilna at the rate of about fourteen miles a day; from Vilna to Vitebsk, and on to Smolensk, at the rate of twelve miles a day; to Moscow at the rate of ten miles. The Russians, under Barclay, in retreat covered about ten miles a day, except from Vitebsk to Smolensk, when they doubled the distance. Bagration, from Volkovisk to Smolensk, averaged seventeen miles a day. On the retreat from Moscow to Kovno, the rate was about thirteen miles.

It is worth while to quote almost entire the Bulletin penned by the emperor himself on the eve of leaving the army. Whatever its prevarications, in view of the fact that those were not the days of special war correspondents and telegraphs, and compared with the reports of other unsuccessful campaigns by the commanding generals, it will hold its own.

29TH BULLETIN OF THE GRAND ARMY.

Molodechno, December 3, 1812. Up to the 6th of November the weather had been perfect, and the movement of the army was executed with the greatest success. The cold had commenced the 7th. From this moment, each night we lost several hundred horses, which died in the bivouac. Arrived at Smolensk, we had already lost many cavalry and artillery horses. The Russian army of Volhynia was opposed to our right. Our right left the line of operation of Minsk, and took for pivot its operation the line of Warsaw. The emperor learned at Smolensk, the 9th, this change of line of operation, and guessed what the enemy would do. However hard it seemed to him to undertake a movement in such a cruel season, the new state of things necessitated it. He hoped to reach Minsk, or at least the Beresina, before the enemy; he left Smolensk the 13th; he slept at Krasnoi the 16th. The cold, which had commenced the 7th, gained sharply, and from the 14th to the 15th, and to the 16th, the thermometer marked 16 and 18 below freezing [nearly zero Fahrenheit]. The roads were covered with sheet ice. The cavalry, artillery and train horses perished every night, not by hundreds but by thousands, especially the horses of France and Germany. More than thirty thousand horses perished in a few days; our cavalry was all afoot; our artillery and our transports were without teams. We had to abandon and destroy a great number of our guns, and all our munitions of war and mouth.

This army, so fine the 6th, was very different dating from the 14th, almost without cavalry, without artillery, without train. Without cavalry we could not reconnoitre a quarter of a league; still, without artillery we could not risk a battle and stand with firm foot; we had to march so as not to be forced to a battle which the want of munitions prevented our desiring; we had to occupy a certain space so as not to be turned, and this without cavalry, which would reconnoitre and tie together the columns. This difficulty, joined to an excessive cold suddenly arrived, made our situation a sorry one. Men whom nature had not fashioned stoutly enough to be above all the chances of fate and of fortune seemed overcome, lost their gayety, their good humor, and dreamed of nothing but misfortune and catastrophe; those whom it had created superior to all things kept their gayety and their ordinary manners, and saw a new glory in the different difficulties to be surmounted.

The enemy, who saw on the roads the traces of this horrible calamity which had struck the French army, sought to profit by it. He enveloped all the columns with his Cossacks, who carried off, like the Arabs in the deserts, the trains and the carriages which lost their way. This contemptible cavalry, which only makes a noise and is not capable of driving in a company of voltigeurs, was made redoubtable by the favor of circumstances. However, the enemy was made to repent all of the serious attempts which he undertook; he was broken by the viceroy before whom he placed himself, and he lost large numbers.

Ney, who with three thousand men formed the rearguard, had blown up the ramparts of Smolensk. He was surrounded and found himself in a critical position ; he escaped it with the intrepidity which distinguishes him. Having held the enemy off from him the whole day of the 18th, and having constantly repulsed him, at night he made a movement by the right flank, crossed the Borysthenes, and upset the calculations of the enemy. The 19th the army passed the Borysthenes at Orsha, and the Russian army, tired, having lost many men, there stopped its attacks.

The army of Volhynia moved by the 16th on Minsk and was marching on Borisov. Dombrovski defended the bridge-head of Borisov with three thousand men. The 23d he was driven in and obliged to evacuate the position. The enemy thus passed the Beresina, marching on Bobr ; Lambert's division was the vanguard. The 2d Corps, commanded by Oudinot, which was at Chereia, had received the order to move on Borisov, to assure to the army the passage of the Beresina.

The 24th, Oudinot met Lambert's division four leagues from Borisov, attacked it, beat it, made two thousand prisoners, took six guns, five hundred wagons of the baggage of the army of Volhynia, and threw back the enemy to the right bank of the Beresina. . . . The enemy found safety only in burning the bridge, which is more than three hundred fathoms long.

Still the enemy occupied all the crossings of the Beresina. This river is forty fathoms wide. It was floating a great deal of ice, and its banks were covered with marshes three hundred fathoms long, which made it difficult to cross. The enemy's general had placed his four divisions at different outlets, where he guessed the French army would want to pass.

The 26th, at the point of day, the emperor, after having deceived the enemy by different movements made during the day of the 25th, moved on the village of Studianka, and at once, despite a division of the enemy and in its presence, had two bridges thrown over the river. Oudinot crossed, attacked the enemy, and followed him fighting two hours ; the enemy retired on the bridge-head of Borisov. . . . During the whole day of the 26th and the 27th the army crossed.

Victor, commanding the 9th Corps, had received orders to follow the movements of Oudinot to form the rearguard, and to contain the Russian army of the Dvina, which followed him. Partouneaux's division was the rearguard of this corps. The 27th, at noon, Victor arrived with two divisions at the bridge of Studianka.

Partouneaux's division left Borisov at night. A brigade of this division which formed the rearguard, and which was charged to burn the bridges, left at 7 o'clock in the evening ; it arrived between 10 and 11 ; it sought its first brigade and its division general, who had left two hours before, and which it had not met on the route. Its search was vain : it became anxious. All that has been since ascertained is that this first brigade, leaving at 5 o'clock, lost its way at 6, turned to the right instead of turning to the left, and marched two or three leagues in this direction ; that at night and nearly frozen it rallied on the fires of the enemy, which it took for those of the French army; thus surrounded it was captured. This cruel mistake made us lose two thousand infantry, three hundred horses and three guns. The rumor runs that the division general was not with his column, and had marched alone.

The whole army having passed by the morning of the 28th, Victor held the bridge-head on the left bank; Oudinot and behind him all the army were on the right bank.

Borisov having been evacuated, the Armies of the Dvina and of Volhynia got into communication ; they concerted an attack. The 28th, at the point of day, Oudinot notified the emperor that he was attacked ; a half an hour afterwards, Victor was attacked on the left bank. The army took to arms. Ney moved in the rear of Oudinot and Mortier behind Ney. The fighting became lively : the enemy wished to turn our right. Doumerc, commanding the 5th division of cuirassiers, and who made part of the second corps remaining on the Dvina, ordered a charge of cavalry to the 4th and 5th regiments of cuirassiers at the moment when the legions of the Vistula were engaging in the woods to pierce the centre of the enemy, who were beaten and put to rout. These brave cuirassiers broke in, one after another, six infantry squares, and routed the enemy's cavalry, which came to the relief of his infantry : six thousand prisoners, two flags and six guns fell into our hands. On his side, Victor charged the enemy vigorously, beat him, made five or six hundred prisoners, and held him beyond cannon-shot from the bridge. . . . In the combat of the Beresina the army of Volhynia suffered much. Oudinot was wounded ; his wound is not dangerous : it is a ball he received in the side. The next day, the 29th, we remained on the battlefield. We had to choose between two routes, that of Minsk and that of Vilna. The route of Minsk passes through the middle of a forest, and uncultivated marshes, where it would have been impossible for the army to subsist. The route to Vilna, on the contrary, passes through very good country. The army, without cavalry, feeble in munitions, horribly fatigued with fifty days' march, carrying along its sick and the wounded of so many combats, needed to reach its magazines. On the 30th headquarters was at Plek-shenizi ; December 1, Staiki ; and the 3d at Molodechno, where the army received its first convoys from Vilna.

All the wounded officers and soldiers and all which was in the way, baggage, etc., were moved towards Vilna.

To say that the army needs to reëstablish its discipline, to repair itself, to remount its cavalry, its artillery and its material, is the result of the statement just made. Rest is its first need. Material and horses have arrived. Bourchier has already more than twenty thousand remount horses in the different depots. The artillery has already repaired its losses. The generals, the officers and the soldiers have suffered much with fatigue and want. Many have lost their baggage on account of losing their horses, a few by the ambushes of the Cossacks. The Cossacks took a number of isolated men, geographical engineers who were sketching positions, and wounded officers who marched without precaution, preferring to run risk rather than to march in order and in the column.

The reports of general officers commanding the corps will make known the officers and soldiers who most distinguished themselves, and the details of all these memorable events.

In these movements the emperor always marched in the middle of his Guard, the cavalry commanded by Bessières, and the infantry commanded by Lefebvre. His Majesty has been satisfied with the good spirit that his Guard had showed ; it has always been ready to move wherever the circumstances demanded; but the circumstances have always been such that its simple presence sufficed, and it was never necessary to put it into action.

Berthier, Duroc, Caulaincourt and all the aides-de-camp and the military officers of the house of the emperor always accompanied His Majesty.

Our cavalry was dismounted to that degree that we had to reunite the officers who had kept a horse, so as to form four companies of a hundred and fifty men each. The generals performed the functions of captains, and the colonels those of subordinates. This sacred squadron, commanded by Grouchy and under the orders of Murat, did not lose the emperor from sight in all the movements.

The health of His Majesty has never been better.

French Imperial Cuirassier.